The Fear Fix

SOLUTIONS FOR EVERY CHILD'S

MOMENTS OF WORRY, PANIC AND FEAR

SARAH CHANA RADCLIFFE

Collins

Published by Collins, an imprint of HarperCollins Publishers Ltd.

First edition

HarperCollins books may be purchased for educational, business, or sales
promotional use through our Special Markets Department.

HarperCollins Publishers Ltd.
2 Bloor Street East, 20th Floor,
Toronto, Ontario, Canada
M4W 1A8

www.harpercollins.ca

Library and Archives Canada Cataloguing in Publication
Radcliffe, Sarah Chana, author
The fear fix : solutions for every child's moments of worry,
panic and fear / Sarah Chana Radcliffe.

ISBN 978-1-44341-591-0

1. Fear in children. 2. Anxiety in children. I. Title.
BF723.F4R33 2013   155.4'1246   C2013-902275-9

Printed and bound in the United States of America
RRD 9 8 7 6 5 4 3 2 1

CONTENTS

CHAPTER ONE

Panic, Worry and Fear

"Look, Ma! No hands!" shouts little Jimmy as he rides his bike down the driveway toward the main road. "STOP! STOP!" screeches Mom, chasing after the bike and finally managing to grab the handlebars just as the vehicle is sliding past the edge of the driveway. "What is wrong with you, James William Henry? Have you no fear at all?" she reproaches her son. "You could've got yourself killed!" At least Mom had the good sense to feel fear!

THE VALUE OF ANXIETY

A fearless child is not a good thing. In fact, it's a very dangerous thing. Feelings of anxiety are there to protect us, to help us be vigilant enough to protect ourselves. The sixteen-year-old high school girl who feels secure and comfortable walking alone through an unlit park at midnight is a risk to herself. She needs to be a lot more worried.

But how worried is worried enough? We want our kids to have just the right amount of fear, not a drop more or less. We often want them to be afraid of whatever we're afraid of: robbers ("Keep the front door locked, for goodness' sake!"), fires ("Would you please remember to turn off the burner when you take the pot off the stove?"), financial loss ("If you spend it all now, what will you do when your summer job ends and you've still got your car insurance to pay for?"), sickness ("Yes, you *do* need to wear your coat") and safety ("Don't even *think* about skateboarding without your helmet, young man!"). If they don't share our fear of these things, we consider them to be reckless and naive and in bad need of a serious injection of fear chemistry. Only we don't want them to get hurt in the process of learning their lesson. We worry about them.

FLOODED WITH FEAR

> Child: *I'm not going. I want to stay home.*
> Parent: *But Jory has been to our house so many times already. He wants you to come play at his house this afternoon. His mommy will be there and I'm sure they'll have some nice cookies at snack time. You'll have a good time!*
> Child: *I'm not going.*
> Parent: *I'll take you in the house and stay with you for a little while until you feel comfortable. How will that be?*
> Child: *No. I'm not going!*
> Parent: *But I already told Jory's mom that you'll be there. You don't want them to be disappointed, do you?*
> Child: *I DON'T WANT TO GO! I DON'T WANT TO GO! I'M NOT GOING! WAAAAHHHH! YOU CAN'T MAKE ME GO! I'M STAYING HOME. WAAAAHHHH!*

A truly frightened child is no fun to deal with. Intense fear triggers the release of adrenaline and other hormones—the fight-or-flight emergency chemistry of the brain. This homegrown pharmacy generates enough power to turn weaklings into strongmen—think of stories of women who lift up cars to save their trapped child underneath. Emergency chemistry is meant to be life-saving, helping us to flee from burning buildings or to fight tigers, should we need to. There is no need to waste precious moments thinking what to do; adrenaline propels us to action, unleashing the brain's powerful survival instincts. Run, thrash, scream, lash out, talk fast, make no sense, just go for it—this is adrenaline and terrified children are filled with it. Was that a temper tantrum you just saw in the playdate scenario above? Not at all. That was the emergency response system arriving to save the child's life: "NO, HE WON'T BE GOING, YOU BETTER BELIEVE IT!"

HELPING CHILDREN THROUGH FEAR

All children, teens and adults experience fear and its cousin, worry. There is, after all, reason for fear at every age and stage of life. First-time experiences, traumatic events, unstable world forces, devastating natural disasters and so many more perfectly alarming events confront us all. Instant digital access to every local and nonlocal crisis only seems to have increased the fear that even children are experiencing these days on a regular basis. In addition, everyone has their own unique demons. Rational or otherwise, we and our kids fear rejection, failure, humiliation, loss and other invisible forms of torture. Yes, some of us are more fearful than others, and some have enough fear to be formally diagnosed with an anxiety disorder (something that we will explore further in this chapter). Like adults, all children experience the entire gamut of fearful feelings: panic, irrational fear, worry, terror, overwhelm, doubt, confusion, insecurity and every other flavor of fear. To be human is to be scared. Because this is so, parents need to know how to help their kids through fear, whether those kids are tiny toddlers, rambunctious grade schoolers, tough-looking teens or even young adults. *The Fear Fix* will give you skills that you can use in your home. Whether your child is just a "worry wort," is suffering from an anxiety disorder or is experiencing temporary mild, or even intense, anxious feelings, you will be able to offer a variety of calming techniques to help restore her emotional balance.

CHRONIC, INTENSE AND OVERWHELMING FEELINGS OF FEAR

What is the difference between a child who feels anxious and a child who "has anxiety"? As we have already seen, *every* child and teen experiences anxious feelings along with the whole range of other emotions that all people experience. Moreover, very young children experience more fear than other people, and while most grow out of those fears by the time they are school age, those who have an "anxious nature" may remain more fearful throughout life. However, when a child's fear is so intense or so frequent that it affects his ability to function well (or happily) at home or school, the child might have more than an anxious nature; he might have an anxiety *disorder.*

FEAR VS. DISORDER: HOW TO TELL THE DIFFERENCE

Since it can be important to identify the existence of an anxiety disorder, let's get a better idea of the difference between the fear that every child feels and the fear that a child with an anxiety disorder feels. To do this, we'll look at two nine-year-olds: Carly and Karen. Carly is afraid of spiders. She doesn't like to go into the basement of her house because she knows that spiders lurk there. If she sees a spider indoors or outdoors, she shrieks and runs in the other direction. Karen is also afraid of spiders. She is so afraid of them that she obsesses about them all day long, worrying that she might see one. She walks the long way to her classroom daily in order to avoid the more convenient route where she once saw a spiderweb. She refuses to play outside in the summer because she might see a spider in the grass. She'll never go back to a friend's house once she's seen a spider or spiderweb on the friend's property. If she does actually spot a spider, Karen has a complete meltdown, screaming, crying and hyperventilating. Karen's life—her choice of activities and her habits—is severely impacted by her fear of spiders. Upon professional assessment, Karen may be deemed to have a *phobia*, whereas her friend Carly would be described as having a *fear*. A phobia is a type

SARAH CHANA RADCLIFFE

of anxiety disorder; a fear is a frightened feeling. Although a fear can be quite intense, if it does not have a serious negative impact on a child's life, habits or emotional well-being, it will not be classified as a disorder.

If you're wondering whether your child's anxious feelings may be part of a larger mental-health syndrome, speak to your doctor or arrange for a psychological assessment. In addition, it's always advisable to seek professional advice if you notice:

- fear, worry or anxiety that makes it very difficult or impossible for your child to engage in normal, age-appropriate activities, such as doing schoolwork, taking tests, participating normally in the classroom, making friends and socializing, being in a car (or bus or plane), bathing, submitting to medical and dental procedures, staying alone (age-appropriately), accomplishing tasks in a normal time frame, learning to drive, sleeping away from home, dating, learning to swim, or doing anything else that her peers are capable of doing
- fear, worry or anxiety that routinely interferes with your child's ability to fall asleep, stay asleep or achieve restful sleep, or that leads to frequent disturbing nightmares
- fear, worry or anxiety that results in chronic physical distress like stomachaches, headaches, body aches, bed-wetting or other types of physical health issues
- fear, worry or anxiety that leads to unhealthy coping mechanisms (like avoiding people, places or things) or addictive or compulsive activities like obsessive rumination (the child is unable to stop worrying); engaging in unnecessary, unusual or time-consuming behavioral rituals; abusing substances (like drugs or alcohol); engaging in activities in a compulsive way (doing anything excessively); engaging in skin-picking or hair-pulling; or engaging in any other compulsive behavior or habit
- chronic worry that causes distress to your child or to

yourself or other family members because of its intensity or frequency

- any fear that reaches such an overwhelming intensity that it is accompanied by an inability to function normally or by aggressive or violent behavior or by a panic attack (feelings of panic plus fight-or-flight-induced symptoms like dizziness, chest pain, difficulty breathing, pounding heart, chills or hot flashes, nausea, trembling, numbness, fear of going crazy, an intense desire to flee, or fear of dying)

All of these kinds of fear and any other type of overwhelming fear should be assessed by a mental-health professional. When an anxiety disorder does exist, professional treatment offers the fastest and most profound resolution of anxious feelings. In the following chapters, we will look at some of the criteria for specific types of anxiety disorders. These sections will further help you identify the differences between fearful and anxious feelings and anxiety disorders, helping to alert you to symptoms that warrant further investigation.

WHAT CAUSES ANXIETY?

Fear is the normal and appropriate reaction to dangerous circumstances. As we noted earlier, lack of appropriate fear can be dangerous in itself. On the other hand, healthy fear can lead to life-saving behaviors like taking appropriate precautions ("I always wear a reflector when I'm walking in the dark because I'm afraid cars won't see me when I'm crossing the road") and appropriate reactions ("I heard some odd noises outside, so I quickly locked the front door"). Even worrying a little can sometimes lead to good things ("I was worried I wouldn't do well on the test, so I stayed up all night studying and guess what? I got an A+!"). However, there is definitely such a thing as too much fear. This is fear that is counterproductive, that decreases performance rather than enhances it, that causes problems rather than solves them ("I was so scared of saying the wrong thing that I couldn't answer the questions properly. I didn't get the job"). This is the sort of unnecessary and even harmful fear that *The Fear Fix* aims to help.

But why do kids feel too much fear? What causes them to worry when there's nothing to worry about, or makes them completely freak out when there's really no cause? To a certain extent, everyone is vulnerable to this sort of "misfiring" of the anxiety signal. Each one of us has a sore spot or two that triggers unnecessary fear chemistry. However, misfiring can be caused by many things, including learning to be scared based on previous traumatic or unpleasant experiences or having an inborn "loose wire," a tendency to shoot fear chemistry through the system more readily or more intensely. Indeed, the tendency to have more frequent and more intense anxious feelings seems to run in families and is thought to have a genetic basis. Moreover, an overload of anxious feelings is often seen in kids and adults who are prone to other mental-health syndromes (like depression or Asperger's disorder, for example), further supporting a biological link. In addition, it is known that environmental factors can affect the course of both normal anxious feelings and the more disruptive anxious feelings found in anxiety disorders. For instance, for those who are sensitive to them, certain foods can increase anxious feelings; many people become anxious upon consuming sugary foods or caffeine-laden beverages, and some people become anxious when they eat gluten-containing foods. In fact, any child can be sensitive to any environmental factor, including foods of all kinds, fluorescent lighting, medicines, perfumes and other substances. In some young people, this sensitivity can stimulate mild anxious feelings, and in some, it can stimulate overwhelming anxiety. In addition, all kids can *learn* to be afraid through regular exposure to fearful significant others (like parents). Those who are genetically vulnerable may be more deeply affected by the fear of those around them, just as this group tends to be more negatively affected by frightening movies, scary stories and traumatic news events.

Selecting the appropriate interventions for the treatment of frightened and anxious feelings depends to a certain extent on understanding their source. Obviously, if medications, foods or other substances are stimulating your child's anxious feelings, you will want to make environmental adjustments or address your child's sensitivity when that is an option. Ditto for scary movies and stories. If your own expressed worries are contributing to your child's sleepless nights, you can almost certainly ease up on expressing those concerns out loud. If your child's anxious thoughts and feelings are the consequence of unmanaged stress, negative mental and emotional habits (inborn or learned) or a lack of healthy coping strategies, you can help him correct these patterns (and I'll show you how to do so shortly). If an anxiety disorder is in place, you will want to add professional treatment to your own arsenal of home-based fear fighters.

In general, the home-based interventions found in *The Fear Fix* can be used with all children and teens to help address all levels and intensities of frightened feelings. *The Fear Fix* offers a wide range of fear-soothing techniques so that if one strategy isn't effective, there's another that can be tried. Some strategies are targeted to a narrow focus: the immediate relief of a very specific fear or worry. Others help to lower the child's overall stress level and emotional reactivity, helping to reduce the tendency toward anxious feeling and thinking in the future. Some techniques are designed to change mental and emotional habits—to change the brain itself—to uproot chronic patterns of fear and anxiety. No one intervention works equally well for all kids and all fears at all times; through the process of trial and error, you and your child will eventually discover which "fear fixers" fix his frightened feelings best. This smaller, unique set of interventions can then be called upon repeatedly to address unsettled, frightened feelings that occur not only in childhood and adolescence but throughout life.

THE PARENT'S JOURNEY THROUGH A CHILD'S FEAR

As a parent, you are intimately involved with your child's fears. After all, your child turns to *you* to help make her frightened feelings go away. Parents are the child's "Rock of Gibraltar," the ultimate fortress, the source of all security. If *you* can't make that fear disappear, then all is lost. Unfortunately, it is not only the child who feels that way; parents too may feel that their child's emotional survival depends on them. When they can't soothe their youngster's fear, they themselves often become overwhelmed.

But what is so overwhelming about a child's fear? Like a baby's cry, fear signals the sort of distress that is difficult to ignore. In fact, in both cases, parents themselves feel distressed until the child's distress is completely resolved. The problem is that parents are often unable to help their child completely resolve worried, frightened or panicked feelings. For this reason, parents frequently feel helpless in the face of their child's fear. They can find no pill, no food, no activity and, quite often, no words that will make the anguish cease. Moreover, although it will eventually wane on its own, the fear is almost certain to return, bringing with it a new wave of trauma for all involved.

In addition, parents fear the implications of their child's fear. A fearful child is, after all, not coping well. Whatever it is that the child is afraid of—bugs, tests, new experiences, rejection, failure, separation, the darkness of night, rabbits, robbers, terrorists—it overpowers the youngster. She dissolves into tears, paralysis, rage, hysteria or just endless, pitiful whining. The confident and self-assured child or teen is nowhere to be found; a quivering, quaking, troubled child stands in her place—even if only temporarily. Parents suffer along with their youngster, aching for the child's pain. If their child feels fear frequently or intensely, parents often start to worry about her future. Will she be limited, hampered or unhappy? How will the fear negatively impact the child's entire life?

Ironically, parents' fear of the fear can reduce their effectiveness in soothing their child's agitation. In their own desperation to help, parents can sometimes be forceful, ordering a child to "snap out of it" or "grow up" or using threats ("Either get on that elevator or I'm leaving you right here!"). They urgently, and understandably, want the child to turn the fear off. Of course, the child can't do it. An equally common intervention used by concerned parents is to offer rounds of reassurances, which utterly fail to soothe the youngster. This well-intentioned strategy comes naturally to most of us and can actually be redesigned to be effective (as we will see in Chapter Two). However, in its original form—basically, explaining to the child why there is no need for fear or worry—the technique virtually guarantees the return of the fear. Both parents and kids then experience the added frustration of being unable to end the cycle of fear.

YOU AND YOUR CHILD'S FEAR

Fortunately, *The Fear Fix*, with its large array of effective fear-fighting tools, provides a way out for both parent and child. You will never have to feel helpless again in the face of your child's fear. Knowing what to think, what to say and what to do will give you the confidence that will inspire your child's confidence. From a calm, equipped and centered place, you will be able to help your child move through the chemical, biological, emotional, relational, full-body, out-of-body experience we call fear. In doing so, you'll bring your child home to his own calm, equipped and centered place—the safest place on earth.

SARAH CHANA RADCLIFFE

CHAPTER TWO

What You Can Say

Child: *I don't want to go on the elevator.*
Parent: *Don't be silly. Elevators are fine. Come on, just get on. I haven't got all day.*
Child: *No. It could get stuck. I've heard stories of elevators getting stuck.*
Parent: *It's not going to get stuck! Just get on already—we have an appointment with Dr. Sanders and we're late as it is!*
Child: *I'm taking the stairs. (She runs down the hall, looking for the stairway.)*
Parent: *You are being ridiculous! Get back here right now!*

It can be hard to know just what to say in the face of a child's fear. A lot of fears seem silly to those who don't have them. It's tempting to just tell a child to "get over" a fear that doesn't make any sense. However, parents usually find that such an approach not only fails to remove the child's fear but also creates relationship stress. How, then, should a parent respond to a child's irrational fear (e.g., the fear of clowns)? For that matter, how should a parent respond to a child's reasonable fear (e.g., the fear of a school bully)? The ideal response will:

- build and strengthen the parent-child relationship
- help diminish the fear and increase feelings of security
- foster the child's overall emotional health and well-being
- help reduce the occurrence of fearful feelings in the future

What is that response? It is *naming the child's feeling.*

Giving the child's fear a name is akin to offering it a friendly greeting—a welcome mat, if you will. Instead of slamming the door on fear ("Go on, get out of here!"), parents can open the door to this emotion, giving the clear message that fear is welcome here. In case you're wondering why anyone would want to welcome fear, it is because doing so is an absolutely necessary step in the healing process. By comparison, imagine that your child has a bleeding wound. If the child runs off, you cannot clean and bandage the wound. Getting the child to feel safe enough to come to you is the only way you can help heal the torn tissue. It's the same thing with fear: You can't address it if you can't get it to come close enough. You have to find a way to make the fear "feel comfortable" with you; giving it a name is one way of befriending it. The name acts as a door-opener, a communication strategy that invites further discussion. "You're afraid?" Mom can ask, inviting the child to say more, to explore the feeling further and to let it run its course. Remember, fear will *not* go away just because it is told to, gently chided, cruelly mocked or enlightened with facts and figures. It *will* go away, however, when you invite it in and encourage it to tell its tale.

FEAR IS A WAVE

What is it about welcoming and listening to fear that helps it to dissipate? It all makes sense once one understands that all feelings move in a wave-like motion. A feeling may start off small, rise to a high peak of intensity, dwindle down again and finally fade away. This is true for feelings of joy, sadness, grief, anger, rage and, of course, fear. From small fears to big panic attacks, all fear follows the same wave-like movement.

As long as fear can complete its wave, it will heal fully. To see why, let's switch metaphors for a moment. Let's picture a wick or a stick of incense. Either of these can be lit to burn. As long as there is still some physical material left (a little bit of string in the wick or a little bit of wood in the stick of incense), the material can be lit again and again. However, when all the string or wood has burned completely to ash, there is nothing at all left to light. In the same way, when a particular fear pathway burns along its entire length (as it does during the wave process), then the pathway has burned up completely and there is nothing left to "light" anymore. If, for example, someone had a neural pathway in his brain that maintained a program called "fear of public speaking," he could burn that pathway up completely. Then, public speaking engagements would no longer be able to light the fire of fear in his brain. On the other hand, if this person stops the fear in its tracks (by refusing to engage in public speaking, for example), the fear-of-public-speaking neural pathway still remains in place in his brain. Every invitation to speak in public will have the power to trigger the feelings of fear. But the situation is even worse than in the case of the wick or stick of incense because, in the case of a neural pathway, each time the fire is lit, it enlarges and strengthens the fear pathway, as we shall soon see. In other words, not only does the neural pathway for fear *not* diminish and dwindle away, it actually gets bigger and stronger from use.

Let's return to our wave now. The wave properties of fear account for the power of cognitive-behavioral therapy to successfully eliminate obsessions and compulsions in the clinical disorder of fear called obsessive-compulsive disorder (OCD). As Dr. Paul Munford points out in his manual *Overcoming Compulsive Checking*, anything that *stops* the progression of the wave *maintains* the fear. The very activities that put a quick end to an anxious feeling— behavioral routines and rituals, mental magic (thinking "magic words" and the like), distraction, avoiding the subject or object that is feared, using logic to argue the fear away, and seeking and receiving reassurance—all of these fear-stoppers are really fear-*builders*. Because they prevent the fear from completing its wave, the fear remains locked into the wiring of the brain. And then, there's the bad news we learned above: instead of diminishing over time, the fear grows bigger and bigger due to the effect of constant practice. Every time the fear is triggered, it is as if the brain is learning and practicing the scared feeling. It's the same process when we learn to play the piano really well: we use the piano-playing pathways over and over again as we practice, practice, practice. This is how we learn to play our fear really well. The more we "do fear"—the more we trigger fear—the more naturally, quickly, mindlessly and expertly fear will come to us. Therefore, preventing fear from completing its wave and burning up its pathway ensures that fear will always be available to be triggered, which in turn, ensures that it will grow over time.

While this dynamic certainly holds true for the fear found in OCD, it also holds true for the regular fears, worries and anxieties that all kids and adults experience. This is why people who have supposedly overcome their fears are sometimes shocked to experience a return of the old frightened feelings. Even though they may have learned new responses and built new neural pathways, the old ones were never completely destroyed. This could happen, for instance, if a person learned a set of public speaking skills that gave him the confidence to talk in front of a crowd. Now he has a "confident" neural pathway for public speaking and a "panicked" pathway still in place as well (albeit buried somewhere beneath the new one). The panicked pathway could suddenly be triggered by some unexpected event—a look on someone's face in the audience or the color of the room in which he is speaking or anything else. Fortunately, it can be surprisingly easy to remove the remnants of a fearful pathway so that nothing is lurking in the recesses of the subconscious mind. Parents can help their children do just this once they know the differences between the kinds of interventions that stop the movement of fear and those that facilitate it.

UNINTENTIONAL FEAR STOPPERS

Parents can accidentally contribute to stopping the movement of fear when they are party to any of the fear-stopping processes described earlier by Dr. Munford. Of course, the child herself may discover that certain thoughts or activities provide fear-stopping distraction. Using these strategies, the child accidentally prevents her fear from completing its wave. Once they know how, parents can help their child learn how to release fear rather than repress it.

However, in their attempts to help, many parents currently employ variations of the other fear stoppers: distraction, helping the child to avoid the subject or object that is feared, using logic to argue the fear away and, our all-time favorite, offering reassurance. We will examine many alternatives to these common interventions in the coming pages. For now, we will simply note that it is all too easy for parents to fall into the trap of shutting down their child's fear by giving it a reception that inadvertently discounts, corrects, invalidates, minimizes or otherwise denies the right of the fear to exist exactly as it is. The fact that parents do all this with perfectly good intentions ("I just wanted to show him that there's nothing to be afraid of") doesn't help. All attempts to turn fear off have the same unfortunate effect no matter how parents express it. "There's no reason for your fear"; "You don't need to be afraid"; "You shouldn't be afraid"; "There's nothing to be afraid of"; "Don't be afraid"; "No one else is afraid"; "Only babies are afraid" all have the same effect. The message to the child is that he's feeling something that he needn't and shouldn't be feeling. The child doesn't have the permission and, most important, the *assistance* to explore her frightened feeling further. Consequently, there is no opportunity for the feeling to move along and complete its wave.

EMOTIONAL COACHING

Now let's look at what parents *can* do to help their children clear worry, panic and fear out of their neural pathways once and for all.

We will examine many strategies throughout the remaining chapters. Right now, we will start with a verbal intervention called *emotional coaching*. Drawn from the work of John Gottman in his book *Raising an Emotionally Intelligent Child,* this technique has been shown to enhance the parent-child relationship, increase the child's emotional and physical well-being and improve academic and social performance while giving the child tools to soothe his own fear and other types of emotional distress.

Parents can use emotional coaching to help their child take fear all the way to its conclusion. This powerful technique helps a youngster to express and release emotions verbally. When a child or teen can talk about his feelings of fear, the fear can rise and intensify, then ultimately diminish and disappear. Parents help this process along by naming and accepting the child's feelings *without trying to change them.* Remember: the natural parental tendency is to try to calm a child's fear, that is, to change the anxious feeling to a calmer one. In emotional coaching, the parent leaves the fear exactly as it is. It can be quite challenging for parents to do this, as it is so counterintuitive. Here's an example of what emotional coaching might sound like as a parent acknowledges his child's feeling:

I know you're scared.
Are you worried?
You seem concerned.
It's terrifying.
Of course you're frightened!
You're worried about it.
You seem nervous.
Are you afraid?
Sounds like you're not sure.

Expanded versions of emotional coaching simply add more information about the feeling:

I know you're scared. There's so much at stake here.

Are you worried? It's hard waiting.
It's terrifying—there's absolutely nothing you can do.
Of course you're frightened! Pain is a scary thing.

A dialogue might sound something like this:

Child: *I don't want to get a needle! It's going to hurt!*
Parent: *I know you're scared. No one likes pain.*

Emotional coaching ends after the feeling is named. It ends with a period. Look at all the examples above; each one ends with a period. *Emotional coaching never contains the word "but."* Parents, however, have a tendency to want to soften the blow by using a "but" in order to quickly comfort the child. They are inclined to say things like:

> *I know you're scared, but really, it's not going to hurt that much.*
> *I know you're worried, but you'll see, it will turn out just fine.*
> *I know you're nervous, but believe me, you've got what it takes!*

The problem with these well-intentioned "buts" is that they take the child away from his fear too quickly. It must be emphasized again and again (because this goes against all of our instincts), that the child must be encouraged to feel all of his fear in order to release it fully. Fear that is stopped too soon is unlikely to complete its wave. Indeed, the word "but" causes the first part of the sentence—the part that welcomes the frightened feeling—to be dropped from consciousness. A sentence that says, "I know you're afraid, but everything will turn out fine," gets translated in the brain only as "Everything will turn out fine." All the words before the word "but" will be effectively ignored, leaving only the reassurance intact. We've already seen that reassurance perpetuates, rather than releases, fear. *It doesn't stop the fear; it only stops the movement of fear.* This is the exact opposite of what needs to happen in order for the fear to clear out. Fear needs to move along its wave, building to a crescendo and then diminishing more and more until it is completely gone. Here's what's likely to happen when a parent adds a "but" to a child's fear of pain:

> Child: *I don't want to get a needle!*
> Parent: *I know. No one likes pain. But don't worry, it really doesn't hurt that much.*
> Child: *Yes, it does! It kills! I've had needles before—they burn!*

Instead of being soothed by the "but," the child may feel that the parent doesn't understand the issue sufficiently. He then escalates in an attempt to make his fear more comprehensible. He expresses the fear more intensely, rousing himself up as he tries to rouse up the parent's sympathy and support. Had the parent in this example just left off before the "but," saying, "I know. No one likes pain," the child probably would have whined once or twice more and then just ended the conversation in resignation. Resignation sometimes signals the end of the fear cycle. The child has taken fear as far as it goes and then agrees to succumb to the inevitable—in this case, pain.

Naming and Accepting the Fear in Order to Release It

So what is the correct way to offer emotional coaching? There are really only two simple steps: (1) name the frightened feeling and (2) pause for a moment before saying any other words. To see how these two steps are used, let's look at the following two conversations. In the first dialogue, Mom responds to her teenager's fear the way most parents do, using simple reassurance instead of emotional coaching. In the second dialogue, Mom uses emotional coaching.

Normal Parenting

Child: *I've been having a lot of headaches recently. Do you think it could be a brain tumor?*
Parent: *It's probably just stress—you haven't had enough sleep lately and you had all those exams.*
Child: *Yeah, but the pain is really strange. It's not like my usual headaches. I think something could be wrong.*
Parent: *It's probably nothing serious. Most headaches are just from stress.*
Child: *But sometimes headaches can be caused by a tumor.*

Emotional Coaching

Child: *I've been having a lot of headaches recently. Do you think it could be a brain tumor?*
Parent: *You sound worried.*
Child: *Well, I'm not so worried. But a little. Could it be a tumor?*
Parent: *I don't know—are you scared?*
Child: *Well, a little. No, not so much. It's probably just from staying up too late.*

You might find it hard to believe that a terrified child can turn around so quickly just because her parent accepts her fear. The truth is that it is often surprising how quickly fear can be resolved when it is just accepted. The above conversation is a true dialogue between an eighteen-year-old girl and her mom. The only difference in what actually happened is that the mom used a few more rounds of reassurance than were shown here. None of it helped, of course. All of the variations of "it's probably just stress" and "it's probably nothing serious" did nothing to stop the fear and, instead, left it firmly in place.

Those rounds ended with the teenager still worrying that she might have a serious health condition. Then the mom remembered to try emotional coaching and the conversation proceeded exactly as you see it above, with the teen concluding that lifestyle factors are probably causing her headaches.

Emotional coaching facilitates cognitive and emotional restructuring. When we hear ourselves saying something that doesn't sound quite right, we fix it. The parent facilitates cognitive restructuring by being a "sounding board," or a receptive listener. The parent uses emotional coaching to allow the fear to move freely, without trying to stop it. As a result, the fear moves up all the way to "my headache is due to a life-threatening condition" and back down to "I probably need more sleep." In many cases, emotional coaching is all that is needed to help a child completely resolve a feeling of fear.

Naming Feelings Decreases Resistance

Wouldn't it be great if all fear disappeared just because a parent accepted it without judgment? Unfortunately, the act of naming a child's feelings—while extremely beneficial—isn't always enough to completely resolve a fear. Often, other interventions will be required as well. If the parent has taken the time to name the child's feelings *first*, however, the child will often be much more open to any suggestion or strategy the parent then applies. Consider the following dialogue:

> Child: *I don't want to go to the party because I hardly know anyone who is going.*
> Parent: *Yeah, that can be uncomfortable.*
> Child: *I won't have anyone to talk to and I'll feel weird.*
> Parent: *Hmmm.*
> Child: *I'm going with Carey, but she's going to drop me once we get there and start talking to everyone else. I know her.*
> Parent: *You'll be left standing alone.*
> Child: *Definitely. I'm staying home.*

SARAH CHANA RADCLIFFE

In this case, the child has chosen avoidance as a solution to fear. The problem is that avoidance increases fearful feelings (as we'll learn more about later). Mom wants to help her daughter deal with her anxiety in a different way. Fortunately, her emotional coaching session has put her in exactly the right place for helping. By naming and accepting her child's feelings, she has shown herself to be a safe, nonjudgmental helper. Her daughter has felt comfortable in sharing her uncomfortable thoughts and feelings, letting her mom into her private space—just as someone might invite a friend into her home. Now that Mom is inside, she can make a suggestion.

> Parent: *Yes, I guess you could stay home. Or maybe you could go for a short time and just see what happens.*
> Child: *That's not a bad idea. Yeah, I could go for a few minutes and if I don't feel comfortable then I can come home. Thanks, I'll do that!*

Can a child really make such a quick come-around? Absolutely! When the parent has taken the time to accompany the child down her anxious neural pathway, the child *can* readily accept a suggestion. This won't always happen, mind you. The child's fear may be so intense that it requires further interventions before the youngster can confront it behaviorally. On the other hand, if the parent makes suggestions *before* allowing the child to express her fear fully, it is virtually guaranteed that all of the suggestions will be refused outright even if the fear does not require further treatment. Consider this alternate scenario in which Mom rushes into her daughter's house, so to speak, without being invited:

> Child: *I don't want to go to the party because I hardly know anyone who is going.*
> Parent: *Why let that bother you? You can always check it out and then leave if you want to.*
> Child: *Nah, I won't have anyone to talk to and I'll feel weird.*

Parent: *You never know till you get there. There might be people there you know.*
Child: *I'm going with Carey, but she's going to drop me once we get there and start talking to everyone else. I know her. I'll be left standing alone. No, I'm not going.*
Parent: *You're not even giving it a chance?*
Child: *Nope. I'm staying home.*

Why doesn't the daughter accept her mother's wise advice in this second scenario? Because Mom hasn't earned her place as "trusted adviser." She is offering advice from the position of an outsider, one who doesn't necessarily "get it." The conversation then has the feeling of a struggle or an argument. The act of patiently naming feelings moves parents in close to their child's inner world, putting them in a position from which suggestions can be offered *and* received.

Adding Problem-Solving to the Picture

Some children have stickier brains than others. Once they get onto a worry or fear, they simply replay it over and over without processing it. In other words, nothing moves, even when the parent provides emotional coaching. Consider this dialogue, for example:

Child: *Why do we have to go on the plane? I don't want to fly!*
Parent: *I know, honey. I know you aren't comfortable on planes.*
Child: *So why do we have to fly? Let's just go by boat!*
Parent: *I wish we could do that for you, sweetie. It would just take way too long—we can't do it; we have to fly. I know you're scared.*
Child: *So let's not fly!*

As you can see, the conversation isn't really going anywhere. However, it's not going anywhere *bad* either. When a child is feeling fearful, the adrenaline that is being generated in his system can all too easily be channeled into anger. Remember, adrenaline is the *fight-or-flight* chemical. Children (and their parents too) can suddenly find themselves in the throes of a tantrum when they are feeling overwhelmed by fear. Had the parent not gently welcomed her son's anxious feelings, the he might have felt both scared and enraged instead of just plain scared. Here's what can transpire when the parent just delivers the facts instead of acknowledging the feelings:

Child: *Why do we have to go on the plane? I don't want to fly!*
Parent: *Because that's the only way we can get there.*
Child: *I hate planes! I'm not coming with you!*
Parent: *You don't really have a choice in the matter.*
Child: *(Screaming at the top of his lungs) YES, I DO. I'M NOT GOING AND YOU CAN'T MAKE ME. I HATE YOU! I HATE YOU!*

Even when it doesn't make a fear go away, naming a child's fear helps prevent it from escalating while it simultaneously strengthens the parent-child bond. We saw earlier that emotional coaching can make a child more open to a parent's suggestion. However, a parent's first suggestion may not be acceptable to a child. When that's the case, emotional coaching can also make the child more open to a problem-solving process—the process whereby the parent and child work together to figure out what sort of compromises, interventions or strategies might help in a given anxiety-provoking situation.

In this case, let's say that Dad wants to do some problem-solving with his fearful daughter. Imagine the conversation happening as follows:

Child: *Why do we have to go on the plane? I don't want to fly!*
Parent: *I know, honey. I know you aren't comfortable on planes.*
Child: *So why do we have to fly? Let's just go by boat!*
Parent: *I wish we could do that for you, sweetie. It would*

*just take way too long. We can't do it; we have to fly. I
know you're scared.*
Child: *So let's not fly!*
Parent: *I understand how much you really don't want to
get on that plane. Since we are going on the plane, the only
thing I can suggest is that we try to find a way to make the
plane ride more comfortable for you.*
Child: *Like what?*
Parent: *Maybe we could take you to Dr. Palmer to help you
with your fear of flying. He teaches kids tricks to feel more
relaxed up there in the sky.*
Child: *I don't want to go to a doctor.*
Parent: *You don't have to go to a doctor if you don't want
to. Would you be interested in reading about things people
do to feel better on airplanes? There are books and plenty
of stuff on the computer.*
Child: *No.*
Parent: *Okay, that's fine. Do you have any ideas? What do
you think would help?*
Child: *Nothing.*
Parent: *I know, honey. You don't think anything can make
you feel happier on a plane. You may be right. The only
thing I can tell you is that I used to be scared to fly too,
and then I learned a few things to help and now I am not
afraid at all. In fact, I love going on a plane. I can show you
the things that I learned if you'd like.*
Child: *Show me.*

Again, because the parent took the time to first welcome and
accept the child's feelings, the child became less resistant and even
engaged (albeit a bit reluctantly) in the problem-solving process. At
the end of the back-and-forth, the youngster actually agreed to let
Dad teach her a thing or two about conquering fear.

Points to Remember

- Go slowly with your child's fear: take the time to name feelings and accept what the child is saying without correction or comment *before* offering advice and solutions. You may have to name feelings and listen without comment for a number of minutes. One short line of listening is probably not going to be sufficient—your patience with the process increases its effectiveness.
- Calm your own fear of your child's fear by remembering that your child's fear moves in a wave-like fashion; your calm support will help your child's fear move forward, up, down and away.
- Practice emotional coaching as much as possible. There are many more interventions that you will be learning in *The Fear Fix*, but they all begin with this skill.

DEALING WITH A CHILD'S INTENSE FEAR

Children's fears can be very intense, threatening to overwhelm not just the child but also the parent. Emotional coaching will help a parent negotiate any conversation about feelings, helping to calm and slow down feelings in both the parent and child. Here is an example of a highly anxious young adult who is sharing his feeling with his mom:

> Child: *What if I don't get into medical school? I've worked so hard at this. This is my third rejection letter and there's only two schools left that are considering my application. I'm cracking up. I can't take the pressure. If I don't get accepted, I'm going to kill myself.*

How does a parent deal with this kind of fear? An untrained parent might fall apart when she hears such words, thinking, "Kill himself? Did he say he was going to kill himself? I can't believe this! What will I do? I've got to call someone, talk to someone. Someone please help me, my son said he is going to kill himself. Good grief, what should I do?" Feeling frantic herself, the parent may attempt to intervene in the direct, frontal-attack way that rarely helps:

Parent: *Now listen here! You will not be killing yourself, do you hear me! It's not the end of the world if you don't get in! You can try again next year or be something else. Don't you ever talk about killing yourself—do you understand what I am saying! Nothing is that important—nothing!*
Child: *(Thinking to himself: You just don't get it, do you.)*

This scenario is probably as scary as it gets. However, even this young man's desperate panic can be addressed effectively by a parent who knows how to welcome, name and accept feelings.

Child: *What if I don't get into medical school! I've worked so hard at this. This is my third rejection letter and there's only two schools left that are considering my application. I'm cracking up. I can't take the pressure. If I don't get accepted, I'm going to kill myself.*
Parent: *(Touching the child lightly on the shoulder and speaking quietly) I know, Michael. You've done everything that anyone could do. It's so hard waiting this out. It's so scary thinking that you may not get into a program this year, after all this.*

Emotional coaching can end in the "middle of nowhere"—the parent doesn't have to work hard to tie up loose ends, move the conversation forward or resolve anything. Emotional coaching allows the *child* to resolve things. The parent's *pause* invites the child to do the work.

In the above case of strong emotion, does the parent have to address the child's threat of suicide? Unless the child has shown suicidal tendencies before this conversation, his poor choice of words is most likely just that: a very poor way to express strong, anxious feelings. When fear overwhelms a person, the adrenaline hijacks the frontal lobes of the brain, causing the person to say "stupid" things—things they don't really mean and often regret. The earlier in life that a parent starts naming a child's feelings, the less likely it is that the child will resort to extreme or dysfunctional ways of expressing emotion when highly stressed. The parent will have to use her judgment in this case—her knowledge of this child's way of communicating and thinking. If the parent is at all concerned that the child is feeling a dangerous level of desperation, then the conversation needs to include a recommendation for professional assistance. For instance:

> Parent: *(Touching the child lightly on the shoulder and speaking quietly) I know, Michael. You've done everything that anyone could do. It's so hard waiting this out. It's so scary thinking you may not get into a program this year, after all this.*
> *If the pressure is feeling too much to bear, we can get you some help. Dr. Mandel is a good resource—he can make a referral to someone who's helped other people get through really tough times like this.*

The more intense a fear, the more important it is for the parent to use emotional coaching. Intense fears require successful interventions, and the parent's use of emotional coaching dramatically increases the likelihood that any subsequent intervention will be successful. Keep in mind that your child's professional helper (counselor, doctor, therapist) will generally begin treatment by using techniques very much like emotional coaching. When it comes to children's fears and worries, parents can often ward off visits to mental-health professionals by simply learning to listen to their child in a more "professional" manner. When your own skill set is insufficient to keep your child safe, however—the child's fear does *not* abate, he is not speaking or behaving normally or he is threatening to hurt himself—be sure to access the appropriate professional services. Remember that *overwhelming* fear is indeed overwhelming. Your child will need help restoring his balanced state of mind.

REASSURANCE PREVENTS THE HEALING OF FEAR

For most parents, emotional coaching is not a natural technique. Chances are that they themselves were *not* raised by parents who used this particular strategy. In fact, it is much more likely that their own parents offered encouragement and reassurance in the face of their fears. While well-intentioned, these interventions can never calm fear for more than a couple of seconds. What they *do* do is increase the likelihood that the fear will return again and again. Let's see why it is important to avoid greeting anxious feelings with reassurance. Consider these sample dialogues:

Child: *I don't want to go to Kelly's house. She has a dog.*
Parent: *Don't worry; it's just a little dog and I know that dog—he's very friendly.*
Child: *I don't want to see the dog.*
Parent: *Honey, that dog wouldn't hurt a fly—honestly. It's the nicest dog in the world.*
Child: *I don't like it!*

Child: *I'm afraid I'm going to make a mistake when I sing my solo.*
Parent: *Don't be silly—you know that song inside out.*
Child: *I know, but I get scared when there's an audience.*
Parent: *They'll love you. There's nothing to be scared about.*
Child: *I'm so nervous I feel like I'm going to be sick.*

Child: *My hair doesn't look right.*
Parent: *It looks fine.*
Child: *It looks weird. I can't go out like this.*
Parent: *I'm telling you that it looks just fine. You're imagining things.*
Child: *I don't know what to do: I have to leave now and I haven't got time to fix it!*

In all of these examples, the parent is rejecting the child's anxious feelings. The first child is worried about seeing a dog, the second is afraid of making a mistake, and the third is concerned that her hair looks odd. In each case, the parent attempts to draw the child *away* from the anxious feeling using reassurance. Here's the problem with that approach: the child cannot heal a feeling that she cannot hold. Let's use a metaphor to understand this more fully. Suppose a child has dialed the wrong number. Mom takes the phone away from her and says, "You should dial such and such number instead." However, Mom is holding the phone now—not the child. The child can't dial at all and therefore cannot correct the error.

A child owns her own feeling and only she can change it. When helping your child to change a feeling, you must let her continue holding her own feeling so that she can make the necessary changes. This is true whether the child discovers the error herself or whether you point it out to her. Let's look at cases in which the child discovers her own error while the parent leaves the "phone in her hand" by either naming her feelings back to her or just accepting what she says.

Child: *I don't want to go to Kelly's house. She has a dog.*
Parent: *Yes, she does. Are you scared of the dog?*
Child: *Yes. I don't want to see it.*
Parent: *You don't want to see it. It's scary.*
Child: *Not so scary. Just a little scary.*
Parent: *Yes, it's a little dog, so it's just a little scary.*

Child: *Can you ask Kelly's mommy to stay in the room with us if the dog is there?*
Parent: *Sure, I can do that.*

Child: *I'm afraid I'm going to make a mistake when I sing my solo.*
Parent: *Are you, honey?*
Child: *Well, I get scared when there's an audience and then I can't concentrate.*
Parent: *Oh, I see.*
Child: *Maybe I should sing it in front of the family for practice.*
Parent: *That's a good idea.*

Child: *My hair doesn't look right.*
Parent: *Doesn't it?*
Child: *It looks weird. I can't go out like this.*
Parent: *Hmmm.*
Child: *Don't you think it looks weird?*
Parent: *What's important, honey, is that you think it looks weird.*
Child: *Oh, it doesn't look that bad, I guess. I've got to go. Bye.*

You can see that anxious thoughts and feelings can diminish rapidly when the child is allowed to hold them and work through them on her own, using the parent as a sounding board. By using emotional coaching, the parent has allowed the frightened feelings to follow their wave up to the top and down again. The fear clears. It's no good for *you* to have the right answers and solutions to your child's anxieties; your child must have them inside her own brain. In this way, and only in this way, does the correction take place where it needs to be. The child rewires her anxious brain with calm thoughts and feelings as she begins to think and feel differently. The very act of finding or creating soothing ideas and emotions is what wires them in. Unless you are a very unusual brain surgeon, there is no way you can take the calmness from your own brain

SARAH CHANA RADCLIFFE

and wire it into your youngster's brain. What you *can* do, however, is help position your child to do the wiring that needs to be done. You are doing exactly this when you offer emotional coaching.

REASSURANCE INCREASES FEAR

Here is another reason why reassurance should be avoided: it can actually *reinforce*, and thereby increase, anxious thinking patterns.

> Child: *I'm so scared I'm not going to do well on the test!*
> Parent: *Don't worry, you always do great.*
> Child: *Yeah, but this test is going to be really hard—the teacher warned us!*
> Parent: *You'll do great anyway. You always do.*

Now, if the child always does great, why is he so nervous? How come Dad is so relaxed and confident about the outcome but the child hasn't noticed his own pattern of success? The answer may lie in the dialogue itself. If we trace the emotional experience in this dialogue, we'll see that the child starts off feeling nervous and agitated, then receives reassurance, then acts nervous again, then receives more reassurance. At the next test, the same thing happens. In fact, it is likely to happen on the occasion of every test for the rest of the child's life. The child's brain is being trained in anxious rumination by the parent's calming, reassuring response.

Here's how it happens: A good-feeling communication is to the brain what candy is to a child—yummy! Just like giving a candy to a child can reinforce whatever the child was doing just before receiving it, giving a compliment to someone reinforces whatever they were doing just before receiving it. If a child got a candy for being quiet at the bank, then the child will tend to be quiet at the bank in the future. If a person got a compliment or any other kind of good-feeling communication (like reassurance) for expressing a frightened feeling or insecure thought, then the person will express—and actually feel—more frightened feelings and insecure thoughts.

Now, you might argue that emotional coaching also feels good to the child. And I would have to agree—it certainly does feel good to be completely understood. However, emotional coaching has an unpleasant edge to it as well. Precisely because it fails to offer reassurance, it tends to leave a child feeling "unfinished," slightly uncomfortable and still in some distress, as in the following conversation.

> Child: *I'm so scared I'm not going to do well on the test!*
> Parent: *Feeling worried about it, honey?*
> Child: *It's going to be really hard—the teacher warned us!*
> Parent: *Hmmm.*

If the parent stops there, absolutely holding back all cheerful words of reassurance and comfort, something rather strange tends to happen: the child is quite likely to reassure *himself*. For instance, he may say something like, "Well, I usually do pretty well, so hopefully I will this time too." Why is the child likely to comfort himself? As we saw earlier, one reason is that there is a tendency to engage in cognitive restructuring as a result of hearing oneself think. That is, we hear our own nonsensical thoughts and recognize the nonsense of them. We correct them, bringing them more in line with reality.

However, another reason that the child will most likely reassure himself is that there is an "itch" to end our thoughts happily, to resolve a problem. Human beings have an urge to tie up loose ends and make everything come out right, not unlike the happy ending of a movie or the harmonious notes played after discordant chords in a piece of music. If the *parent* doesn't provide the happy ending by offering reassurance, the child will often want to resolve it himself. The child's own reassurance is called *self-soothing*, and it has both short-term and long-term effects. In the short run, self-soothing calms the youngster down. In the long run, each occasion of self-soothing helps contribute to the building of a calmer brain, one that falls into fewer and fewer anxious thoughts over time.

SARAH CHANA RADCLIFFE

RESPONDING TO REASSURANCE SEEKERS

Some kids actually fish for reassurance. Take Zoe, who likes to follow Mom's household rules, including the rule that cookies are only for *after* dinner. On Monday, right after dinner, Zoe reaches into the cookie jar and says to Mom, "I can have a cookie now, right?" Mom says, "Yes, you can. It's after dinner." On Tuesday, right after dinner, Zoe says, "I can have a cookie now, right?" and Mom says, "Yes." On Wednesday, Zoe reaches for her after-dinner cookie, looks at Mom and asks, "I can have a cookie now, right?" Now, if Zoe was three or four years old, this behavior would be considered a normal manifestation of the learning process. But Zoe is eight and she's a very bright little girl. She *knows* the answer to her question and is not asking for information but rather for *reassurance*. If Mom continues to take her question at face value, answering each time it's asked, Mom will be giving Zoe relief from a slightly anxious sensation, thereby accidentally strengthening the anxious thought process. Now let's see what it would sound like if Mom refrained from reinforcing the anxious feeling:

> Child: *I can have a cookie now, right?*
> Parent: *You know the answer.*
> Child: *I can, right?*
> Parent: *You tell me.*
> Child: *I can.*
> Parent: *See, I knew you knew the answer.*

Now the parent has reinforced the child's feeling of trusting her own judgment. This will serve the child a lot better. When children ask unnecessary questions—questions they either know the answers to or could easily figure out if they just thought about it for a minute—they increase their own anxious feelings. They want an outsider to provide them with the settled feeling of certainty. As we've seen, feelings are an inside job; these kids have to learn how to give *themselves* a comfortable feeling of certainty. This feeling, the

"I can trust myself" feeling ("I can trust my own gut instinct" or "I just know"), is essential for optimal functioning. Each person needs to have access to her own inner guidance and inner knowing. This gives a person the security to step into the world and do whatever has to be done. Those who trust other people's inner guidance more than they trust their own are left feeling constantly anxious and uncomfortable. They hesitate to make a step. This slows them down and limits them while it leaves them in a perpetual state of stress. By sending unnecessary questions back to the child ("What do *you* think?"), parents help the child locate her own mental, emotional and neural paths of certainty. Being sent back with this question again and again helps the child to strengthen and expand these "knowing" pathways.

GREETING ANXIOUS FEELINGS CALMLY

A child's anxious feeling can be catchy. As a result, parents may respond in an equally anxious manner to a child's expression of worry, insecurity or fear. The adult may start to panic, firing off chemistry that makes it almost impossible to go slowly in order to listen and learn. This may result in an irritated, impatient response to the child's fear, or it can cause an overly deep concern. Let's see how showing a bit too much concern can backfire. In the following dialogue, Mom's ears perk up anxiously as soon as her daughter starts to complain about feeling fat.

Child: *I think I'm getting fat.*
Parent: *Really? You think you're getting fat? Why? Are your clothes not fitting you properly?*
Child: *Everything fits, it's just that I feel fat.*
Parent: *Well, I hope you aren't developing an eating disorder or something. You look perfectly fine to me.*
Child: *I'm not developing an eating disorder, but look at my legs; they look gross.*

SARAH CHANA RADCLIFFE

Parent: *You know, you're really scaring me. I don't see anything wrong with your legs. I think you should talk to Dr. Steinman. He'll let you know if you're getting fat or if you're getting neurotic.*
Child: *I'm not talking to Dr. Steinman! I'm going on a diet and I'm going to do leg exercises.*
Parent: *This is too much. I'm calling Dr. Steinman right now.*

This parent's intense concern over a small comment reflects the parent's own fear. The parent has made a mountain out of a molehill, a diagnosis of pathology based on one little remark. Possibly, the parent has read too many articles or watched too many programs on adolescent eating disorders, or perhaps the parent is just anxious by nature. Whatever the reason for the panicked response, the parent's attitude to the remark gives the child the impression that crisis and disaster lurk behind every corner. The conversation could have been handled easily with some basic emotional coaching:

Child: *I think I'm getting fat.*
Parent: *You're feeling fat?*
Child: *Yeah, my legs look gross.*
Parent: *You think so?*
Child: *Yes. I'm going on a diet and I'm going to start an exercise program.*
Parent: *Okay.*

How can the parent just end this with "okay"? What if the child really has a distorted self-image and is at the beginning of a severe eating disorder? The parent in this second scenario needs more time and reason for concern before jumping to conclusions. It's possible that the teen will diet for a week and exercise twice and then forget the whole problem. On the other hand, the child might start starving herself and exercising for three hours a day, continuing for several weeks straight with no sign of letup.

Should the latter scenario occur, the parent will then develop the appropriate concern and take the appropriate steps to arrange for a medical intervention.

Now, it's all fine and dandy to tell parents not to get all worked up about small things like a child's anxious moment. However, what if the parent *is* all worked up about it? What if *you* feel frightened when your child expresses insecurity and fear? Knowing that your fear won't help your child is not going to help *you*. But there are some steps you can take that can help both of you. If you feel anxious when your child expresses fear, note your anxiety to yourself. For instance, you might think, "Uh-oh, I don't like the sound of what she's saying. I am starting to feel uncomfortable." Use emotional coaching to respond to your child. This will slow down the conversation and help you to manage your own fear. Make a note to yourself that you will express your fear to your child later (this means at least one hour after the particular conversation has ended).

If you are still feeling anxious at the end of the conversation, use some of the techniques in *The Fear Fix* to restore your peace of mind. When you are feeling calm again, begin problem-solving: talk with a spouse, friend, relative, professional or other person to get an outside opinion; use the Internet to gather information and resources; call your doctor or do whatever you need to do to begin the helping process. Keep in mind that you have time. Everything doesn't have to be worked out over a twenty-four-hour period. There are very few dire emergencies in parenting, but even if this is one of them, you'll do better addressing it from a place of emotional centeredness than from a place of inner hysteria. As they tell you on airplanes, take care of yourself before you take care of your child.

EMOTIONALLY EMPOWERING THE MINIMALIST GREETING

Although fear always deserves a compassionate reception, it is important to be aware of the power of parental attention. Too much interest in a child's fear can inadvertently reinforce that fear, leading to an increase in frightened feelings. What constitutes too much interest? Consider the following scenario.

Parent: *Say hello to Mr. Khan, Liam.*
Child: *(Looks down and says nothing)*
Parent: *(To Mr. Khan) Oh, he's just shy—aren't you, Liam?*
Don't feel like talking much today, right? Feeling a little
bashful? Don't worry, Liam, Mr. Khan is a very nice man.
Are you sure you don't want to shake hands with him?
Look, Mr. Khan wants to shake hands with you!
Child: *(Looks down and says nothing, tries to hide behind*
the parent)
Parent: *Oh, I know, you're scared, right? You don't like*
talking to strangers, right? Well, that's really a good thing,
you know, because you never know who to trust these
days—isn't that right, Mr. Khan? Still, when Mommy or
Daddy is here, you don't have to be afraid, Liam. Are you
still afraid? You're a very shy boy, aren't you?

Attention is a funny thing. It doesn't matter whether the attention feels good or feels bad; it reinforces behavior in both cases. Poor little Liam is getting so much attention for his social fear that his parents might as well have offered him prizes for refusing to say hello. The results would have been the same: a lot more insecure social behavior. Here is an example of offering too much attention to fear through misplaced compassion:

Child: *Now that Daddy isn't with us, I'm scared to sleep*
alone in my room.
Parent: *Are you, honey? I understand. Why don't you come*
sleep in my bed, then? We'll keep each other company and
you won't have to feel scared anymore.

What could be more rewarding than being able to cuddle with Mom all night? Will this new privilege help the child learn to be comfortable in the house without Dad? No. As long as the child isn't comfortable in her own room, she's not fully relaxed in the house without her father. Mom wants to ease her daughter's pain and so offers to remove it by removing the problem. "Afraid to sleep in your own room? Then you don't have to sleep there." However, making the problem disappear robs the child of the opportunity to master it. Of course, on occasion you may need to temporarily avoid a frightening situation because you cannot help the child through it at the moment. For example, you might be at a friend's house with your child who is terrified of dogs. The barking of your friend's dog is throwing your child into hysteria, but you and your friend are trying to concentrate on the details of an event the two of you are planning. You've only got a small window of time today, certainly not enough to divert your attention to your child's fear of dogs. In this case, moving the dog out of the room is the most practical solution. What's important is that this does not become the entire strategy for handling the child's fear. It is just a temporary emergency stop-gap, to be followed with a program that actually addresses the fear (see, for example, "Gradual Exposure" in Chapter Three, page 73). Addressing it requires that the child be allowed to feel her fear. It is the parent's support *during* the anxious moment that can help the youngster to master it. This support can involve emotional coaching and problem-solving. Here's an example:

Child: *Now that Daddy isn't with us, I'm scared to sleep alone in my room.*
Parent: *Are you, honey? I understand. What can we do to help you feel more comfortable in your room?*

As you see, welcoming fear can be a short process. However, *pacing* is everything. The few words of emotional coaching need to be uttered s-l-o-w-l-y. "Are you, honey? I understand." *Pause* and nod sympathetically. It is this magical pacing that empowers the words, transforming them into heartfelt emotions rather than cold, robotic observations. These two patterns of speech are universes apart. The slow, sympathetic expression of feeling is processed at a different brain-wave level than the curt, factual utterance. The former has the power to heal; the latter has the power to alienate. Indeed, when parents use the *right* words (e.g., "I know you feel afraid") with the *wrong* tone, they accidentally end up conveying something like "I know you feel afraid, but I don't care much and, anyway, you are making a big deal out of nothing, so let's find a solution already." Children invariably protest, demanding that their parents stop naming their feelings back to them. When your child starts screaming, "Stop it! Stop saying that!" in response to your attempts at emotional coaching, it's not because the child doesn't want to be understood. Rather, it's that your emotionally empty words are insulting her painful feelings. Emotional coaching that is delivered in a quick, matter-of-fact manner is not emotional coaching at all, precisely because it fails to address emotions. Emotional coaching is *emotional*, carrying authentic parental feelings of empathy and compassion. For some sorts of frightened feelings, the emotional tone of the parental remark will be sympathetic. For others—for example, when the child is actually panicking—the emotional tone will be appropriately intense. In either case, the effectiveness of the parent's few words depends totally on how successfully the parent manages to convey real feeling. Hint: it is easiest to convey true emotion when we run the child's emotion through our own bodies *before* we name it. For instance, before acknowledging a child's fear of being alone, remember a time when *you* felt this kind of feeling, and feel it for just a moment. Then name it for the child. "Yes, it feels scary right now." Because you yourself felt a touch of this fear, your communication will now be and sound authentic, allowing it to effectively release or shift the child's emotion.

The minimalist approach involves using a few truly empathic words of emotional coaching, followed by initiating a search for solutions. The brevity and low-key nature of the response can help calm both parent and child.

LISTENING TO FEAR

It can be very challenging for parents to just listen. It seems so passive. Parents usually want to *help*. Very often, they do this by giving advice, providing information and showing kids how to do things. Parents see themselves as active teachers, which can make it hard for them to do emotional coaching. Emotional coaching is not about teaching but rather about *listening*. Emotional coaching addresses feelings, whereas teaching ignores the fear itself, appealing instead to the child's logical brain. When the *feeling* of fear is not addressed, it cannot be helped along its wave. It stays right where it is: inside. Let's look at a typical dialogue in which a parent gives input instead of listening passively:

> Child: *Do you think I should start taking driving lessons?*
> Parent: *Sure—if you feel ready.*
> Child: *I'm not sure if I'm ready.*
> Parent: *Well, don't rush yourself. It's a big step.*
> Child: *But everyone in my class already has their license.*
> Parent: *That doesn't matter. You may not feel ready yet and you don't have to compare yourself to anyone else.*
> Child: *I honestly don't feel like doing it.*
> Parent: *That's totally fine. You don't need to drive. You're still very young. There's no rush. Some people never drive.*
> Child: *Well, I want to drive sometime.*
> Parent: *Of course. But that doesn't mean that you have to take lessons this year.*

You might wonder why this dialogue isn't a good example of accepting and naming the child's fear—a case of the parent just reflecting back what the child is saying. If you read it quickly, it looks like that. But slow down and read it again; you'll see that the parent does *not* reflect back what the child is saying but rather gives her opinion. Look, for example, at this pair of sentences selected from the dialogue:

Child: *I'm not sure if I'm ready.*
Parent: *Well, don't rush yourself. It's a big step.*

The parent hones in on the child's fear of taking driving lessons, giving him permission to honor that fear. The parent is not *reflecting* at all but rather *advising* (in this case, making the suggestion that it's best not to rush into lessons). If the parent had just named the child's feelings, the dialogue might have sounded something like this:

Child: *I'm not sure if I'm ready.*
Parent: *You don't know if it's the right time yet.*

Similarly, look at these two lines from the dialogue:

Child: *But everyone in my class already has their license.*
Parent: *That doesn't matter. You may not feel ready yet and you don't have to compare yourself to anyone else.*

Again, the parent is not reflecting but rather *teaching* (in this case, teaching the child that he doesn't have to compare himself to his classmates and, again, that he has the right to honor his fear). Parents can respond to their child's comments by doing a lot of different things: teaching, offering an opinion, correcting, agreeing, disagreeing and so on. Although there is a place for each of these interventions when necessary and at the right time (i.e., *after* naming feelings), none of them are examples of naming feelings, accepting feelings, reflecting feelings or allowing feelings. If the parent had simply reflected back what the child was saying in our example, the dialogue might have sounded like this:

Child: *But everyone in my class already has their license.*
Parent: *You're feeling like the odd man out.*

Although these differences in parental responses are so subtle as to seem almost insignificant, they can actually have an impact on the child's level of fear. Remember: reflecting back a feeling allows the child to hear himself and to make adjustments in his own brain. Giving information and guidance short-circuits that process; the parent rather than the child has the answers. Moreover, telling the child how to deal with the frightened feelings is really a lesson in how to work with those kinds of feelings. The parent in the first dialogue is teaching the child to avoid the frightening activity. Perhaps this is the parent's own way of dealing with frightening situations. A different parent might have advised the child to face his fear head on and sign up for driving lessons. Either way, however, the child has not been helped along in his own ability to feel and respond to fear. Although there is certainly a place for problem-solving and finding solutions to frightening feelings, this place always occurs *after* the feelings have been acknowledged and *after* the child has been invited to offer ideas.

GREET FEAR ONCE OR TWICE AND THEN PROBLEM-SOLVE

As we saw earlier, excessive attention can reinforce feelings of fear. Talking about the same fear over and over again is another way of offering too much attention.

Ten-year-old Ashley has been picked on by some kids in her class and now she is afraid to go to school. Although only her feelings were hurt, Ashley is a sensitive child who is eager to avoid further insult. Mom feels very protective of Ashley and so, *every single day* after school, asks her how it went:

> Parent: *How was it today, honey? Did anyone bother you?*
> Child: *They looked at me funny.*
> Parent: *That's not nice! You must have felt terrible!*
> Child: *Yes. I don't want to go to school tomorrow.*
> Parent: *I know, honey. It's hard having to see those kids every day.*

Mom is a concerned and loving parent. She shows interest in her daughter's problem by checking in with her and staying on top of the situation. Moreover, Mom has great listening skills; throughout this dialogue she carefully gives her child emotional coaching. In fact, Mom is only making one mistake: she is searching for a problem, inadvertently inviting her daughter to focus her attention on negative, scary happenings. The daughter did not approach Mom to complain about the events of the day. While it is possible that the youngster didn't raise the subject because she felt uncomfortable discussing her difficulties, it is also possible that she simply had a decent enough day that she temporarily forgot to complain about the one or two annoying incidents she experienced. If she did indeed forget, that would be great. After all, in any given day there are far more positive moments than negative ones, and it would be better if the youngster could focus her attention on what's right with life rather than on what's wrong. Of course, human beings rarely do that (at least, not without being trained to do so). Instead, they tend to search out and focus on the difficulties, setbacks and problems that they face. When Mom acts like the most important news of the day, every day, consists of what went wrong for one or two minutes, Mom is unintentionally teaching her daughter how to join in on humanity's bad habit of focusing on the negative. Ashley will eventually learn that she should be paying close attention to scary feelings and disturbing incidents; she will learn to be vigilant for negative emotions. In addition, she will likely come to bond with Mom around the sharing of bad news, learning to talk about the upsets of the day before Mom even has a chance to ask her how things went.

Now, to be fair, it *is* possible that Ashley is really having problems with the troublemakers at school every single day. It is possible that she is unhappy and bothered by this regular assault. And she is entitled to emotional support from Mom. While it is important to be able to listen compassionately to a child's worry or fear, repeated listening to the same worry or fear without directly addressing the fear is *not* useful. Parents sometimes say, "I do emotional coaching every single night for my child's bedtime fears, but he's still afraid!"

Exactly my point. Emotional coaching is not a technique that is to be used alone repeatedly. Two times is usually enough and then it *must* be combined with other strategies.

For instance, if the problem can be solved, it should be solved. Emotional coaching plus various types of problem-solving approaches would be appropriate. If it can't be solved, however, then the child's focus of attention needs to be shifted so that she can lead a happy life. For example, if the child is bothered by the world situation but the parent can't (for some reason) fix the world situation, the child will benefit from employing strategies that increase her peace of mind *despite* the world situation. This is the essential message of the Serenity Prayer, held dear in Twelve Step programs. "Grant me the serenity to accept the things I cannot change and the courage to change the things I can." Parents can show a child how to move her own attention away from negativity and strengthen positive resources and coping skills. In future chapters, we will explore many strategies that you will be able to offer your child; what's important is to convey through your own selective attention that you are not so much interested in the worry as you are in the way to resolve it.

CONFRONTING FEAR

While some people pay excessive attention to scared feelings, some take the opposite approach: they try to minimize them out of existence in a well-intentioned desire to make them disappear. Some do this by providing a fast rescue (as we saw earlier with the child who was afraid to sleep alone in her room), while others do it by ignoring them, downplaying them or otherwise waving them aside. These latter strategies that involve discounting the child's fear as not that serious, or at least as not deserving of much attention, are particularly dangerous. They can lead to the child becoming so overwhelmed that the fear then multiplies to the level of a true phobia. The following story exemplifies what can happen when a parent pushes her child into confronting a fear without first providing the appropriate emotional support and practical preparation:

> *My mother knew I was afraid to swim in the deep end,*
> *but she figured the quickest way for me to get over my fear*
> *was to force me to just do it, so she actually pushed me*
> *into the water! I knew how to swim enough not to drown,*
> *but I struggled and gasped my way to the edge of the pool*
> *in a state of terror. I was so traumatized that I avoided*
> *swimming at all for many years afterward.*

Parents need to find the middle path, neither prematurely forcing confrontation of fear nor becoming complicit in its avoidance. In upcoming chapters, we will explore many techniques that accomplish this goal. Parents are truly in a unique position to help their kids negotiate frightened, worried and anxious feelings and, by doing so, to help them exit the loop of perpetual fear.

INTERRUPTING THE CYCLE OF FEAR

What is perpetual fear? It is a fear that returns again and again. Basically, it is a fear that has failed to complete its wave and therefore continues to be available to be triggered. Interestingly, ignoring a child's fear doesn't guarantee that it will complete its wave. For instance, the swimmer in the above example was left to contend with his terror on his own. One might think, then, that the terror would be the full expression of the fear and thus cure it once and for all. What we saw, however, was that the youngster became even *more* afraid than before. This is because too much fear caused a release of chemistry that actually interfered with the learning process. Trauma-based fear (overwhelming fear) is fear that does not complete its wave at all but rather loops around endlessly. In order for fear to complete its wave, it needs to be *supported and modulated*. A movement of a tolerable amount of fear along its pathway can completely resolve the feeling.

When the fear is stopped from moving or when it is allowed to move way too fast for comfort, it is unlikely to resolve. Without parental assistance, some fears are going to be left to just this fate.

Do parents *always* have to help their child's fear? No. Some fears will just go away on their own. However, while it is true that the fears of preschoolers are especially likely to eventually dissipate on their own, spontaneous remission of fears becomes less and less likely as the child grows older. A three-year-old's fear of cats is far more likely to melt away without outside help than the same fear in a thirteen-year-old or a twenty-three-year-old. Moreover, the intensely fearful three-year-old is less likely to overcome all her fears on her own than a three-year-old with just one or two small issues. Even so, all three-year-olds benefit from parental assistance just as much as any other age group; parents can help make the experience of fear more tolerable *and* they can help prevent the expansion of fear. Unfortunately, as we've already noted, many unaddressed fears tend to spread over time, increasing in both intensity and quantity.

We saw earlier how the disorder of anxiety known as OCD clearly shows the pattern of fear expansion. Because parents often fail to recognize early symptoms of OCD, they sometimes accidentally aid and abet the process of expansion. In the following example, Mom unwittingly contributes to the enlargement of her son's fear:

> *Little Eli doesn't like the look of his plate—it seems to have a spot on it. He tells Mom he won't eat off it, and Mom, suspecting nothing out of place, simply offers him a new plate. Eli looks that one over carefully and then agrees to use it. At the next meal, however, Eli examines his plate and again finds an unacceptable "spot." Again, Mom innocently hands him a new plate. This time, Eli finds the second plate unacceptable as well. Mom is tired of running back and forth for plates, so she instructs Eli to get his own plate. Eli is happy to do so. Soon, however, Eli is finding "spots" on his cups. He has to go through a number of cups and plates at the beginning of each meal before he finds*

those he can use. Mom ignores his activity. She barely
notices when he begins to check the cutlery as well, but
finally realizes something is wrong when Eli starts asking
for disposable plates, cups and cutlery so that he won't
have to check the cleanliness of everything. In fact, this is
just the beginning of Eli's journey into OCD.

Mom was on the right track when she refused to continue to bring more plates. However, in allowing Eli to go get new ones himself, she accidentally became an accomplice to his anxious process. She allowed her son to stop his wave of anxious feeling by replacing the offending place settings. What she actually needed to do was help him survive those feelings by insisting he eat from the same plates that everyone else in the family was managing to eat from. The microscopic "spots" he had been identifying were not significant to any other member of the household, and therefore they needed to lose their power for him as well. This could not happen as long as he avoided them. Mom will have to find ways to help Eli confront his fear without being overwhelmed by it. As we shall see, there are many tools she can use to do just that.

BEING EMOTIONALLY PRESENT

Your children will be experiencing many fears that they won't discuss with you. You will not be able to anticipate all of them or help your child through all of them, but there are many that you can address if you are willing to do so. Moreover, you can create a climate that facilitates open discussion and emotional awareness, which will help your children step forward with worries and fears that are on their mind.

I used to lie in bed trembling. My father would be chasing
my younger brother around the house with a belt. He'd
eventually catch him and beat him badly. For some reason,
Dad had something against Ryan. He never touched me.

But he might as well have; I'm sure I suffered just as much as Ryan did—listening to his helpless screams just tore me apart. No one in the family ever spoke about what was going on. I just assumed that this was life and we had to cope.

Yes, and perhaps that explains why the writer is such a heavy drinker to this day. But one might wonder: Where was his mother? Was she there but just as much a villain as Dad? Although that is certainly possible, it is more common that one parent is out of control, while the other one feels terrified and helpless to do anything about it. In such scenarios, the parents may struggle for years until they finally get help or get divorced. Meanwhile, the children are suffering. Interestingly, however, a little emotional support can go a very long way. Had this fellow's mother come to him after the terrifying episode to initiate a discussion of feelings, he likely would have grown up emotionally healthy, despite the dysfunctional aspects of his household. Here's what Mom could have said:

Parent: *You must be terrified when this happens! This is so awful. I'm sorry we are going through this, honey. I'm so sorry for Ryan and so sorry for you. I'm scared too, but I want you to know that I am working on this. I'm trying to do something about it. You must feel so deeply saddened having to listen to all this yelling and screaming and crying. I know it really hurts both of you terribly.*

Of course, it can be excruciatingly difficult for parents to talk to their kids about feelings that they feel guilty about inflicting. Parents may avoid raising the subject of emotional pain when that pain is being caused by their own actions, their marital conflict, their conflict with others, their divorce or their remarriage. They hope that if the kids don't raise the subject, there is nothing that has to be talked about. Nothing could be further from the truth. Children are *children;* they are not the ones who are equipped to lead the house emotionally. That is the *parent's* job. The parent must go to the child when the parent knows that fear and upset are surely present. Children can look perfectly normal on the outside, while inside they are tormented by anxiety and grief. If parents don't help a child to release these feelings, they can remain inside, growing larger over time. By the time the youngster is a young adult, it often happens that feelings of overwhelming anxiety begin to surface in the form of panic attacks or other symptoms. Many times, this is nothing more than the buildup of childhood sadness and hurt that have not been named and released. However, adolescents and young adults don't always seek the help of a mental-health professional at this point; many of them turn to alcohol and drugs or compulsive behaviors (such as self-harm and eating disorders) to relieve their pain instead.

No matter what life stresses your child has experienced, you can help him remain emotionally healthy and resilient. At times, this may mean providing your child with appropriate professional help. At other times, your own skills will be sufficient to help your child clear feelings of distress and angst, preventing the buildup that can lead to mental-health and addiction problems later on. In all cases, the healing process begins with *you*—not your child. You take the lead by initiating communication about the difficult things going on in your family life. In fact, it is your job to talk to your child about disturbed and scary feelings if your child is either *experiencing* or *witnessing* any of the following kinds of events:

- shouting matches or unpleasant arguments between you and the child
- fighting between you and your partner or ex-partner
- separation or divorce
- fighting (involving any two or more people) that the child has overheard
- illness of anyone close to the child, including yourself, a family member, a teacher, a neighbor, a family friend or a classmate
- death of a person in the child's life (no matter how close or distant the relationship)

- job loss of either parent
- anyone's intense or alarming display of emotion (e.g., suicide threats, threats of violence, abusive rages, hysteria or crying)
- sibling abuse (chronic mistreatment by one or more siblings)
- financial cutbacks or lifestyle changes
- any significant changes, such as moving houses or changing schools

This is not a comprehensive list but rather a sampler of intense life stressors that *always* affect children. Remember: your child may not be a skilled communicator, but it doesn't matter if he shares his feelings with you or not. By speaking about worry, fear and anxiety as if these are normal, expected phenomena in certain situations, you are teaching your child that painful feelings are a normal part of life and nothing to be ashamed of, afraid of or rejected. By telling your child what you think he may be feeling, you are also illustrating that you understand and you are available for emotional support. Never worry about guessing wrong when it comes to your child's feelings: your child will appreciate your effort to understand and will simply offer a correction. Here is a great example of supporting a child through a very stressful family event:

While visiting the family for Dad's fortieth birthday party, Adam's grandfather has a health incident—a possible stroke or maybe even a heart attack. He lies on the floor with all the adults gathered around him in a panic. Some are calling the police, the fire department and the ambulance service. Within minutes, emergency personnel arrive on the scene and Grandfather is rushed off to the hospital. Dad and Uncle Jon go with him, but the other family members are still milling around the house. There is lots of commotion for a while, while the grown-ups mobilize their response. Adam watches all this from the sidelines, knowing that it is

*best if he stays out of the way for now. Later that evening,
the child—in shock but silent—is playing on the computer
when Dad enters the room.*

Parent: *(Putting a hand gently on child's shoulder) That
was really scary today, wasn't it?*
Child: *I dunno.*
Parent: *All of those ambulances and everything—fire
trucks, too. I can tell you, I was scared.*
Child: *(Clicking away on the computer)*
Parent: *I was really worried there for a while. I didn't know
what happened. It was so confusing.*
Child: *What did happen?*
Parent: *Well, the doctor said that Grandpa had a minor
heart attack but that he's going to be all right. He's just
resting now.*
Child: *(Clicking away on the computer)*
Parent: *Those kinds of events are really scary because they
make you worry about whether the person is even going to
live. I was afraid that something really bad was happening,
like Grandpa was going to die or something. Did you feel
like that too?*
Child: *Yeah.*
Parent: *Yeah. I'm pretty tired from all that stress today. I'm
happy it wasn't so bad in the end, but I'm really tired. How
about you?*
Child: *Yeah.*

In this dialogue, we see that the child is not a sophisticated communicator. However, the father has done a masterful job of presenting a feeling-word vocabulary, naming the important feelings that anyone might be expected to feel in this kind of highly alarming situation. The child has benefited immensely even without his own participation. Growing up in such an emotionally intelligent atmosphere, the child is likely to develop good emotional regulation and communication tools before he leaves this home.

Of course, some children are very communicative when it comes to their feelings. They will have no trouble joining in the discussion and, in fact, doing so will help them to process and release their fears. As Dr. Dan Siegel explains in his book *The Whole-Brain Child*, talking about the details of a frightening event helps to move the event out of the emotional centers of the brain into the calmer thinking and remembering sections. The emotional "charge" from the event is thus neutralized, and the child will not store the experience as a long-lasting trauma. Being traumatized means being stuck. The traumatized child is stuck in time, constantly replaying a small section of video (the recording of a particular upsetting event) in the back of his mind—there is no "off switch." The video itself is stuck in one moment of time and doesn't continue running past that moment to the end of the movie (i.e., to the part that shows that the child has survived the event and life has moved forward). Moreover, the ever-running video acts as an energy drain on the system, depleting resources that the youngster could otherwise use for active living. When the child is invited to talk about the event, it is as if the movie is finally allowed to finish playing. It becomes unstuck. The event now feels finished and "over." (We will learn more about traumatic fears and their resolution in Chapter Ten.)

When frightening or disturbing events occur anywhere in your child's life, take the lead in talking to your child about feelings. Assume that frightening events are frightening and that your child needs your emotional support and guidance in managing his fear.

HELPING YOUR CHILD PROCESS FEAR

Children need help to process (unpack and resolve) all their fears, from their little worries to their traumatic nightmares. Without that help, their bodies often carry it for them until they're old enough to find help for themselves. This means that tense children (like tense adults) are likely to experience their unprocessed stress physically and emotionally. Depending on their genetic vulnerabilities, they may suffer headaches, stomachaches, compromised immune systems or other physical manifestations of stress. Like grown-ups, they may have sleeping problems (insomnia, nightmares and early wakening), mood issues, nervous habits and emotional disorders. By the time they are adolescents, however, young people often discover a form of temporary release from uncomfortable feelings of stress, anxiety and worry: mood-altering substances and activities.

More independent now, teens learn that they can calm their nerves with a range of dysfunctional activities such as bulimic eating patterns, anorexic eating patterns, pornography, sexual addiction, cigarettes, alcohol, drugs, gambling, self-harm and other unhealthy behaviors. Once a teenager's brain experiences the temporary relief engendered by such activities, the youngster can become "hooked." Children whose fear stems from high-conflict family life, abuse and traumatic incidents are particularly vulnerable to discovering the power of mind-numbing substances and activities. However, any child who has high levels of anxiety, frequent fear or chronic stress— even if only because of inborn genetic tendencies—is definitely at risk. There is a natural drive to relieve this sort of internal discomfort by whatever means works.

These teens often become adults with dysfunctional and destructive self-soothing habits and lifestyles. As long as a person has not been shown how to relieve anxious, uncomfortable feelings using natural, healthy strategies—no matter how old she may be—the body will attempt to regulate agitated emotions through manifesting physical or mental illness or addictions. You can help your child develop comfort and skill in dealing with her emotional world. No matter what challenges your child may face, your presence and your willingness to acknowledge and accept her feelings lays the foundation for a lifetime of healthy emotional regulation.

Having learned what you can *say* to your frightened child, let's now turn our attention to what you can *do* to further help alleviate her fear.

CHAPTER THREE

What You Can Do

Mom and Dad take nine-year-old Lindsay, her friend Karlye and five-year-old Sam to the amusement park. Lindsay and Karlye have been looking forward to the outing for weeks. Sam has only been to an amusement park once before, when he was a toddler, so he isn't really sure what to expect. As soon as the group enters the park, they are approached by a costumed character, a giant, friendly-looking red bear, eager to shake everyone's hands. As the bear reaches out to Sam, the little boy screams in terror and runs to hide behind Mom. Even after the bear apologizes and moves on, Sam continues to sob, pleading to be taken home. Mom uses emotional coaching, acknowledging that Sam has been badly frightened ("Was the bear scary, honey? You felt scared, right?"). However, Sam, hysterical and inconsolable, refuses to calm down; he continues crying loudly and begging to go home.

FEAR-SOOTHER TOOL KIT

Parents need to have a selection of interventions they can employ when their children experience strong fear. There is no one technique that will help every child every time. In fact, parents may have to try a few different strategies even during one child's single episode of frightened feelings. In this section, we will explore some of the tools that parents can call upon to help their child through moments of panic, worry and fear. In subsequent chapters, we will see how these tools and their variations can be used to address specific types of frightened feelings.

As we saw previously, emotional coaching can sometimes stop a fear in its tracks. This technique is always the first strategy to employ. If it puts an end to your youngster's fear—great. If not, its use will at least position you to be more effective when employing additional strategies. Now we will look at additional strategies that you can use—things you can *do*—when your child or teen is feeling afraid.

THE POWER OF PARENTAL PRESENCE

One foundational fear-soother is Parental Presence. Frightened children naturally seek comfort from their parents—hiding behind them, holding onto their legs, grabbing their hands, begging to sit or lie with them and so on. Even teenagers, when feeling insecure, panicked or worried, will seek proximity to their parents. Like younger kids, they often feel that being near a parent is protective and calming. Teenagers will run home to their parents when there is a crisis at school (like a shooting) or elsewhere in their world (like a terrorist attack). Similarly, when they feel panic about anything (a bad dream, a painful dental procedure), they will seek the calming presence of a parent. Indeed, parents are seen as protective by children of all ages, even when they are, in reality, powerless. Frightened children want to be near their parents before surgery, even though the parents can do little but stand by, and children want to be near their parents during a thunderstorm, even though the parents cannot stop the loud clap of thunder or the terrifying electrical show in the sky. Parents can even be protective in the child's eyes when they, themselves, are the source of fear: a child will sometimes cling to a parent who has just frightened him by shouting.

Because Parental Presence can be so powerfully soothing, it can be purposely employed to address a child's fear. However, parents must be careful that they don't accidentally encourage *avoidance* when they are using their own presence as a tool. For example, a frightened child or teen may wish to sleep in the parent's bed or bedroom. While Parental Presence will inevitably calm such a child, it will also be instrumental in maintaining the child's nighttime fear. A child cannot develop security by avoiding a feared stimulus (like a lonely bedroom); he can only become secure with such a stimulus when he develops coping strategies that work in the presence of that stimulus.

For example, a child can learn to overcome fear of being alone in his room. If he sleeps in his parent's room, however, his frightened feelings will be calmed only *for that night*. But the fear of his own bedroom still exists and will manifest again the next night and every night after that. If he uses a strategy that calms him down in his own room, on the other hand, then he will become calmer and calmer over time until there is no more fear left.

Instead of using Parental Presence to help a child *avoid* his fear, parents can use Parental Presence to help a child *address* his fear. For instance, they can use Parental Presence to help a child get used to sleeping alone in his own room. They can say to a young child, "I'll stay with you for ten minutes while you are getting ready to fall asleep. I have to leave after ten minutes whether or not you are sleeping." What does this accomplish? Parental Presence helps the child:

- feel secure enough to fall asleep in his own bed, in his own room
- get familiar with all aspects of his own room—the feel of the bed, the smell of the sheets, the sounds in the room, the effects of lighting and shadows and all other features
- develop a ritual for falling asleep in his own bed

Children can often learn to fall asleep quickly because they don't want to be awake after the parent leaves the room. It's fine for parents to pick any time period for offering their presence that works for them—it could be twenty or thirty minutes or longer. Perhaps the parent wants to read, knit or work on a laptop while the child is drifting off into slumber. But if the parent can only afford five or ten minutes, then that will have to do. No matter what amount of time is chosen, however, it will be reduced over time (normally over the course of a few weeks): ten minutes becomes seven minutes, then five minutes, then three, then one and then the child will be capable of falling asleep *without* Parental Presence. By the time Parental Presence is withdrawn, the child will have incorporated the feelings of security within his own being and will be able to fully self-soothe.

HELP YOUR CHILD FACE HIS FEAR BY OFFERING
PARENTAL PRESENCE IN THE FEARED SITUATION.

REDIRECTING ATTENTION

In order to experience fear, a child must focus her attention on a scary stimulus—either a scary thought, a scary image or a frightening scene in front of her. When a child focuses attention on peaceful, safe and happy thoughts, images or scenes, she'll feel calm and happy. The same is true for adults, of course. Try it for yourself: picture yourself (i.e., focus your attention on an image of yourself) in a flaming plane that is taking a nosedive—what sort of feeling does that generate? Now picture yourself lying on a beautiful sandy beach under bright blue skies and palm trees. What sort of feeling does that generate?

Let's consider a teenager who is worrying about whether her relationship with her boyfriend is ending. She's on the phone with her girlfriend, rehashing the details of a recent conversation she had with the young man, trying to figure out what each word meant and what each sigh signified. Does it mean he's interested in someone else? Or is it just that he's preoccupied with tryouts for the team? Why did he sound bored? Could he have been tired? His choice of words was odd—why did he say it that way instead of the other way? And she goes on and on, angst pouring out of every cell of her body. Suddenly, the doorbell rings: it's a delivery man bringing a package of clothes that the girl ordered from her favorite online store. She tells her friend that she's *got* to go: "I've been waiting for this package *forever*, and I can't *wait* to open it. Call ya back later!" And with that, the teen dives into the package, trying on this and that with complete focus, pleasure and satisfaction. What happened to all the worried feelings?

The worry is only there if the young lady puts her mind to it—literally. We'll explore the process of worry and its treatment in great detail in Chapter Five, but right now, we'll just highlight the point that we do have some control over what we choose to attend to. Even if a scary thought "pops" into our mind, we can then choose to nurture it with more attention or to turn our attention elsewhere (e.g., to our shopping cart).

Parents can help their frightened children use the power of focused attention. They can do this by helping the child to *redirect* her attention, moving it away from scary thoughts, images and scenes to more comfortable sorts of stimuli. As Dan Siegel points out in his book *The Whole-Brain Child*, this movement of attention is also a movement within the brain itself. The mind can guide attention away from the emotional centers (such as the fight-or-flight center within the amygdala) to the calmer centers (such as those in the thinking and planning centers, like the frontal cortex), and also from the emotional right brain to the logical left brain. Allowing attention to rest longer in calm sections of the brain actually *builds* more neural pathways in those sections, leading, over time, to a *calmer brain*.

Redirecting Attention begins, as usual, with emotional coaching. Emotional coaching—the naming and accepting of the child's fear—readies the child for further interventions by creating a strong parent-child connection in the moment and by relieving some of the intensity of the current emotion. After acknowledging the fear, the parent can help the child move her attention to a good-feeling stimulus.

Parents of toddlers naturally and routinely redirect their kids. However, they don't always do it in the healthiest way for the child. Let's look at a typical scenario in which a parent uses old-fashioned distraction:

> Mom has put Sean in his stroller and has walked him and the babysitter down the driveway. Mom is about to drive off to work, and Sean is about to spend the morning with the new babysitter. At first, Sean doesn't get it, but then the little wheels in his head start to go around and he realizes what's coming. He starts to whine, "Mommy! Mommy!" Mom points to a shiny red tanker passing their house just at that moment (thankfully) and says, "Look, look, Sean! See the big truck? Wow! Isn't that a great truck?" Sean looks up and is, indeed, mesmerized. Mom takes the opportunity to say a quick good-bye and turns toward her car, just as the babysitter picks up the conversation about the truck and pushes the stroller rapidly along the sidewalk.

From a certain point of view, we might say, "Mission accomplished!" Sean stopped crying and didn't feel the pain of Mom's departure. However, like many common antianxiety strategies, this sort of distraction solves a problem in the moment while potentially creating a longer-term problem for the future. Distraction does help move the child's attention away from a frightening stimulus to a happier, calmer one. However, pure distraction is not a recommended intervention. The easiest way to see why is to imagine the following conversation between a husband and wife:

> Wife: *I'm really worried about my job. I love this job—I've never loved a job so much in my life—and now they're about to let ten people from our department go, and I know that I'm in a vulnerable position. I'm really scared.*
> Husband: *Hey, did I tell you about that really funny email Phil sent me?*

Clearly, the husband's attempt at distraction is a horrible way to respond to his wife's feelings! You can just imagine what she might say next. Interestingly, toddlers, kids and teens experience very similar emotions to those of adults. If *you* don't like it, chances are good that your youngster of any age also doesn't like it. Therefore, if *you* don't like your feelings being completely ignored, you can be sure that your child won't like it either. However, the problems with using pure distraction go beyond the child not liking it. Using this technique can inadvertently *retard* a child's emotional intelligence, making the child less attuned to his own feelings and the feelings of others, thereby leading to a poorer overall developmental prognosis. High emotional intelligence is correlated with better social skills, better physical health, better mental health, better behavior and better academic performance. The most powerful way that parents can foster emotional intelligence in their kids is to welcome, name and accept the child's feelings—in other words, use the technique of emotional coaching. Instead of avoiding a child's frightened feelings, go right to them. Instead of being afraid of or uncomfortable talking about these kinds of feelings, give them a name. Instead of trying to ignore or push away frightened feelings, welcome them with validation and compassion.

Now let's look more closely at what was wrong with the husband's use of distraction and compare his responses to Mom's responses in dealing with little Sean:

- The husband didn't acknowledge his wife's feelings at all. Notice that Sean's mother also did not acknowledge Sean's feelings at all.
- The husband's emotional tone was totally disconnected from his wife's emotional tone; he was all cheery while she was clearly distressed. Sean's mom, too, was all upbeat, while her little boy was experiencing distress.
- The husband's distraction had absolutely nothing to do with the subject at hand and so was far worse than a minimization of his wife's feelings—it was a complete denial of those feelings, as if she had never expressed her fear at all. Sean's

mother distracted in a similar way, randomly pointing out a truck, which in effect, constituted a complete denial of her son's previous communication of anxious feelings. (Although all her son had said was "Mommy! Mommy!" the parent clearly understood from her knowledge of him, his body language and his tone of voice that the communication actually meant something like "Mommy, please don't leave me alone with this strange woman!")

Unlike distraction, Redirecting Attention has the following characteristics:

- It begins with emotional coaching: acknowledging, welcoming and naming the distressed feeling.
- Its sympathetic tone shows compassion for the person's fear.
- Attention is redirected to a stimulus that addresses the feelings of fear by comforting that fear.

If the husband in our example were to use the technique of Redirecting of Attention on his wife, the dialogue might sound something like this:

Wife: *I'm really worried about my job. I love this job—I've never loved a job so much in my life—and now they're about to let ten people from our department go, and I know that I'm in a vulnerable position. I'm really scared.*
Husband: *Yes, that sounds pretty overwhelming. I can see why you're so worried. I know how much you love that job, and of course you don't want to lose it. This must be really hard for you.*
Wife: *Yes, it's awful. I can't stand the waiting. The tension is killing me. I feel like my whole future rests on this.*
Husband: *Yeah, that's really hard—to have to wait for something like this, something that can change everything*

overnight. You know, I'm wondering if there's something we can do to help take your mind off it, to give you a little break. I know I can't make this go away for you—I wish I could—but do you think it would help if we went out and saw that movie we've been talking about? I heard it's completely engrossing. Maybe it will give you a couple of hours when you don't have to think about this.
Wife: *Yes, we might as well go. I'm just driving myself crazy and there's nothing I can do about it anyway. Yes, let's go.*

In this example, the husband welcomed his wife's feelings with emotional coaching and then offered to help her to think about something else for a couple of hours as a way of taking a break from scary thoughts. He effectively helped her attain some relief from anxious rumination while providing the kind of emotional support that would make her love him forever. (Emotional coaching helps create and maintain strong bonds between people.) Now let's see how Mom might have helped Sean through his separation anxiety using the same technique of Redirecting Attention:

Sean: *Mommy! Mommy!*
Mom: *Yes, Sean—are you worried that Mommy is leaving?*
Sean: *Mommy! Stay, Mommy!*
Mom: *Yes, sweetie, I know you want Mommy to stay. Elicia is going to take you to the park now because Mommy is going to work.*
Sean: *No! Mommy! Stay!*
Mom: *I know it's hard, honey. Would it help if Mommy gave you a lollipop to take to the park? Would that be better?*
Sean: *Lolli!*
Mom: *Okay, here is a lollipop for you to eat while Elicia takes you to the park. Mommy will be back soon.*

Have a nice time, you two!
Sean: *Lolli.*

In this case, Mom has acknowledged that Sean has real feelings—feelings that are valid. She names the feelings, showing that she is not afraid of them, that they have names and that they are, in fact, very normal and acceptable. She then teaches Sean that when a person has a painful feeling like fear, Redirecting Attention (in this case to a sugary treat) can take the edge off that feeling. Now some people might wonder whether Mom isn't teaching Sean to drown his real feelings in sugar. They might worry that Sean will turn to food whenever he is feeling upset, sad, mad, scared or otherwise stressed, starting on a lifelong struggle with obesity.

The truth is that a small treat can be helpful in soothing upset emotions *on occasion.* Perhaps you yourself have taken a bit of chocolate or a cup of tea when you've felt nervous or anxious in some way. In my opinion, it is fine for parents to offer food treats as a distraction *sometimes,* providing they offer a wide range of other sorts of comforting distractions at other times. If a parent *only* uses food to shift a child's attention, there is indeed a chance that the child will become an emotional eater with some sort of disordered food issue later in life. What other sorts of soothing distractions can parents offer a fearful child? Consider the following dialogues, each of which offers a different way to redirect the child's attention:

I know you're scared to get the needle. No one likes pain, even if it's a short pain. (For a younger child) Would it help if we went to the park right afterward? (For a teen) Would it help if we walked around the mall afterward?

I know you're worrying about the move, honey. It's really hard to leave everything behind. You're going to be sad for a while—there's no way around it. (Pause . . .) Meanwhile, would you like to take your mind off it for a bit? Should you and I watch that really funny TV show you love? At least we could laugh for a little while.

I know you're scared about what's going on with Grandma—we all are. We love Grandma so much. Still, there's nothing we can do right now except say our prayers for her. And you know Grandma wouldn't want us to be sitting around thinking sad thoughts all night. How about I read you a couple of chapters of your favorite book tonight? Maybe that would give your brain a little rest from all the worry just before you fall asleep.

It's so hard to wait for those results! I know you're anxious. How about I give you a nice foot massage? It will relax your whole body and mind and maybe even let you sleep a little tonight.

You're really scared from that movie, aren't you? It was so creepy! Do you think it would help if you did something physical right now to help get rid of that bad feeling— like taking a long hot shower to wash it away or going to the park with your sister to play a really fast game of tag (which she'll love)?

All of these examples show the kinds of situations in which the Redirecting Attention technique can be very helpful: *situations in which there is fear that cannot be removed by changing the situation itself.* The child *has* to get the needle, the family *is* moving houses, Grandma *is* facing some sort of health crisis, the teen *will* be writing the examination, the parents *are* going out for the night and so on. The child's fear is understandable but painful. Comforting and calming it with redirection of attention can provide at least temporary relief and a regrouping of energies. Even for circumstances in which the fear will inevitably return, temporary relief is valuable as it helps reduce the overall internal emotional pressure. Unrelenting, unrelieved and unsoothed fear can lead to a buildup of overwhelming feelings that can eventually trigger some sort of meltdown or breakdown. This can take many forms ranging from excessive irritability all the way to inability to function. Taking routine breaks from unavoidable stress is a protective practice that parents can encourage when they redirect their child's attention.

....

IN STRESSFUL AND FRIGHTENING SITUATIONS THAT ARE INESCAPABLE, HELP YOUR CHILD MOVE FEAR BY REDIRECTING ATTENTION.

....

MOVE FEAR WITH FACTS

In some cases, parents can provide a new way of understanding a situation so that the situation becomes less frightening to the child. Again, parents often instinctively try to apply this technique in order to calm their child. Here are three versions of "natural" attempts to use factual information to calm a fear:

Child: *I'm not going to the picnic—there might be bees there.*
Parent: *Don't worry. You don't bother them and they won't bother you.*
Child: *I'M NOT GOING!*

Child: *I'm not going to the picnic—there might be bees there.*
Parent: *You can't stay indoors all summer. Everyone's going—you can go too.*
Child: *I'M NOT GOING!*

Child: *I'm not going to the picnic—there might be bees there.*
Parent: *Bees are more interested in flowers than they are in you.*

Child: *I'M NOT GOING!*

Notice that each dialogue leaves the child unimpressed: she's still not going.

As we've already discussed, emotional coaching is always a necessary first step, helping prepare the child for whatever *next* intervention the parent employs. Notice that none of these examples contains emotional coaching. Let's add emotional coaching to one and see what happens:

> Child: *I'm not going to the picnic—there might be bees there.*
> Parent: *Are you afraid you might get stung?*
> Child: *Yes! I hate bees! I'm not going near them!*
> Parent: *Yes, a lot of people don't like bees. No one wants to get stung. Of course, you can't stay indoors all summer. Everyone's going—you can go too.*
> Child: *I'M NOT GOING!*

Hmmm. Emotional coaching doesn't seem to have changed this child's mind. Why didn't it help her accept the logical statement? The reason lies in the nature of the logical statement.

Offering truisms does not alleviate fear. Yes, it is true that the child can't solve her problem by staying indoors all summer. Saying so, however, does not provide any comfort at all. In fact, none of the factual, true, logical statements in the examples above would soothe fear even if they had all been preceded by emotional coaching. We saw earlier that the technique of Redirecting Attention only works when it is used to *directly address* feelings of fear. Similarly, Moving Fear with Facts requires that the facts *directly address the feelings of fear.* Consider this dialogue:

> Child: *I'm not going to the picnic—there might be bees there.*
> Parent: *Are you afraid you might get stung?*

Child: *Yes! I hate bees! I'm not going near them!*
Parent: *Yes, a lot of people don't like bees. No one wants to get stung. Of course, you can't stay indoors all summer. So you're going to need to know what to do about bees when you see them.*
Child: *I don't want to see them!*
Parent: *I understand. If I could remove them from the world for you, believe me, I would! Since I can't do that, the next best thing is learning what to do about them. There's two things we can look at: The first is how to avoid getting stung. The second is what to do if a bee does sting you. Let's you and I go to the computer right now and look up both of those things.*

This little conversation will be followed by a complete lesson (available on www.about.com, by the way) on bee management. The child will learn about which colors and odors attract and repel bees and wasps. He will learn how to dress, move and stand to avoid getting stung. He will also learn what to do in the case that he does get stung—which actions quickly reduce pain and swelling. The child will now have the kind of information that directly addresses his fear and, in many cases, this will drop the fear down at least a couple of notches—hopefully, close enough to zero to allow the child to agree to attend the picnic.

The key characteristic of the technique of Moving Fear with Facts is to use facts that offer practical help in dealing with whatever negative outcome the child fears. Moving Fear with Facts offers much more than simple reassurance. When a parent says, "Don't worry—bees aren't interested in you," she is primarily providing reassurance along with a small fact. On the other hand, the facts provided in the Moving Fear with Facts technique either provide practical solutions to feared outcomes or provide enough strong, new information that the child can see the whole situation in a more positive light. In our example of the fear of getting stung, Mom's new facts equip the child to prevent or handle the feared situation. The child is empowered, hearing that "bees don't like dark colors or the smell of eucalyptus oil, so wear your black T-shirt and navy pants and rub a little eucalyptus oil on your arms and neck. If a bee stings you, gently push the stinger away with your finger or get an adult to push it away with a credit card. Put ice on it to stop it from hurting and ask an adult for more help."

In subsequent chapters, we will see how this technique of Moving Fear with Facts can be used to address various specific fears.

USE THE MOVING FEAR WITH FACTS TECHNIQUE TO
OFFER COPING STRATEGIES FOR PREVENTING OR
DEALING WITH FEARED OUTCOMES.

INCOMPATIBLE RESPONSE

Parents can sometimes elicit an Incompatible Response in their child—an emotional reaction that cannot coexist with fear in the same moment. For example, someone can be very afraid or they can feel completely safe, but they cannot feel completely safe and very afraid at the same moment in time. Feelings of safety are incompatible with feelings of fear.

In a sense, the techniques we've seen so far—Parental Presence, Redirecting Attention and Moving Fear with Facts all produce *emotional* responses that are incompatible with feelings of fear. Parental Presence, for instance, elicits feelings of security. Redirecting Attention elicits feelings of comfort. And Moving Feelings with Facts elicits feelings of confidence (once the child is armed with fear-reducing information). Now, in this section, we will look at an Incompatible Response that produces a *physical* reaction that is the opposite of the physical sensations of fear.

Fear produces brain chemistry that puts the body on high alert. Muscles are tense, eyes are sharply focused, the heart beats quickly and breathing is rapid and shallow in order to fire up the system for fight or flight. Digestion is put on hold, and the stomach may be primed to empty (hence nausea, "butterflies" and diarrhea). Blood flow is directed to larger muscles (sometimes leading to tingling in the extremities, temperature changes, light-headedness and dizziness). Choking or difficulty breathing can result from the changes occurring in the lungs and heart. Then, something really interesting happens: the brain *notices* that the body is in emergency mode. It's as if the brain is saying to its energy regulation department: "Hey guys, he's tightening all his muscles and breathing shallowly—something very bad must be happening. He needs help! Send him some more adrenaline quick!" Once the extra adrenaline arrives, the person's heart will beat even faster and harder. His brain will note how hard his heart is now working and will repeat its instructions: "Hey guys, there's still danger out there—his heart is beating wildly—send him more adrenaline!" And so on. This is all great when the person really *does* need adrenaline because of an actual threat that must be dealt with. Now the person can run for his life or, if necessary, push, punch, pull or lift his way out of danger. When there is no external threat, however, vast amounts of energy are pumped through the body with nowhere to go and no way of being released. This results in overwhelming physical sensations that commonly instill intense fear in the sufferer, with the person feeling as if he is having a heart attack, is dying or is going crazy. (Children, teens and adults are often able to break the adrenaline cycle once they learn that their physical sensations are just the result of fight-or-flight chemistry that isn't needed for fleeing or fighting right then.) The excessive energy also creates an urgent need to *move fast*—hence the strong urge to escape from the current location (even though nothing dangerous is happening there).

The complete opposite kind of physical experience is a deeply relaxed body: limp muscles, soft eyes, slow pulse with deep, slow breathing. A relaxed jaw tells the body to tell the brain to tell the emotional regulation department, "Hey guys, stop sending the emergency chemistry—everything seems fine now!" Depending on what the body is doing (and also on what the mind is thinking about), the brain might also issue instructions to turn on specific peaceful, calming chemistry. This will increase physical sensations of calmness.

A positive feedback loop ensues: as the brain notices how calm and relaxed the body is, it will continue to send more calming chemistry. As the person notices how wonderfully relaxed his body is feeling, his mind and emotions will also relax more and more.

In upcoming chapters, we will learn much more about this biofeedback loop between body and mind, and we will explore many techniques that children can employ on their own to turn the fear down and turn the calm up. For now, the important point to note is that *a person can use his body to change his mind.* A relaxed, calm, slow physical sensation is incompatible with the tight, tense, rapid sensations of fear. Parents can help their child relax the body. There are two ways to accomplish this: (1) the parent holds the child in a way that calms the body or (2) the parent directs the child or teen to hold himself in a way that calms the body.

There are many, many ways to help the body relax physically. In this section, we'll look at only one intervention: the Heart Hold,* a technique for relaxing the heart center. Just as it sounds, the heart center is located on the trunk of the body, around the area of the heart and solar plexus—above the stomach and below the neck. To relax the heart center, one needs to draw one's attention to that area of the body. This can be done by touching it—putting the hand firmly over the center of the chest or pressing two fingers firmly into the center of the chest bone, right in the middle of the chest, about three or four finger-widths above the indentation of the breastbone, a point on the body known as CV17 (Central Vessel #17) to acupuncturists—its Chinese name "Sea of Tranquility" says it all. Hold the heart center in this way and breathe very slowly and rhythmically. (As one becomes more familiar with this center, it becomes possible to stimulate it just by putting one's attention on it, without touching it directly.) "Holding the heart" while breathing slowly relaxes the heart center—the middle of the body, where frightened and stressed

---

* This technique and its variations have been described by many practitioners from various health disciplines. See, for example, *Acupressure for Emotional Healing* by Michael Reed Gach.

emotions tend to be held. When the heart center is relaxed, the breath slows down even more, without conscious effort. The calming heart sends messages to the brain that all is well, causing the brain to release chemicals to the body that produce even more deeply relaxed physical sensations, perpetuating the cycle of mental and physical relaxation. The child moves away from agitated, frightened feelings to a calm, coherent state of being.

Here is how a parent might apply this technique when dealing with a very frightened small child:

- Hold the child close, pressing one of your hands firmly on the center of his chest. (If you like, you can place your other hand on top of the pressing hand and press even more firmly.) Continue pressing for two or three minutes to allow the pressure to have its effect.
- *Optional*: Ask the child to feel your hands pressing—this will draw the child's attention to the heart center and intensify the calming effect, slowing the breath even more.
- *Optional*: If the child is calming down enough to follow instructions, you can ask him to breathe slowly. As the child calms down more and more, ask him to think about a happy thought (a pet, a treat or an activity).

The following dialogue is an example of how the technique might be taught to an older child or teen. As usual, the parent begins with emotional coaching before moving on to the technique itself.

Child: *I'm so nervous! What if I do something stupid? What if I get fired the first day of my first job?*
Parent: *I know—it's scary when you start something new. Everyone probably feels scared on their first day.*
Child: *But I think they made a mistake hiring me. I'm not really qualified. I have no idea what I'm doing!*
Parent: *It's hard when you're just starting and you really don't have experience, and everything is new and strange.*

You seem really anxious and uncomfortable. Would it help if I showed you a quick calming technique just to take the edge off?

Child: *Yes, show me! I feel like a basket case!*

Parent: *Just firmly press into the center of your chest with two hands, like this—or make a fist and press it firmly in the center of your chest, or if you prefer, you can just press firmly with the fingers of one hand like this (parent demonstrates pressing the fingers of one hand into the center of her own chest). Now keep pressing and slow your breathing down, in and out, in and out slowly. That's right. Good. Keep pressing and breathing like that for a couple more minutes. . . . How do you feel now?*

Child: *A little better. Thanks, Mom!*

As with all other interventions, this heart-centered Incompatible Response will not work for all kids all the time. This particular technique sometimes completely eradicates a state of anxiety, sometimes provides a short relief from the anxious feeling and sometimes does nothing at all. You don't know how it will work until you try it.

Incompatible Response includes *any* technique that calms the physical body. As I already mentioned, there are *many* kinds of techniques that can accomplish this, and we will explore several in Chapter Four. However, most of them require that the user has already "installed" the calming program into his brain before calling on the technique when actually feeling fear. For instance, breathing techniques can be very effective in calming the physical body once a person has practiced them regularly for a long time. On the other hand, a frightened person who has previously used breathing techniques very rarely or never will usually be unsuccessful in using them to calm down in his current anxious moment. Similarly, deep muscle relaxation can be very effective—once it has been "installed." However, this technique isn't particularly child-friendly as it requires significant training. Fortunately, there are easier ways to help a child relax the body, and we'll explore these in upcoming chapters.

USE OR TEACH THE INCOMPATIBLE RESPONSE USING THE HEART HOLD TECHNIQUE TO HELP CALM VERY ANXIOUS FEELINGS AS NEEDED IN THE MOMENT.

GRADUAL EXPOSURE (A.K.A. BABY STEPS)

Gradual Exposure involves helping a child to overcome a specific fear in small, gradual steps. In order to use this technique, parents need to conceptualize a behavioral goal, like saying hello to visiting relatives, as a series of mini-skills. A child who won't talk to the relatives can be encouraged and supported to play or stay in a nearby room (as opposed to retreating to a bedroom on the second floor whenever relatives come to visit). The next step might be having the child hang around (albeit silently) in the room that the visitors are in, staying at a comfortable distance from them. The child's next step might be staying closer to the parents and visiting relatives without saying anything. Then, staying nearby, nodding and smiling might be the last step before the target behavior of saying hello when greeted. Once parents have conceptualized steps for a target behavior, they are ready to guide the child through them using the Gradual Exposure technique. The technique involves encouraging and supporting the child at each step, ensuring that the youngster feels relaxed and comfortable before moving on to a subsequent step.

For example, suppose a family is renting a cottage near a lake for a couple of weeks in the summer. One child is afraid to go into the lake when the family goes to the beach. The parents allow the child to just play on the sand while the other kids in the family go into the water to play and swim. The next day, the parents lay their blankets down closer to the water's edge and the frightened child plays there near them. The day after that, the parents lay their blankets down *very* close to the water and the child plays there, getting splashed occasionally as other kids run in and out of the lake. The day after that, the parents "forget" the blankets and sit themselves down on the sand at the edge of the water with their feet resting in the water and getting wet, and their child plays right at the water's edge. After a few days of playing at the water's edge, the child gets her feet wet too. Eventually, the child is playing in the water with her siblings. The parents have successfully assisted their child in overcoming her fear using Gradual Exposure.

As usual, the Gradual Exposure process begins with emotional coaching. When appropriate, Parental Presence can also be employed as part of the procedure. When it will be helpful, it is also possible to employ an Incompatible Response within the Gradual Exposure protocol. For instance, the previous scenario showed a child who was afraid of the water. The parents would have started their "treatment" by naming and accepting the child's fear ("I know, honey, you're scared of the water. That's okay. Why don't you play on the sand right here beside us?") By inviting the child to play near them, the parents are providing Parental Presence on the beach near the water—that is, within the parameter of the child's fear. They used the Gradual Exposure process by moving closer and closer to the water's edge until the child found herself getting her feet wet. From there, the youngster ended up splashing happily in the water.

However, suppose things didn't go quite so smoothly. Let's imagine, for instance, that once the parents got very close to the water's edge, the child started to feel panicky. In that case, the parents might have employed the Incompatible Response, either holding the child's heart center or showing her how to do so herself. Once the child calmed down, the parents could use more Parental Presence to walk with her along the water's edge, and then they could go a little farther into the water—again, holding the heart center if the fear started to rise. They could hold the child's hand in the water as she splashed around, then let go of her hand and let her splash freely while they are standing right near her. Eventually, they would move farther and farther away, until the child was able to splash happily with her siblings while the parents remained on the sandy beach.

Even with extra support, however, it is not always possible to make a child feel comfortable in the face of her fear. In fact, when a child's fear is truly overwhelming, she may resist the parents so strongly that no amount of Heart Holding is going to help. As you read on, you will discover other strategies that might be helpful in such a situation. However, it is also possible—particularly when the child is past the normal fearful preschool years—that she needs an even more carefully graduated Gradual Exposure, in some cases guided by professional intervention. Be sure to seek professional assessment when at-home techniques do not relieve your child's fears. Professionals have specialized tools in their tool kit so that no child has to endure the discomfort of unmanageable fear or worry or carry the trauma of those feelings forward into their adult lives.

USE GRADUAL EXPOSURE TO GRADUALLY, STEP BY STEP, BUILD FEELINGS OF SECURITY WHEN YOUR CHILD IS AFRAID TO ENGAGE IN AN ACTIVITY.

USING POSITIVE IMAGINATION

- We generate fear through what we imagine will happen.
- We generate fear through how we imagine what will happen.

Let me explain. We saw earlier that a child was afraid to go on a picnic because of what he imagined would happen there—he *imagined* that he would get stung by a bee. When this youngster created a visual image of the picnic outing in his mind, he saw grass, flowers, kids, picnic baskets, food, bees, and a bee that would sting him. This is a clear case of generating fear through what we imagine will happen. Here are more examples of generating fear through what we imagine will happen:

> *The dog will bite me.*
> *The plane will crash.*
> *The new kids will reject me.*

My boyfriend will drop me.
I'll fail the test.
I'll look ridiculous.

We imagine that what will happen will be *bad*.

But we also have a tendency to imagine that *how* things will happen will also be bad. Once the child imagines that he has been stung by a bee, he imagines that the experience will be unbearably painful. He sees himself swelling up with life-threatening allergic responses. He imagines that the bee sting will lead to an excruciating and dangerous condition. This is a case of generating fear through how we imagine what will happen. With this sort of fear, we expect that something challenging is going to happen and we imagine that it will happen very badly. Our scenarios are always "worst-case scenarios." Here are some more examples of this imaginative process:

Challenge	Negative Imaginative Process
Having surgery	It will be very painful and there will be complications
Leaving home for the first time	I will be lonely, rejected, lost and overwhelmed
Deciding between two academic programs	I'll choose the wrong one, I'll hate it and I'll be stuck in a horrible place for the next four years

Negative images fill the minds of fearful kids and teens. In fact, frightening images are the main ingredient of many types of fear. However, images are just images—*they aren't real*. As such, they are open to manipulation. Why generate a scary image when you can generate a comforting one? The most common reason is habit.

A person of any age can get into the habit of creating frightening scenarios in his imagination. However, scary pictures tell the brain that there may be a problem. The brain responds by sending fight-or-flight chemistry and—well, by now you know the rest!

In this section, we will explore one of the most important tools for the management of fearful feelings: Positive Imagination. You will learn how to use your own imagination to help your child through panic, worry and fear, and you will also learn how to teach your child to access Positive Imagination on his own. The ability to access Positive Imagination will be called upon again and again in the use of a variety of fear-busting strategies.

Positive thoughts and images can provide a powerful antidote to specific fears and anxious ruminations. They are, after all, a type of Incompatible Response. Happy, silly, funny, optimistic, relaxing or otherwise good-feeling thoughts and images generate wonderful, positive feelings that are incompatible with fear. Positive thoughts and images can undo a frightened feeling.

Aiden was just about to lie down on his bed to play with his gaming device when he suddenly spotted a big, fat, hairy spider. He called hysterically for Mom and the following scene ensued:

Child: *MOMMY, THERE'S A SPIDER ON MY BED! GET IT OFF! GET IT OFF! GET IT OFF! HELP! MOMMY, COME! COME RIGHT AWAY, MOMMY! COME!*
Parent: *(Entering the room with a tissue in hand, standing with hands on hips, using a deep, threatening voice in her best imitation of a pirate or warlord of some kind) Let me see that little bug, that slimy intruder—how dare it enter our private domain! I will make it pay for its insolence! Bug! Show your nasty, ugly face to me. I must finish you off! (And with that, Mom scoops the bug into her tissue and escorts it dramatically to the toilet. Turning to her child, she continues) I have made him walk the plank, sire. He will not disturb you again.*
Child: *Good!*

Although the imaginary game might seem a bit violent to some people, as a mother of five boys, I assure you that it will not lead to pathological development! Little boys (and some little girls too) find courage in pretending that they are fierce pirates, brave soldiers, strong firefighters or powerful superheroes. Of course, Mom could have just caught the spider in the normal way. But that wouldn't have been nearly as much fun, nor would it have shown the child how to use playful imagination to deal with fear. Everything that parents say and do is a model for their child. When Mom enters the "brave soldier" mode in the face of a fearful object, the lesson is not lost on the child. On the contrary, the child internalizes the notion of "bravely fighting the spider enemy." When parents demonstrate the use of Positive Imagination to conquer fear, children will very often copy their strategy.

In fact, that is exactly what Aiden decided to do when he spotted the second scary bug that particular afternoon. He copied Mom's show, pretending he was a tough pirate, and started yelling pirate-talk at the bug as he scooped it up in a tissue and threw it down the toilet. Satisfied with his prowess, he congratulated himself on vanquishing the enemy and then continued on with his normal activities.

Of course, scary images needn't be vanquished—they can actually be befriended using the power of imagination. Let's see what happens when another bug-hater, three-year-old Jordi, spots some sort of multi-legged creature creeping across the driveway:

Jordi: *(Panicking and shouting)* BUG! BUG! BUG!
Mom: *(Looking at the bug and speaking in a sugary sweet voice)* Why, hello there, Mr. Buggy! How are you today?
Jordi, did you say hello to Mr. Buggy?
Jordi: *(Copying Mom)* Hello, Mr. Buggy. How are you today?

Mom then takes Jordi's hand and guides him to his stroller. Catastrophe has been averted once again.

Bugs and animals can be transformed from enemies into buddies. Monsters can be shrunk until they fit nicely in the palm of a hand.

SARAH CHANA RADCLIFFE

Strange locations can morph into strange galaxies. Anything is possible with a little Positive Imagination.

Here is another example of teaching imaginative self-soothing skills through demonstration:

Anna is in the hospital and it's time for her parents to go home for the night. Anna feels lonely and scared. Mom uses emotional coaching to acknowledge her daughter's feelings, after which she employs comforting Positive Imagination. Remember, all fear-fighting tools come after emotional coaching.

Parent: *I know you don't want Mommy and Daddy to go home. You don't want to stay here in the hospital by yourself. It's lonely and scary. When we go, we'll leave our pet guards with you. See the corner of the room there, up near the ceiling? There is Morgrid, the Protector Puppy smiling at you—do you see him? He'll make sure you're safe. And see that other corner up there? There is Fatrilla, the Protector Princess—do you see her waving at us now? She has magic powers and will save you from all harm. And look at this corner above us—there is Humril, the Jokester. He's laughing and laughing—just listen to him, he's so funny. He wants you to be happy here! And over there in that corner is Sprig—that friendly little urchin with the big, colorful wings. She is singing you a lovely lullaby right now. I can hear it—can you? Oh, and look at all the lovely fairies flying over your bed. They are carrying our love for you in their little bags and sprinkling it all over you. It's all pink and warm and fluffy. Can you feel it?*

We have to go now, sweetie, but all of these helpers will stay with you to help you have a nice sleep. We'll see you in the morning.

Obviously, parents themselves must have a playful nature and an active imagination in order to teach their kids how to use these tools.

However, don't worry if you are short on both. Take your fantastical ideas from storybooks and fairy tales, children's classic movies (think old Walt Disney animated classics—they have everything you need!), modern fantasy movies, your kids' computer games, the Internet or anywhere else. Lots of other people have vivid imaginations, so you really don't have to invent all the happy, healing images yourself.

Positive Imagination doesn't always have to have a silly or playful side. It can just be plain old positive. Negative, frightening and overwhelming images can be replaced by images that are more pleasant and comfortable. Here's how a parent might employ regular Positive Imagination with an adolescent:

Child: *I've got way too much work to do: an essay due next week, an exam in two days, an oral presentation in four days, another exam two days after that . . . There's no way I can do all that. I'm just going to fail everything!*
Parent: *Wow! That is a lot! I can see why you're stressed!*
Child: *In order to do everything, I'd have to stay up twenty-four hours a day, every day, for the next two weeks.*
Parent: *I suppose that's one solution. There is another one, you know.*
Child: *Like what?*
Parent: *Like just pretending that there is only one task to do. Instead of thinking of having to do four things— the essay, the two tests and the oral presentation—just pretend you only have to do one thing. Since you have an exam in two days, for instance, you can just pretend that's all there is: an exam in two days. Then, when you've finished writing that, you can just pretend you have one presentation to prepare. When that's all finished . . . well, you see what I'm getting at, right?*
Child: *Hmmm. It's not a bad idea. It's actually a lot less pressure. You know what? I'm gonna give that a try. I only have one exam . . . not bad . . . not bad at all.*

SARAH CHANA RADCLIFFE

In this example, the parent could see that the youngster was overwhelming himself with a frightening image of an unmanageable task load. By offering the teen a simpler image of the tasks ahead— essentially, *the picture* of only one task to be done at a time—the teen could calm down and both feel and function a whole lot better.

A final but important use of Positive Imagination is in super-charging the power of belief. One of the most powerful fear fighters is faith. Those who believe that they are always benevolently guided and protected can and do call on their faith to get them through terrifying times and frightening circumstances. Many children discover the power of faith after a long journey of suffering and struggle, but parents can definitely help shorten the course of this learning period and offer the gift of education *before* strong faith is needed. Because the imagination of children is naturally strong, they often respond extremely well to the use of Positive Imagination to enhance their own sense of being supported and protected through danger, uncertainty, painful experiences, loss and other intensely stressful conditions. Parents will speak the language of their own faith and belief system when teaching this material. Here is one example of how a parent taught her child faith-based Positive Imagination tools:

> *My eight-year-old daughter is quite shy. We've moved cit-*
> *ies a couple of times already, and now, on our third move,*
> *Emma is very nervous about starting her new school. I've*
> *seen her when she's in an uncomfortable social situation—*
> *she just stands by herself, not making eye contact with*
> *anyone and looking like she's going to cry. My heart breaks*
> *for her. Emma believes in God and prays every night. She*
> *told me last week that she asked God to help her make*
> *friends at her new school, but she was still very frightened*
> *about going. I told her to remember that God was with her,*
> *that she didn't have to face the new kids all alone. She said*
> *she "knew" that but it didn't help make the fear go away.*
> *I thought it would help if she used her imagination to help*
> *her feel God's presence. She could then turn her "knowing*

*that she was safe" into "feeling that she was safe." To be
honest, this is what really works for me when I'm feeling
anxious. I told her that she could picture being supported.
I gave her three ideas: When entering her new classroom,
sitting at her desk, walking in the hallways and standing
in the schoolyard, she could picture being sheltered under
God's wing (an expression from the Psalms that we read
at bedtime). Or she could picture herself surrounded by
protective angels. Or she could picture one guardian angel
standing beside her the whole time. Emma loved all of
these ideas and said she would use them at school. When
she came home from school a few days later, I asked her
how things went. She said that she felt safe and happy
the whole time because she pictured the spiritual protection we had spoken about. The pictures, far more than the
words and the knowledge, made her feel safe inside her
very core. I know she'll be using these images of protection
for the rest of her life.*

Will using Positive Imagination strategies always calm a child
down? Of course not. There is no one strategy that always calms
down every child. For instance, little Aiden might have screamed at
his mother to stop pretending she was a pirate and just kill that spider already! Little Anna might have protested that she didn't see any
little pet guards and that she still wanted her parents to stay with
her all night. Both kids could have remained inconsolable. The teenager could have argued that the idea of pretending there is only one
task is just plain dumb, because there are really so many tasks. And
young Emma might have felt way too anxious to generate powerful
images of spiritual protection. But sometimes, these techniques will
work little miracles. You don't know till you try. Even when a child
doesn't appear to go for the strategy, he may still be absorbing the
idea into his brain, where it can be called upon in future times of
need.

USE POSITIVE IMAGINATION TO HELP YOUR CHILD
THROUGH FEARS THAT ARE CAUSED OR INCREASED BY
THE USE OF A VIVID NEGATIVE IMAGINATION. INSTALL
POSITIVE PICTURES TO COUNTERACT THE EFFECTS OF
THE NEGATIVE PICTURES THAT THE CHILD IS CREATING.

CHAPTER FOUR

What Your Child Can Do

Children and teens frequently experience anxious feelings. At their age, most face more tests and performance challenges at school alone than they will ever face again. They deal with social pressures, bullies, rejections and broken hearts. They listen to their parents fight. They often experience destabilizing upheaval in their family life, and the older ones among them must deal with uncertainty in their educational and career paths. And of course, like everyone else, they have to deal with ugly insects, bumpy airplane rides, terrifying lightning storms, sudden crises and disasters, and the world situation. And this is only a tiny sampling of the seemingly infinite triggers to panic, worry and fear.

Most of the time, kids will experience their anxious feelings when their parents aren't around. Therefore, one of the biggest gifts parents can give their children is the skill of emotional regulation—the ability to calm and soothe one's own fearful state.

EMOTIONAL REGULATION

Emotional regulation is the ability to change the way we feel. It may seem odd to think that we can choose when, how much or even whether to feel our fear. But this is exactly what we can do when we know how. A child may be in a situation in which feeling intense fear will be counterproductive—for instance, the child may be about to give a solo performance in front of his whole grade. He'll want to turn that panic down several notches so that he can perform properly. Even when we have real reason for fear, being flooded with feelings of panic can be counterproductive. We may inadvertently freeze on the spot rather than run for our lives or help a person who urgently needs that help. Consider the following scenario:

> *A fifteen-year-old girl is babysitting her eight-year-old nephew. They are sitting together at the kitchen table, having a little snack. Suddenly, while holding a cookie to his mouth, the little boy falls backward off his chair, lands flat on his back, stares blankly and motionlessly up at the ceiling and starts bleeding from his ear. The teenager, experiencing a surge of emergency chemistry in her bloodstream, screams loudly and runs around the room, shouting, "OH NO, OH NO, OH NO, OH NO! WAKE UP, NOAH! WAKE UP! NOAH! WHAT SHOULD I DO? PLEASE, NOAH, GET UP! PLEASE, SOMEBODY HELP! PLEASE HELP!" She wastes precious minutes in this state of fluster and panic before she finally focuses enough to realize that she should call an ambulance and other adults for help.*

While her fear is fully justified, it is not useful in this situation. It would be a lot better if she could quickly pull herself together to think about what she needs to do. If she had been trained in first aid, she would have automatically and immediately shifted away from emotional functioning (feeling her fear) into intellectual functioning (drawing on skills and behaviors learned in the first-aid course). However, even if she hasn't been officially trained, she can shift her attention away from fear toward active problem-solving—when she knows how to regulate her emotions.

EMOTIONAL REGULATION VS. EMOTIONAL HEALING

Before we examine techniques for emotional regulation, it is important to know when to use such techniques and when to use other strategies instead. Here is a simple example that can help clarify the matter: Suppose a grown woman has been having regular, intense headaches. She tries to relieve the pain in numerous ways: she uses over-the-counter medications, avoids certain foods, employs massage, has acupuncture treatments, wraps a pressure band around her head and rests as much as possible. Using these techniques, she is able to reduce the pain significantly and even the frequency of the attacks. However, after suffering many weeks of pain that must be managed, the woman makes an appointment to see her doctor. The doctor runs all sorts of tests but doesn't find an obvious physical cause for the headaches. The doctor asks the woman, "Is there any significant stress in your life right now? Is something bothering you?" The woman bursts into tears and says she hates her job. The doctor gently suggests she should find another job—perhaps the headaches are a result of the chronic stress she is under. The woman follows the doctor's orders and, sure enough, her headaches disappear completely.

Similarly, a young person can learn to regulate anxious feelings, reducing their intensity and frequency. Sometimes, this will be all that can be done. However, some anxious feelings are more like tension headaches: symptoms of underlying stress. Often, children suppress other negative emotions, feeling that they are not "nice" or not acceptable or, for some reason, cannot be spoken about. Those feelings then stay submerged while anxious feelings (or headaches, stomachaches, tantrums or other kinds of symptoms) pop up instead. For instance, a child can develop increased anxiety in reaction to his parents' recent separation or in response to his mother's new full-time job. Perhaps the child is really feeling anger but cannot express it properly. It is even possible that he, himself, isn't aware of how much anger he is feeling. In fact, a surprising number of very nice people feel inordinate amounts of fear, worry and anxiety. Many of these people have not learned to accept and release their real, justified feelings of stress, upset and rage. Of course, anxious feelings do not always stem from unprocessed stress, but because they sometimes do, it is important to *always* give anxious feelings the opportunity to express themselves. In this chapter, we will look at ways of doing just that. Releasing anxious feelings and the stress that underlies them is called *emotional healing*, whereas soothing and calming anxious and stressful feelings is called *emotional regulation*. Children and teens need emotional regulation techniques to help them function during the day and sleep well at night. They need emotional healing strategies in order to help reduce and prevent anxious feelings from occurring in the future.

LEARNING AND PRACTICING EMOTIONAL REGULATION

Lots of *adults* lack the skill of emotional regulation. Under stress, they disintegrate into rage, panic or despair. No one ever taught them how to calm themselves down. Fortunately, you do not have to leave *your* child deprived of the self-soothing skills that can protect and comfort her throughout her life. Every fear-buster in this book can be part of your child's emotional regulation toolbox. Some of them, as we shall see, can be used on the spot without prior training. However, many of the most powerful fear-busters require that the person know how to use them *before* she needs them. Teaching a child or teen how to use these skills is no different from teaching her to swim before taking her to a beach. A good swimmer will not only survive in the water but will actually enjoy being there. An untrained person, on the other hand, can drown in that same ocean. Most parents realize the value of teaching their kids to swim, but far fewer realize how important it is to equip children and teens with emotional regulation skills. Being able to call on emotional regulation tools not only calms stress and fear and saves wear and tear on the body, but also allows a person to lead a happier, healthier and more successful life.

START WITH THE BREATH

The first emotional regulation tool we will examine is the use of the breath. *Breathwork,* as it is sometimes called, has been shown to accomplish much more than ease fear. A huge body of research has established that purposeful use of the breath can make people healthier, calmer, happier, more creative and smarter. Fortunately, anyone who can count to one can learn how to use the breath to change his emotional state. That is why Breathwork is so well-suited for children and teens.

As I previously said, breathing techniques can be used to calm anxious feelings *once they have been "installed."* "Installing" this tool means creating a circuit in the brain that wires a specific breathing pattern to a very calm, secure, deeply relaxed emotional state. Although certain patterns of breathing can lead to this kind of pleasant state, they certainly do not automatically do so. When a person breathes slowly, he may start to calm down emotionally and physically. However, if he happens to be extremely agitated at the time when he starts breathing slowly (e.g., he is having an MRI and tends to be claustrophobic) and if he hasn't yet installed this pattern of breath, then, slow as his breath may be, it can definitely fail to calm him down.

Indeed, in the first several weeks of using a new breathing pattern, many people do *not* experience feelings of calm. In fact, they might feel bored, restless or even agitated. If they persist in practicing the breathing pattern, however, they will soon find that these kinds of uncomfortable feelings are replaced by pleasant, relaxed feelings. The longer they continue practicing, the more they will find that the breath is able to trigger feelings that are more and more pleasant and more and more deeply relaxed. Once it gets to the point where the breath triggers a very deep feeling of calm and relaxation (that is, it has been successfully installed), it can be effective at turning off the adrenaline emergency response and helping to promote feelings of calm even in frightening and highly stressful situations, restoring emotional and physical balance. Breathwork is a form of Incompatible Response once it has been installed, since it is not possible to feel calm and relaxed as well as tense and frightened in the same moment.

Installing a breathing pattern means forming a neural network in the brain—a little pathway that links the breathing pattern with calm feelings. In order to build such a network, a person needs to use the breathing pattern regularly—ideally, daily, even if only for a minute or so. Breathing patterns become more effective in reducing tension and anxious feelings the longer they are used in a person's life. (Starting Breathwork in childhood gives a person the most relaxed brain ever!) Teaching a child to "breathe himself to sleep" is one easy way of building the relaxation wiring into the youngster's brain.

TEACHING YOUR CHILD OR TEEN HOW TO INSTALL A BREATHING PATTERN

To help your children install a breathing pattern, ask them to do the following:

- Select a breathing pattern (see options starting on page 90).
- For the first month, practice the breathing pattern for at least one minute at a time, at least two times a day. Practicing for longer periods or more often is also fine. One of the practice sessions should be at bedtime, just prior to falling asleep. After a month, children can use the breathing pattern as many times a day as they like, breathing for as many minutes as they like, but at least once a day, for at least a minute or so.
- *Optional*: Older kids and especially teens (and parents too) often find longer breathing sessions very valuable, because they can significantly reduce and prevent stressful and anxious feelings. Regular practice of a breathing pattern for five or more minutes daily has an extremely positive impact on physical and emotional well-being. (There is an enormous body of research establishing the power of relaxation

techniques such as meditation and Breathwork to prevent disease of all kinds and improve all areas of intellectual, mental, physical and emotional functioning.] Continue forever for optimal results!

There are countless ways of doing Breathwork. Some breathing patterns increase feelings of calm and relaxation, while others increase energy and focus. In this section, we'll look at a number of calming breaths. You can ask your child to try each of these and pick a favorite to practice on her own. In order for the breathing pattern to become effective as a tool in times of true fear, it is best for your child to stick with *one* favorite breathing pattern for daily practice.

Herbert Benson's Relaxation Response

Dr. Herbert Benson, author of *The Relaxation Response,* developed this simple yet powerful breath pattern. It consists of an "in" breath through the nose and an "out" breath through the nose. On the out breath, the person thinks the number *one.* That's all there is to it. To teach this pattern to your child, ask her to breathe normally through her nose. Then ask her to continue breathing normally but to think the number *one* on the out breath. The child can think the word *one* or see the numeral *1* or hear the sound "one." It doesn't matter how she does it. Tell her that if thoughts pop into her mind, she should just let them pass by like clouds—she shouldn't get involved with them. She should just gently return her attention to the number *one* on the out breath. Continue for one or more minutes.

Coherent Breath

The Coherent Breath is a balanced in and out breath without pauses. When a child breathes in for four seconds and out for four seconds without pausing at the top or bottom of the breathing cycle, he is breathing a Coherent Breath pattern. This pattern has been found by many researchers to have powerfully positive effects on the heart and brain. Besides providing calm energy to the user, it helps build sections of the brain that regulate will power, enhance intuition and problem-solving and increase attention. Teens and adults should be able to breathe in for five or six seconds and out for five or six seconds to get these and other emotional, mental and physical benefits.

Here's how to teach this breath to your child: Ask your older child or teen to watch the seconds hand moving on a clock or wristwatch. Instruct him to breathe in for five seconds, then breathe out for five seconds, breathe in for five seconds and out for five seconds, along with the movement of the seconds hand as it makes its way around the clock (i.e., breathe in when the seconds hand reaches the 12 on the clock face and breathe out when it reaches the 1, breathe in at the 2 and out at the 3, and so on, completing six breaths in one minute.)

Younger children have smaller lung capacity and require a shorter breath (some older kids and teens may do better—at least at first—with a slightly shorter breath as well; adjust as necessary). To help your younger child establish a shorter inhale and exhale, you can do the counting out loud to get him started. (Look at the seconds hand of a clock to help yourself with pacing your counts one second apart and then begin saying out loud in a gentle tone of voice, "In-two-three-four, out-two-three-four, in-two-three-four, out-two-three-four," and so on for one full minute.)

Alternatively, use one of the many breathing apps available for smartphones and tablets. Some use a visual guide like a metronome, which can be set for any desired number of seconds. This means that the exhale can be set to twice as long as the inhale in order to induce feelings of deep relaxation (perfect at bedtime), or it can be set to the same number of seconds as the inhale, thereby creating a Coherent Breath that induces feelings of alert calm (excellent for test-taking and performance demands). One current example of this kind of technology available across platforms is the free Breathe2Relax app. There is also the Inner Balance app, which is produced by HeartMath. This program is specifically designed to teach Coherent Breathing using breath pacers and heart rate variability technology. Using this app along with a special sensor device, a teen can easily install the Coherent Breath pattern and also see the exact effects of his breath on his heart. As they say, a picture is worth a thousand words; having this clear feedback provides significant motivation to continue to use the breath to maintain high levels of mental, emotional and physical well-being. (Warning: parents will want to grab the device for themselves!)

There are also non-breathing apps that can be used to train the breath. For example, apps designed to help in the process of meditation or physical exercise sometimes use tones (bells, gongs and the like) to signal a number of set seconds and these can easily be used for breathing practice as well. The regular pacing of the breath is important for the Coherent Breath, but practicing with a training tool or technique once a day even for just a minute or so can help a child breathe more coherently throughout the rest of the day without even consciously trying.

Calm Breath
This rhythmic breath uses an affirmation to strengthen its effects. Ask your child to think, "In-calm," while breathing in and think, "Out-calm" while breathing out (or, if preferred, just "calm" on both the in and out breaths). Continue for a minute or more. The Calm Breath can also be done without affirmations: simply thinking "in" on the in breath and "out" on the out breath also has a soothing effect when done for several minutes at a time.

Play-in-the-Pause Breath
This breathing pattern comes from Thomas Roberts, author of *The Mindfulness Workbook: A Beginner's Guide to Overcoming Fear and Embracing Compassion.* Roberts points out that when we breathe naturally, we pause a little after taking the breath in and we pause a little after letting it out. Just take a moment right now to watch your own natural breathing pattern so that you can identify these two pauses. When you want to teach your child the Play-in-the-Pause Breath, invite her to breathe in to a slow count of three, out to a slow count of three and then just pause. Ask your child to pay attention to how she feels during the pause. The sequence of in-two-three-out-two-three-

pause can be repeated for as long as desired. This is a *very* relaxing breath, one that rapidly calms body and mind. Great for insomniacs!

Mindfulness of the Breath

"Mindfulness" is the practice of being present. It involves being aware of what is happening right now. One can be mindful of the sounds in the environment, of the tastes and textures of food in the mouth, of passing thoughts, of physical sensations in the body and of any other selected target. Being mindful of the breath—a very common focus in the practice of mindfulness meditation—means noticing and experiencing the breath as it enters and exits the body. One can mindfully attend to the breath by simply feeling it entering and exiting from the nasal passages. Or one can attend to the breath by noticing and feeling the rising and falling of the chest or abdomen. If one desires, one can follow the breath as it enters the body, slides down the air passageway in the throat and enters the lungs. For children, the easiest way to practice mindfulness of the breath is to simply notice it entering and leaving the nostrils. Instruct your child to close his eyes and feel the air going in and out of his nose. When he notices that his mind is wandering and he is thinking about something other than the breath, he should just gently return his attention to the breath. He should continue to notice the breath and return to the breath in this way for one or more minutes.

Bonus Anti-Panic Breath

This is not a breath to use daily, but it is one worth teaching to your child, just to have in her back pocket. It can help in moments of high panic. When a child has been using some other breathing pattern regularly, her brain will be ready to use any kind of breath on short notice. When teaching the Bonus Anti-Panic Breath, describe the breathing pattern to your child first, then ask her to try it. The child should breathe in slowly, and then, as she is breathing out, she should imagine that she is blowing up a balloon (or whistling a tune) and pucker up her lips. During actual moments of panic, she should continue the breathing pattern until feeling calmer.

*

I've included only a tiny sampling of popular breathing techniques here—there are many, many more. You can find varieties in books, online resources, and classes and courses on meditation, Breathwork, yoga, relaxation and stress management. When teaching your child a breathing pattern, the most important thing is to convey confidence that this technique will be an effective fear-fixer in times of need. Kids and adults alike tend to underestimate the power of the breath because it seems like too simple a solution to a very serious problem. Your own certainty about the true effectiveness of Breathwork—drawn from medical and psychological research and, hopefully, your own personal experience—will go a long way toward helping your child embrace this intervention enthusiastically. It is also a medical fact that belief in the efficacy of an intervention increases the efficacy of that intervention, so help your child benefit the most from Breathwork by letting him know that millions of people worldwide successfully calm their feelings of intense fear by focusing their attention on their breath.

USING THE BREATH TO ACHIEVE EMOTIONAL REGULATION: THE IMMEDIATE RELIEF OF FEELINGS OF PANIC, WORRY AND FEAR

Concentrating on the breath not only diverts attention away from frightening thoughts and feelings (which is very helpful in itself), it also directly alters physiological processes to induce greater states of calm. A child or teen who uses Breathwork regularly for a brief refreshing pause, for deep relaxation or to prepare for sleep will also be able to use it to effectively calm anxious feelings that arise in the moment. When anxious feelings are strong, however, patience will be required: it can take many minutes of using one's breathing technique before the stressful feelings start to dissipate. Although Breathwork helps the parasympathetic nervous system (calming system) to start working and simultaneously stops the further release of fight-or-flight chemistry into the bloodstream, any fear chemistry that has already been released is still active within the body—it doesn't just suddenly disappear. In fact, this is why people can still be shaking a long time after a near car crash or why they might have trouble sleeping for days after a severe fright. Nonetheless, those who have already installed breathing patterns into their brains are able to hasten the return of normal, calmer feelings in frightening moments. For instance, someone who has not installed a breathing pattern may continue to experience the effects of an aroused fight-or-flight system for as long as thirteen hours after the triggering event occurred, whereas a person who has installed a breathing pattern with daily practice may be able to return to baseline in as little as five minutes after a triggering event. Training and practice make a significant difference.

Even small amounts of stress chemistry take time to leave the system. Therefore, breathing patterns can and should be used for small stresses as well as for full-blown panic attacks. In order to reduce both the buildup and the aftereffects of stress chemistry, advise your child to start focusing attention on the breath *as soon as he starts to feel tense* rather than waiting until feelings of fear become overwhelming. Of course, many children (and adults) are not really aware of early, more subtle feelings of anxiety. By the time they realize they are in trouble, they are already intensely anxious. Giving a child a clear map of how anxiety builds and moves along its wave can help the youngster intervene at the earliest possible time. Here's how to explain it.

Introduce your child to the wave concept, explaining that feelings usually start off small, build bigger and then shrink down to size again. Draw the wave on paper so the child can really visualize this process. Explain to him that using a breathing pattern during the early part of the wave yields quicker and easier results because the breath has less work to do—there's not so much chemistry to deal with yet. When anxious feelings are left to build to a peak, there is a lot of chemistry that the breath needs to deal with, and this will take a little more time and effort. Ask your child to get in the habit of *noticing* the intensity of his fearful feelings—where are they along the wave? On a ten-point scale, a ten is an extremely strong fear—the kind that a teenage girl might experience when hearing a sudden loud banging noise in the house where she is babysitting. It is at the very top of the wave. Again, pointing to the location on the wave on an actual drawing will help the child integrate the concepts best. Show the child where zero will be on the diagram, zero being no fear whatsoever. It occurs before or after the wave. A two or three is just a bit of an uneasy feeling—at the very beginning or very end of a wave. Talk to your child about the intensity of his fearful feelings and have him share his ratings with you when he is feeling anxious or fearful. You can also help your child develop an accurate subjective fear scale by asking about the intensity of different types of fears he commonly feels ("How much fear on the ten-point scale do you feel when you have to stay in the house alone for an hour at night?" "How much fear do you feel when a wasp is flying around you?" "How much fear do you feel when you think about giving your book report?") Tell your child to start practicing a breathing technique when fear is at a two—just to gain practice in moving the fear down. Once the child is able to calm his small fear, encourage the use of the breathing technique in the following kinds of circumstances:

- when the child feels very nervous before an undertaking (e.g., before a performance, examination, procedure or competitive event)
- when the child is physically afraid (e.g., afraid of getting a needle, afraid of a thunderstorm, nervous about getting on a ride at an amusement park, afraid to vomit, afraid to ski down the hill, afraid to put his head under the water, etc.)
- when the child is having trouble falling asleep
- when the child feels physically keyed up or agitated due to stress
- when the child has stress-related pain (like a headache or stomachache) or other physical symptoms

SARAH CHANA RADCLIFFE

- when the child can't stop worrying about something
- when the child has experienced a big fright (e.g., after putting out a fire that he started on the stove)
- when the child is engaged in an activity that provokes anxious feelings (e.g., going to school on the first day of the school year, engaging in any first-time experience, writing a test, giving a book report, asking someone on a date, etc.)

You can see that once a child knows how to employ Breathwork, he has a portable self-help tool, his own personal "chill pill," that can be used in virtually any life situation. The installed breathing pattern can also be likened to a life jacket that the child carries in his pocket, ready to pull out at any time. Sometimes, using this life jacket, the child will be able to float safely to shore—nothing else will be needed. At other times, the life jacket will keep the child afloat while waiting for other rescue measures to arrive—whatever is needed to return the child to feelings of safety and security.

OTHER FOCUSING TECHNIQUES

Despite its merits, Breathwork isn't for all kids—some just can't get into it, can't figure out how to do it or don't have the patience to allow its effects to grow strong enough over time. There is no one fear-buster that works for everyone every time; fortunately, there are many other things that a child can do to take the edge off tense and frightened feelings. Here are more techniques that accomplish the same thing as Breathwork without using the breath as a focus of attention.

Eye Focus (Soft Eyes)

The first technique uses the eyes to change the child's focus of attention. A child who is feeling anxious about an upcoming event is focusing her attention on that event. To get a break from the resultant stress, the child can use her eyes to shift her focus to something that induces feelings of deep relaxation. As for Breathwork, the child must build a pathway in her brain that can turn on what Dr. Herbert Benson calls the Relaxation Response. The Relaxation Response is a wonderful, calm, sometimes even euphoric feeling that takes over one's entire body and mind. It is incompatible with feelings of stress and fear.

Some kids will find it easier to build the relaxation pathway using their eyes rather than their breath. Once the pathway is built, it can be used daily to lower the child's overall stress level and it can also be used in specific situations to increase feelings of calm and relaxation. The eyes can be trained to focus in such a way that the brain automatically turns on the Relaxation Response. Because the focus involves softening the gaze, we'll call this method *Soft Eyes.* You can teach your child how to do Soft Eyes by using a wonderful series of books called Magic Eye.

There are several titles in this collection of three-dimensional stereograms (pictures that pop into 3-D when the viewer softens her eyes in just the right way), but an excellent one to start with is *Beyond 3D: Improve Your Vision with Magic Eye.* Viewing the book is great fun (for kids and adults alike) and, at the same time, it actually trains the brain how to hit the right spot (i.e., the right brain wave frequency) for triggering the release of calming brain chemistry. As soon as the child can see the image in 3-D, her brain will be flooded with good-feeling chemistry. Ask your child to notice what she is *doing* with her eyes when the image becomes three dimensional and how she is *feeling* in her body right at that time. Encourage her to try to hold the 3-D image for as long as possible (and as long as comfortable). The goal is for your child to be able to get into the "zone"—the zone of the Relaxation Response.

If you have an older child or teen who tends to frequently feel stressed, worried or otherwise fearful, explain that looking at the Magic Eye images (or any other stereograms) for a few minutes a day can help the brain become calmer over time. Nowadays, 3-D stereograms are also available as apps for one's phone or tablet, making it easier than ever to practice the Soft Eyes technique throughout the day. In addition, explain that it is possible to soften the eyes in the Soft Eyes way, even when the book or app isn't available. Doing so can help the brain calm down in the moment. Once the child has practiced the Soft Eyes method for a couple of weeks, she should be able to use Soft Eyes in any of the stressful or frightening kinds of situations described in the Breathwork section earlier. When she feels tense, worried or afraid, she should soften her eyes and focus her attention on the feeling inside her brain—the same very pleasant feeling she can generate when looking at a Magic Eye picture. (It helps to try the Magic Eye book yourself, so you'll know the feeling well enough to guide your child's attention to it.)

Although people can learn to soften their eyes without looking at anything in particular, most kids will find it easier to do Soft Eyes if they actually do look at something—anything. For instance, the child can soften her eyes while gazing at her thumbnail (which is conveniently present all the time) or even at a wall. Another portable Soft Eyes tool is a nail-size rose quartz stone. The stone itself can be purchased from science stores, some children's toy stores, crystal stores and online, and shouldn't cost more than a couple of dollars. It can be kept in a pencil case, purse or pocket. It is also possible to purchase a key chain with rose quartz attached to it, which is particularly convenient for the intended purpose. The child simply gazes at the rose quartz the way she has gazed at a Magic Eye picture. The quartz offers visual depth that makes it much easier to get the right Soft Eyes location quickly. (As a bonus, a rose quartz held close to the body can help stabilize the heart center, adding another physically calming effect. Interestingly, children are often intuitively drawn to healing stones and like to just hold them or place them under a pillow, finding them somehow soothing or calming. In fact, children are probably responding to the properties within crystals that science is currently exploring and utilizing.)*

---

* For those who are curious as to how stones might have healing effects, see Dr. Richard Gerber's book *Vibrational Medicine.*

Ear Focus

Instead of using the eyes to focus attention away from fear, a child can use his ears. As with Breathwork and eye focusing, a child who prefers this way of regulating emotion should be encouraged to use it regularly—a few minutes each day—to achieve the most profound results.

The simple technique involves focusing attention on the sounds in one's environment. It is an excellent anti-rumination tool, fondly embraced by many adults. (Try it when walking, standing in line, doing household tasks and so on—you'll quickly appreciate how calming and pleasant it can be.) When teaching the technique to a young child, it's best to do it with the youngster until you are sure he can do it independently. Just before bedtime, ask the child to close his eyes and name a sound that he hears in the environment. The sound can be footsteps in the hallway, the sound of air conditioning or heating coming through the vents, the sound of cars outside the window and so on. It's okay to name the same sounds over and over. Continue naming sounds for a minute or so. With very young kids, you might have to do the exercise in just this way for a number of weeks before you can ask the child to close his eyes and do it independently. For an older child, one or two practice sessions may be all that is necessary before the child can close his eyes and do the exercise *silently*. Teens can skip the out-loud practice sessions altogether and go straight to the silent version of this exercise. When introducing the silent method to a child of any age, give instructions as follows:

> *You can do this exercise with eyes open or closed. Pay attention to the sounds you hear all around you. You can name them if you like, but you don't have to. If you notice that you are thinking about something else, just let the thought pass by like a cloud—stop thinking about it and start listening again to the sounds you hear around you, noticing them one at a time.*

This is a great technique for kids who obsess, ruminate and worry. When they notice that they're thinking unproductive, scary thoughts, they can take a break and focus on the sounds they hear around them. If there are plenty of obvious noises around them (e.g., traffic, kids playing, laughter, music and so on) it will be easy to name or attend to sounds. But even when the environment is quiet, there are always noises that can be attended to. Encourage the child to pretend that he is visually impaired and must rely on sounds in order to navigate the environment. When walking outdoors, the child can concentrate on the sounds of his shoes hitting the pavement. Kids can listen to the sounds of themselves eating and breathing, the sounds of a slight breeze rustling through a small bush, or the sound of an airplane in the distance. While listening, the child cannot simultaneously worry or focus attention on scary thoughts and feelings. This kind of listening is also a form of mindfulness meditation, a practice of enhancing awareness of the events occurring in the present moment. Present-moment awareness tends to soothe and balance the nervous system, providing an immediate break from stress. Used regularly, it helps to build a calmer brain.

Word or Mental Image Focus
Another way of using focused attention to regulate emotion is paying attention to a word, phrase or visual image. This strategy involves moving attention away from frightened feelings and anxious thoughts to a word, phrase or image that elicits a Relaxation Response. It is similar to Breathwork, but different in that the breath itself is not an important part of the process (although it normally slows down by itself during the course of the exercise). The trick is to choose a word, phrase or image that does not produce any internal conflict. While some anxious kids might be able to think words like *calm, peaceful, courage, I am strong, God is with me* and so on, others will find that such words *fight* with their actual feelings of fear, insecurity and worry. For this reason, I suggest that children and teens pick a word, phrase or mental image that naturally elicits a warm, happy feeling.

The choice will be highly personal. Here are some words and images that kids have chosen:

- bunny (or panda bear, koala bear or other favorite animal)
- chocolate bar (or lollipop, ice cream or other favorite food)
- Grandma (or Grandpa, a hero, a role model or someone loved or admired)
- family pet (e.g., bird, hamster, dog, cat)
- rainbow (or lake, stars, sunshine, snowflakes, flowers, butterflies or other natural beauty)
- balloons (or another symbol of celebration and joy)
- imaginary characters (from comics, movies or other media)
- supercalifragilisticexpialidocious (or other funny words)
- new clothes (or accessories, jewelry, shoes or other fashion items)
- tech toys (e.g., a smartphone, tablet, video game, etc.)
- teddy bear (or other stuffed animal, doll or favorite toy)

Teenagers might choose the refrain of their favorite song, a meaningful saying, a personal goal, a happy memory or anything else that makes them feel calm and joyful. One teen said, "When I start to feel stressed, I think of my part in the play at camp, picturing my solo over and over again. In a few seconds, I feel completely relaxed and happy."

To teach this technique, give your child the following instructions (Steps 1 to 3 are optional, to help give a head start on calming down; the exercise can begin at Step 4, if you prefer):

1. Breathe in, counting slowly and rhythmically to four.
2. Breathe out, counting slowly and rhythmically to four.
3. Continue breathing in and out, but count a little slower now.
4. Think of something that makes you feel happy and calm— you can choose a word, a phrase or a mental picture like a memory or an image of something or some place you like. You can think of something that you enjoy, something

good that happened or something that would be wonderful if it happened in the future. For instance, you can think about your favorite dessert, or you can remember the night you won the prize for public speaking or you can think about how nice it will be when we go on vacation next week. Continue saying your word or phrase over and over, or thinking about your happy scene for a few minutes, and notice how your body feels when you do this. If other thoughts pop into your mind, just let them pass by like clouds and return your attention to your words or your happy picture.

Body Focus

This exercise is a little different in that it doesn't directly attempt to instill calmness. Rather, calmness is a natural by-product of body focus. In this exercise, the child pays attention to the way *fear feels* in her body. The child watches the fear without trying to change it in any way. In fact, the youngster takes the attitude of a camera: an objective observer just noting what is happening without passing any judgment one way or the other. Like other practices that cultivate nonjudgmental present-moment awareness, body focus can be considered a form of mindfulness meditation. To help your child do it, instruct her as follows:

1. Close your eyes and try to find where the fear feels strongest in your body. Check your head, face, chest, stomach, legs—even check your hands and feet.
2. When you find where the fear is, just notice what it feels like—whether your body feels tight, or heavy, or light, or if it feels like something is pounding, fluttering, moving or churning, or whether it feels like something is pinching, pressing or squeezing. Maybe something feels like it's tied up in a knot. Whatever it is, just notice it.
3. Now watch the fear as if you are a camera: follow what it

is doing, noticing if it stays the same or changes or moves. Just keep watching it for a few minutes. If you want to, you can describe it to yourself as you are watching—you can say things like "my heart is beating, I'm holding my breath, there's a knot in my stomach, there's a pressure on the top of my head and around my eyes, my lips are squeezing tight" and so on. Just notice all the physical sensations without saying whether they are good or bad. Keep noticing for a couple of minutes and then just end the exercise by taking a deep breath in and out.

4. That's all for now. If you still feel the fear later on, you can watch it again for a few minutes. Do this anytime you feel scared.

Watching fear usually has the effect of causing it to diminish. (For some reason, fear "appreciates" being attended to; once acknowledged or observed, a large part of it tends to melt away.) However, even if the fear stays the same, the ability to *watch* it rather than *react* to it is, itself, a powerful form of emotional regulation. Odd as it seems, a person can actually calmly watch her fear. This brings an element of control to what might otherwise feel like an out-of-control experience of panic or fear. Just being able to watch the fear also reduces the child's fear of fear—and this leads to an overall reduction in anxious and frightened feelings over time.

Heart Focus
The heart can send calming rhythms throughout the body, quickly transforming agitated and anxious states into calm, coherent states. In Chapter Three, we saw how parents can help calm a child's heart center using the gentle form of acupressure we called the Heart Hold. As we saw there, it is also possible to show a child how to do this emotional reset exercise for himself. Show the child how to access the power of the heart in any of the following three ways.

Heart Hold

Apply gentle pressure by pressing two or three fingers into the Sea of Tranquility point in the center of the chest, parallel to the heart (a couple of inches above the base of the breastbone). Hold the point while breathing slowly and gently for a few minutes.

Coherent Heart-Based Breath

Place a full hand (or two hands—one hand on top of the other) across the center of the chest, over the heart, and breathe slowly and rhythmically for a couple of minutes. Make a continuous breath, counting slowly (in-two-three-four, out-two-three-four, in-two-three-four, out-two-three-four) for at least a minute, but longer if possible. Breathe without holding the breath at any point or pausing.

HeartMath

Older kids and teens (and parents) may especially appreciate the app-assisted or computer-assisted heart-based stress-reduction technique called HeartMath (see *The HeartMath Solution* and *Transforming Anxiety*, both by Doc Childre). HeartMath tools and research are also available online. HeartMath devices, such as their smartphone app, help the user improve a measure called heart-rate variability— the beat-to-beat changes in the heart that are correlated with various emotional states. Learning to produce the heart-rate variability pattern that is associated with calm energy allows a person to replace fear (and other negative emotions) with happier and calmer feelings. HeartMath is one of my personal favorite emotional regulation tools, as it is fun, fast and powerful.

All of the above variations of "focusing techniques"—breath focus, eye focus, ear focus, word or mental image focus, body focus and heart focus—help a youngster learn to control his attention. He can then use this skill to prevent, address or quickly recover from high states of emotional discomfort like fear, worry or panic. Long-term use of these emotional regulation strategies helps the child build a calmer brain that is less prone to anxious feelings.

USE IMAGINATION

Now we will look at several other types of techniques that are also effective tools for emotional regulation. The first one is the use of imagination. We saw in Chapter Three how a parent can use the power of imagination to help a child feel less fearful. Now we will see how a child, herself, can use imagination for that same purpose. As I said before, most feelings of fear stem from negative imagination— mental pictures of things going wrong. A child who is afraid to go on a roller coaster, for instance, is at some level imagining that she will suffer injury or disaster on the ride. With such a picture in mind, she will, of course, feel frightened. But what if she pictured arriving safely at the end of the ride? Similarly, a child who is afraid to sleep in her dark room is, at some level, picturing monsters or robbers or other dangerous people coming to hurt her in the night. What if she pictured a protective, impenetrable shield all around her bed so that she could sleep in a dome of safety?

Not all kids can use visual imagination to elicit powerful feelings of safety and protection. However, very few kids even learn that doing so is a possibility! You can teach your child to create safety tools and images and practice using them. A certain percentage of children will find this strategy useful for the rest of their lives—you won't know if your child is in this group unless you give her the opportunity to learn and practice the technique.

Here are some ideas for introducing the concept and value of Positive Imagination to your child:

1. Scary images aren't real, but they can really make you nervous; protective images aren't real either, but they can really make you feel safe.
   - For teens or science-oriented younger kids, you can go further into the biochemical reality of this proposition by explaining: Simply picturing a frightening event generates fight-or-flight chemistry that surges through every cell of the body and causes uncomfortable sensations of

fear that, in themselves, generate even more fear chemistry. Picturing a happy or pleasant scenario similarly sends calming chemistry to every body cell that helps calm and soothe body, mind and emotions.

2. Positive images are more "real" than scary ones. Scary images have a very, very small likelihood of coming true, whereas images of positive outcomes are statistically much more likely and therefore more realistic (e.g., arriving safely at the end of the roller coaster ride is much more likely to happen than is suffering pain or injury on the ride).

   • Again, for the older or more sophisticated crowd, you can explain: It is possible to die in a plane crash, get robbed, get struck by lightning and so on. Picturing these disasters is simply not a good use of one's time. For instance, if a child has to write a ten-page research paper on the life cycle of ants, she should probably spend a certain amount of time researching different kinds of ants, where they live, how they mate, how they die, what they do when they're alive and so on. If the child spends 99 percent of her work time making sure that a single letter t is properly formed in the first sentence of the project, she is not using her time well. It's not that it isn't important to cross the t properly— it's just that some things are not worth spending so much time on, especially when you've got a really big project to do. Similarly, when one is in one's home on a rainy Sunday evening—doing homework, eating dinner, playing around and so on—it's just not a good use of time to concentrate all one's thoughts on getting killed by lightning. Yes, it's possible, but not possible enough to spend time on it. A better use of that time is to pay close attention to the cozy feelings of being sheltered from the storm in a warm, loving home—an experience that is happening for real, every minute of the storm.

3. Scary images poison your body and mind with stress chemicals, causing you harm over time; positive and protective images are good for you in every way, making you stronger, healthier and happier in the long run.

4. Painting scary images is just a bad habit; however, the habit picture stays in your brain unless you create a new habit picture in that same place. For instance, there is a place in your brain that thinks about elevators in a certain, scary way—that is, every time you think of an elevator, you also think of getting stuck in it. Your elevator picture will always contain a picture of you getting stuck in it unless you purposely create a new picture in that place. You could picture an elevator and see yourself getting on and off it safely, for example. But if you don't make the new picture, the old one stays there forever. If you already have a scary picture in your brain about something, you can always change it by making a new good picture. Then you make the new picture bigger and stronger by thinking about it often. This works equally well for pictures that you made up in the first place (like a picture of being robbed when you were never robbed) as for pictures that come from a previous real experience (like worrying about having a car crash because you had that car crash last year).

Instructions for creating positive images are as follows:

- Think of something that you are worried about. Notice the scary scene you are picturing. Notice how that makes you feel (pay close attention to the way your body feels when you think of that picture). Now picture a good scene happening instead. Notice how that makes you feel. For instance, think about giving your book report to the class and picture the kids falling asleep or saying mean things. Now picture them sitting up, listening and asking good questions; see them nodding, smiling and laughing at the funny parts. Spend a few minutes a day practicing creating positive scenes. You can also draw pictures of the positive outcome (like a room full of smiling faces) and place the picture around your bedroom or even around the house where you will frequently see it (e.g., near or on the computer, on the bathroom mirror, on the front closet, etc.).

- Think of something that you are scared of (e.g., dogs, lightning, spiders, etc.). Make up an imaginary defense weapon or shield (like an impenetrable dome, an invisible repellent cream, a protective bodyguard, a digital antidote or whatever). Imagine that you have this protection with you every time you are confronted by your feared object.

Once you have taught your child how to play around with images, you can remind her to draw on them in the moment they are needed:

Child: *I don't want to go upstairs by myself.*
Parent: *I can't come with you right now, honey. Just take your Guard Lions with you.*

TAPPING-IN MEMORIES

Now that you've encouraged your child to access helpful images, you can go a step further. As we just noted, memories are also images—in many cases, visual images. A positive memory can be used to help calm anxious feelings. Let's say that a child is nervous about taking a swimming test. The nervous feelings are overwhelming his brain, making it hard for him to remember that he is a good swimmer who has already passed many swimming tests. In fact, it almost feels as if this is the first test he has ever taken—he cannot access the part of his brain that feels competent. Mom reminds her son that he is a good swimmer, but the information falls on deaf ears. The youngster still feels extremely nervous about the test.

A technique called "Tapping-In," developed by Dr. Laurel Parnell, can help to remedy the situation. Alternately tapping on one's body—the left side, then the right side—stimulates both the left brain and the right brain in such a way as to provide whole-brain integration. Right now, this child's left brain *knows* that he is a good swimmer, but his right brain *feels* intense fear. By stimulating the left and right brain while remembering previous successes, the child will finally have access to his sense of competence. Tapping this way allows the child to both *know* (left brain) and *feel* (right brain) his strength, thereby diminishing his fear.

Let's see how a modified version of this technique works, using the example of a child who is feeling anxious about an upcoming speech he has to give at school. Mom helps the youngster remember a particularly successful talk that he gave last year. She asks him to recall the best part of that talk. Then Mom tells the child to pay attention to that good memory and particularly the good feelings that the memory elicits. She instructs her son to begin tapping on the side of his legs using his fingers or hands, tapping first the left leg and then the right leg. Here's what Mom says exactly:

> *Remember the really good feeling you felt when you gave*
> *that talk? Think to yourself, "Everyone loved that talk!"*
> *See their smiling faces. Feel the warm, relaxed feeling right*
> *inside your chest and all over your body. Notice how relaxed*
> *your forehead feels as you remember the big round of*
> *applause you received. Now, while feeling the good feelings*
> *as much as you can, tap your thighs (or knees, if sitting*
> *down) one at a time, really slowly like this: left leg . . . right*
> *leg . . . left leg . . . right leg . . . left leg . . . right leg (three taps*
> *on each leg, alternating left and right—six taps in total).*
> *Stop tapping now and take a deep breath in and out.*
>
> *Tap again, the same as before, nice and slowly while*
> *thinking about the good feeling you had when you gave*
> *your speech. Remember how well it went and how great*
> *you felt: left leg . . . right leg . . . left leg . . . right leg . . . left*

leg . . . right leg. Stop tapping and take a deep breath in and out.

Let's do one last round of tapping, remembering that really good feeling of giving a great speech and thinking, "They loved my speech": left leg . . . right leg . . . left leg . . . right leg . . . left leg . . . right leg. Stop tapping and breathe in and out.

When you start to feel worried about the speech you are giving next week, just think of last year's talk and how successful it was, while you tap left-right on your legs a few times like we did just now.

EMOTIONAL HEALING: LETTING FEAR TALK

So far, we've looked at techniques for emotional regulation that primarily involve turning attention *away* from fearful feelings. However, as we saw in Chapter Two, turning attention *to* fearful feelings can also help soothe and calm them. You, as the parent, facilitated this process through the act of emotional coaching—gently welcoming and nonjudgmentally accepting your child's feelings. Your child can also learn to welcome and accept her own feelings and, by doing so, help *release* them. The following exercise, adapted from Jeffrey Brantley's Mindfulness-Yes technique, can be practiced before bedtime each day to help "clear the day" of accumulated worries and stress. This practice helps promote a better sleep. It can also be done whenever there is an intense reaction to something going on in the child's life—fear or worry triggered by someone's illness, an upcoming change, a test or performance, a social challenge of some kind and so on.

In this exercise, you will teach your child how to be her own therapist. Offer the following instructions:

Set aside a few minutes to be with yourself and your feelings. Say what you are feeling. For example, you might

say, "I'm mad at Lisa," or "I'm worried about Grandma."
(The exercise can be done out loud with a young child;
older kids and teens can name their feeling out loud or
just think it to themselves silently.) After you name your
feeling, say the word "yes" nice and s-l-o-w-l-y. Continue
naming your feelings for a few minutes until you feel
calmer.

Here is an example of how this exercise might sound in action:

I don't want to participate in English class—I'm afraid I'll
    say something dumb.
Y-e-s.
The teacher will mock me and everyone will laugh.
Y-e-s.
The teacher is so mean.
Y-e-s.
I really hate her.
Y-e-s.
Anyway, I'm not more stupid than anyone else.
Y-e-s.
And if I don't say something once in a while, I'll lose marks
for lack of participation.
Y-e-s.
I'm just going to answer anyway—everyone else does.
Y-e-s.
I don't care if it's the wrong answer.
Y-e-s.

When you are teaching Mindfulness-Yes to an adolescent, you can
offer a more sophisticated version. Ask the child to name thoughts,
feelings and body sensations and follow each with a slow "yes." Your
instructions might sound like this:

I know you're worried about the operation. One way to

help yourself is to name a few thoughts you're having,
following each one with a nice, slow "yes." Then, name a
few emotions that you feel, again following each one with
a nice, slow "yes." Then notice how your body is feeling
and name a few physical sensations, following each one
with a slow "yes." Then start the process again with more
thoughts, feelings and sensations until you feel better.

The beginning of the child's exercise might sound something like this:

I don't want to have surgery.
Y-e-s.
It's going to hurt.
Y-e-s.
I'm going to miss too much school.
Y-e-s.
I'm scared.
Y-e-s.
I feel sick thinking about it.
Y-e-s.
I hate that this has to happen.
Y-e-s.
My head hurts when I think about this.
Y-e-s.
My neck is tight.
Y-e-s.
I feel tense.
Y-e-s.

The child would continue rounds of thoughts, feelings and physical sensations until some or all of the stressful feelings cleared.

Try this exercise on one of your own worries or fears first. It helps far more to know what it *feels* like than what it sounds like! Notice how the exercise helps your feelings flow, moving them out of a painful stuck position so that they can complete their wave. In fact, you might think that the first example dialogue sounds unrealistic, as the child appears to resolve difficult feelings way too quickly. However, Mindfulness-Yes can really work just like that. Alternatively, it might sound to you—if you were able to listen to someone else do the exercise out loud—like she is still feeling upset or stressed at the end of it. However, if you had the opportunity to ask the person about her feelings afterward, you'd likely find that she feels a whole lot better than before.

THE DIARY TECHNIQUE

A child is more likely to recognize his own feelings when he has a daily habit of recording them. You can teach your child how to keep a short daily diary (in a beautiful leather-bound journal or a secure online venue). Encourage the youngster to record the events of his life and particularly his emotional reactions to them. Children aren't born knowing how to use a diary, so don't assume that your child will be able to make good use of this emotional release strategy without your specific instructions. Tell him to record both good-feeling events and bad-feeling events, to search for both kinds as he reviews his day. If he is just starting a diary, ask him to use the same search-and-record process for a fairly brief summary of recent events (the past weeks or months), as well as of long-term events (the highlights and lowlights of his life so far). Then he can start the daily record-ing process fairly up to date. If a child can only make entries every couple of days or even weekly, that's fine too—the main thing is to have a process that invites introspection. Of course, the child needs to know that the privacy of the diary will never be violated. A diary can help prevent feelings from building up to intolerable levels, as the act of putting emotions into words has the effect of releasing much of their negative charge. Take the diary-education opportunity to let your child know that it is always good to discuss one's strug-gles and feelings out loud with someone as well. Let the child know

SARAH CHANA RADCLIFFE

that friends, siblings, parents or even a mental-health professional are available to talk to when there's an upset, challenge or disturbed feeling to address.

AN INNOVATIVE TOOL FOR EMOTIONAL RELEASE: TAPPING

Anxious feelings are often stronger than the logical mind. Even when a child *knows* there's really nothing to be worried about, she can still *feel* very fearful. In the past twenty years, some new mind-body strategies have been developed that have helped millions of people calm their anxious, worried or frightened feelings *very quickly*— often in a matter of minutes. Mind-body techniques address both the left (logical) brain and the right (emotional) brain, helping to achieve the whole-brain healing that results in physical, emotional and mental calm. Although these techniques, in the hands of a skilled psychotherapist, are powerful enough to clear a person's terror and deep-seated trauma from life-threatening events like car accidents, violent attacks, tsunamis and war, they are also simple enough, safe enough and convenient enough to be used in the home as a self-help tool for many everyday stresses and worries.

One of the most child-friendly forms of this sort of mind-body strategy is called "Tapping" (despite the similar name, this is actually a completely different technique from Tapping-In, which we looked at earlier). Tapping can help relieve all distressed feelings, including fear, anger, overwhelm, jealousy, low mood, hurt and sadness. Tapping can also help relieve physical pain such as headaches, joint pain, back pain, stomachaches and other health concerns. In this section, we will look at the use of Tapping only as it relates to the home treatment of frightened, anxious and worried feelings.

Tapping was originally developed by anxiety-disorder specialist Dr. Roger Callahan, who called the process "Thought Field Therapy." The treatment has undergone several modifications by other practitioners over the past twenty years and has been validated as effective in many controlled research studies. Current popular variations are Gary Craig's Emotional Freedom Technique (EFT) and Dr. Patricia Carrington's EFT Choices Method.

All forms of Tapping involve tapping lightly on your own or your child's body while you or your child is thinking about, and feeling, a distressed emotion like fear. Younger children might say the feelings out loud, while older kids can do the exercise silently. As you will see, the child names and pictures her fear at each of eight tapping points. Suppose, for example, that a teenager is afraid she won't know what to say on a date. While using this technique, the youngster will repeat eight times, "I'm afraid I won't know what to say." Please note: If she were concentrating on that phrase eight times *without* tapping, she would actually be practicing her fear, building a larger fearful section in her brain through the effects of repetition. However, if she says it eight times *while tapping*, then she will be breaking up the neural pathway that stores this fear. The end result will be a reorganization of the fear into a set of healthier, calmer thoughts, feelings, physical sensations and action tendencies. Dr. Callahan described this process as a healing of a perturbation or disturbance in the energy system.

The Tapping points are special points along meridian pathways in the body—the pathways that acupuncturists use for the treatment of pain and illness. In fact, Tapping is a form of acupressure for emotional well-being—an intervention that rapidly reorganizes thoughts, feelings, physical sensations and behavior by removing blockages in the energy system. While we don't yet understand all the mechanisms involved in this process, one thing has been clearly substantiated in clinical practice and research: tapping on a fear changes *everything* about that fear both in the moment and for the future. Let's look at an example of the use of Tapping:

Sheri was afraid of mice. She was having breakfast one day, when a small mouse suddenly dashed across the floor. Sheri screamed hysterically as she jumped up on her chair. Mom came running to see what had happened. Though there was no mouse in sight, Sheri was sobbing in terror. *"There's a mouse! Help! Help! There's a mouse!"* In Sheri's brain, the concept of *"mouse"* was stored in four dysfunctional ways: *(1)* Sheri had a cognitive distortion (messed-up belief) that a little rodent was somehow dangerous to her; *(2)* she experienced the physiology of fear as her body released high levels of adrenaline and other fear chemistry; *(3)* she felt the emotions of fear and revulsion; and *(4)* she experienced an instantaneous behavioral reaction to the perceived threat (jumping on the chair automatically).

After one session of Tapping, Sheri's reaction to mice was permanently altered in four ways: *(1)* she no longer had a distorted belief about the little rodents, seeing them now for what they were—little, harmless animals; *(2)* she remained physiologically "normal" in the presence of a mouse, as her brain no longer released fear chemistry; *(3)* she felt emotionally calm in the presence of a mouse; and *(4)* she no longer had an irresistible urge to jump on a chair when spotting a mouse.

Indeed, when Sheri encountered a mouse a couple of weeks after her Tapping session, she remained totally relaxed and settled. *"Mommy, I think that mouse is back. I just saw him run across the dining room."* There was no more hysteria or tears. Sheri was cured!

Tapping can help relieve all types of fear: fear of people, animals, objects or places; fear of doing things; fear of change; fear of failure; fear of rejection; fear of emotional or physical pain; rational fears; irrational fears; worries; anxieties; vague fears; fears caused by traumatic experiences; and so on. It can also release the small or big stresses that might underlie fear. Of course, like any technique, it doesn't work all the time for every single person who tries it. However, it works so incredibly well for so many children, teens and adults that it is definitely worth experimenting with. If your child's fear is intense or if you would rather not learn the method yourself, you can certainly take your child to one of the many therapists around the world who are trained in Tapping techniques. These professionals can often help resolve a child's fear rapidly, and they can also teach the child how to use Tapping independently to manage her own feelings of fear or stress in the future. Tapping-based therapy for children without anxiety *disorders* can often be as brief as a session or two. Even when children do suffer from anxiety disorders, some therapists incorporate Tapping strategies into their treatment plan to augment other interventions. Parents looking for a therapist who uses Tapping techniques should search for licensed mental-health professionals who use Tapping under any of the following names: Tapping, EFT, EFT Choices Method, Energy Psychology, Meridian Psychotherapy or Thought Field Therapy.

How to Tap

The following instructions are a version of the standard EFT protocol developed by Gary Craig. See Appendix A (page 298) for further information, instructions and a sample transcript of how Tapping treatment sounds in action. The strategy is far easier to learn by watching than by reading instructions like those I've included here, so check out our instructional video at www.sarahchanaradcliffe.com.

1. Ask your child to select a fear or worry to work on and rate its intensity between zero and ten (ten being the highest intensity).
2. Have the child tap a few times, using the four fingers of her right hand, on the "Karate Chop point" (on the side of the hand, between the baby finger and the wrist—see the diagram on page 120).
3. Show the child a picture of the eight Tapping points (see the diagram on page 120) or point them out on your body. Ask her to tap lightly on each point on her body while naming, thinking about and feeling the fear. She should tap a few times at each location.
4. After she's finished tapping each of the eight points, ask

the child to take a big breath in and out and just rest for a moment.

After your child has rested, ask her what she is now thinking and feeling. She may have the same feeling as before, only weaker or stronger than before. If so, ask her to rate the current intensity of her fear between zero and ten and then repeat Steps 2, 3 and 4. On the other hand, she may have a different bothersome thought or feeling now. If so, ask her to rate the new thought or feeling and repeat Steps 2, 3 and 4. If she has the exact same thought or feeling with the same intensity as when she began treatment, then change Step 2. Instead of having her tap on the Karate Chop point, have her rub the Tender Spot for a few seconds. (The Tender Spot is located over the left breast, as shown in the diagram on page 120. It should be rubbed clockwise with the right hand—this spot is not tapped.) Then have her complete Steps 3 and 4. Continue until the child rates the fear at zero or simply cannot think about the fear anymore.

The Tapping Points
- top of the head
- eyebrow near the nose
- outer edge of the eyebrow
- under the eye, on the eye bone
- under the nose (in the little indentation over the lip)
- under the lip (in the little indentation on the chin)
- under the collarbone
- on the side of the body, a few inches below the underarm

The Karate Chop Point: This point is on the side of each hand, between the bottom of the baby finger and the wrist.
The Tender Spot Point: On an adult, this point is about two inches below the spot where the neck bones join at the bottom of the neck, and about one inch to the left. On a child, locate a similar point over the left chest. This spot should be rubbed in a circular motion instead of being tapped.

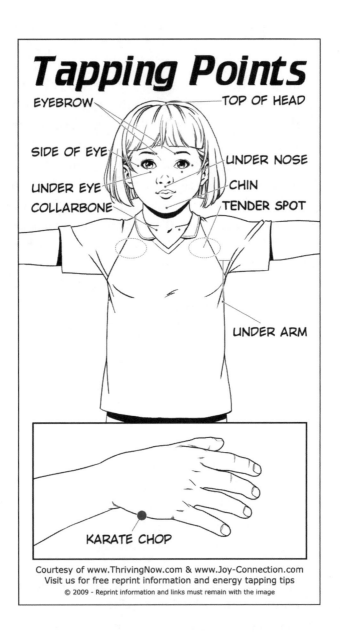

Courtesy of www.ThrivingNow.com & www.Joy-Connection.com
Visit us for free reprint information and energy tapping tips
© 2009 - Reprint information and links must remain with the image

CHAPTER FIVE

Helping Your Child through Worry

Worries about everything;
worries about a specific topic;
worries at night

Worrying is a painful mental habit. Everyone worries occasionally, but some adults and children worry more than others. Moreover, some worry about everything under the sun, while others "specialize"—worrying only about certain specific fears. For instance, a teen who is afraid of public speaking might worry day and night for a week before having to give a major presentation. However, apart from such occasions, this same young person might be relatively worry-free. Whether a child worries frequently or rarely, it's good to know that there are things that can be done to help calm his overactive mind.

Because every worried thought releases bad-feeling chemistry throughout the body, people tend to feel stressed after only a few minutes of worrying. Naturally, parents want to help their worried youngster relax and think good thoughts. Often, they'll tell their child exactly that: "Just calm down, relax and think good thoughts." Wouldn't it be great if this advice actually worked!

Unfortunately, a worrying child cannot simply shut off his noisy brain. From the child's point of view, he has no control over the worry process—rather, worrying seems to be *happening* to him—and he can't stop it from happening, just as a person cannot stop an itch from itching. It's not that he's *choosing* to worry. The worry is invading his brain. From a certain point of view, the way it feels is exactly the way it is. Let's use a metaphor to understand why: Some people love to shop online for books. In fact, many have a "one-click" account at an online seller in order to make the whole experience that much faster and easier. Whenever such a person goes to the site, she receives a greeting on her personalized page: "Hi, Alice! We have some suggestions for you." And then, scattered across the page are many of the kinds of books Alice loves: sock-knitting books, vegan cookbooks, parenting books, technology books, fitness books and biographies of successful entrepreneurs. Gosh! How did the bookseller know that Alice would love these selections? After all, there are thousands, maybe even millions, of books on the site and they managed to pick out a half dozen of Alice's favorite genres.

It's not that they're psychic or just very lucky. In fact, the bookseller didn't make that page at all—*Alice made it herself.* The smart computer figures out her preferences by simply paying attention to what Alice is doing. The website notes which books a shopper tends to click on when searching through the bookstore. It tracks how much time a person spends clicking on those books, and it knows if she's purchasing them. In other words, the website's "suggestions" are based completely on how much attention a person pays to certain kinds of books. Alice's personal home page is a product of everything that Alice has been paying attention to.

Now, if Alice stops paying attention to these kinds of books— she stops buying biographies, for example, and starts buying books on money management instead—guess what will happen? You've got it: eventually the website will stop suggesting biographies and start suggesting money-management and financial planning books instead. Of course, it will take a little while—there will be a delay while the computer waits to see if Alice has really lost interest in the biographical works. But after a time, it records a definite new pattern and stops flashing the old suggestions across her screen.

In exactly the same way, your child's brain (and yours) offers "suggestions" as to what to think about next. When a person wakes up in the morning, lies down at night or leaves a little space in his brain for wandering as he goes about daily activities, the screen appears (inside the mind): "Hi! We've got some suggestions for you!" And then, all his old favorites—the kinds of thoughts and images that he has been paying attention to on a regular basis—pop up on the screen. "Perhaps you'd like to worry about that pain in your stomach. Or maybe you'd be interested in thinking about whether the program will be canceled tonight. Could we interest you in obsessing about whether or not your application will be accepted? How about worrying about what Danny White said about you yesterday?"

On the receiving end, it feels like the thoughts just appeared in the person's mind. We've all had the experience of suddenly finding ourselves worrying about something because an anxious thought just "popped" into our mind. But that's not what really happened at all. That thought only appeared on our screen because we've been paying attention to its genre for quite a while now. When a thought pops into your mind, it only does so because of your personal thinking habits. *Whatever you choose to attend to frequently and intensely is what your mind will offer up.* Worried thoughts will continue to pop into your mind for as long as you choose to "click on them"— in other words, entertain them, reflect on them, repeat them, work with them, engage them and otherwise pay attention to them. This exact same process is occurring within your child's brain as well.

BUILDING A WORRIED BRAIN

Now that we've looked at the book-shopping metaphor, let's look at the process of worrying from a reality-based scientific paradigm. How does *paying attention* cause thoughts to multiply? There are three laws that ensure that worried thoughts will multiply in our brain if we choose to pay attention to them. Dr. Jeffrey Schwartz and Dr. Rebecca Gladding explain these laws fully in their book *You Are Not Your Brain.* Here is a short summary:

1. **Hebb's Law:** Neurons that fire together wire together.
2. **The Quantum Zeno Effect:** Focused attention is necessary for the wiring to occur.
3. **Attention Density:** The more attention the newly wired circuit receives, the bigger, stronger and more active it gets.

In ordinary English, these laws can be rewritten as follows:

1. Pay a lot of attention to a thought.
2. Keep paying attention to that thought, going back to it again and again.
3. When you apply Steps 1 and 2, you allow the brain to literally grow the thought, giving it its own expanded neural territory.

All acquired learning and memory occurs in this way. When we learn something new, impulses travel along preexisting neural pathways (the old "wiring"), making new connections through junctions called *synapses.* The more often the neural impulse travels through a particular synapse from one point to another along a neural circuit, the more efficient the synapse becomes at transmitting the information. With repeated firings through the synapse, information soon travels quickly and easily along the new circuit, eventually becoming automatic. Our thoughts and feelings—good or bad—run on automatic pilot once we practice them enough. We no longer have to "think" them—they just "happen."

Applying these three laws, we see that a person can build many worry circuits in the brain by giving their worried thoughts a lot of time and attention. Now, to be fair, we must realize that everyone's brain has been preprogrammed at birth with the tendency to pay attention to signs of danger. Anything that is problematic, worrisome, frightening or disturbing *will* call out for our attention. This process is in our best interests, helping us to remain vigilant for danger so that we can take steps to keep ourselves safe and healthy. The only problem is that this natural protective tendency can also work against us, causing us to continue to search for problems when there is no more necessity to do so. Repetitive thinking about what can go wrong (i.e., worrying), does *not* help! It just stresses us out.

THE WORRY CIRCUIT IN ACTION

Let's use this brain science to see how eleven-year-old Amy gets caught in a web of worry about going to camp.

> *Amy thinks about camp and starts to worry about how things will be for her there. Her mind fills with unpleasant images: the kids don't like her, the counselor is mean, the food is bad, she misses her dog and her bed. A camp-worry neural circuit is initiated in her brain. Amy tells Mom about her worry, and Mom sits down to talk with her. They talk for about ten minutes, during which time Mom offers reassurance and practical advice.*

One might think that Mom's intervention would cure the worry. However, after their little chat, Amy worries even more. This is not surprising: when Mom and Amy are talking about all the worries, they are, in fact, strengthening the camp-worry circuit due to the quantum Zeno effect—that is, the effect of focused attention. Focused attention holds two activated brain areas (e.g., thinking about camp and thinking about unhappy scenarios like having no friends, missing home, etc.) in place long enough for Hebb's Law to take effect. In other words, camp plus unhappy scenarios becomes a wired circuit in the brain—a circuit that will be easier and easier to access over time.

Nonetheless, just one episode of focused attention on camp-worry will not ingrain a really strong worry habit, just as lifting weights for an hour one afternoon will not build big, fat biceps. On the other hand, repetition of the circuit—coming back again and again to the camp-worry activity—is a good way to form a really strong superhighway of camp-worry in the brain, just as lifting weights for an hour several days a week for months on end will build really big, strong muscles. To build strong neural pathways, we apply the principle of repetition, called Attention Density. Attention Density states that the more times a person allows herself to indulge in worry, the stronger the worrying tendency will become. This is a physical reality: the neural pathways for the worry become more efficient the more frequently the neural impulses are allowed to run their course.

PRACTICE MAKES PERFECT

In short, focusing one's attention on a negative thought or feeling over and over again builds a strong negative tendency in the brain. To put it another way, *the more you worry, the more you will worry.* The more you worry right now, the more you'll be worrying in the future. It's just like learning to play a song on the piano: the more you practice, the more easily and quickly you'll be able to play it in the future because the brain will have acquired a strong, ready-to-run neural pathway. Practice makes perfect.

Now that Amy has a camp-worry circuit in her brain, her brain will go to it every time the topic of camp comes up. Hearing someone talking about camp can trigger the circuit. Looking at a picture of camp can trigger it. Unfortunately, just staring off into space can also trigger it, because the circuit can be activated by daydreaming, relaxing and lying in bed, since the circuit is on Amy's top ten most-visited thought list. Once it is activated, Amy just goes with it and worries. She acts as if she is now a victim of that circuit. She doesn't realize that she has a choice about whether to give attention to the camp-worry circuit. Amy didn't intentionally build a camp-worry circuit in her brain and she doesn't intentionally strengthen it. However, she is certainly unintentionally strengthening it every time she "indulges" in the activity of worrying.

As we have now seen, worrying is an activity—something that a person *does*. Although we say we are worried, what we should say is that we are thinking about unpleasant and scary scenarios. We're not "worried"—we are *worrying*. *Worrying* can be defined as "the act of paying attention to a frightened thought that has popped up." It consists of repeating the thought silently over and over or generating pictures of it. Essentially, worrying consists of focusing one's attention on negative thoughts and images.

We worry by concentrating our attention on what might go wrong in some future event.

> *"I'm worried about whether I'll get accepted into law school" means "I am focusing my attention on an image of myself opening a rejection letter."*

> *"I'm worried about giving my presentation" means "I am concentrating on a picture of myself forgetting my words, communicating poorly and giving an awful presentation."*

> *"I'm worried about Grandma" means "I am picturing Grandma's condition worsening."*

> *"I'm worried about you and Daddy getting divorced" means "I am thinking about what it will be like if you and Daddy get divorced."*

> *"I'm worried that I'll get lost" means "I am looking at an image of myself getting lost."*

> *"I'm worried that I'll forget my lines" means "I am picturing myself forgetting my lines."*

In each and every case of "being worried," a person is not only creating a disturbing image in his mind, but he is also focusing his attention on that image and returning his attention to that image again and again. In other words, the person is using all three physics principles (Hebb's Law, the quantum Zeno effect and Attention Density) to build big worry networks in the brain.

A CURE FOR WORRY

Dr. Schwartz and Dr. Gladding, like many other modern scientists, believe that we can literally "change our minds" using the principles of *neuroplasticity*—the brain's ability to rewire neural pathways to create new patterns of thinking and feeling. (See also Dr. Norman Doidge's book *The Brain That Changes Itself* for a fascinating description of the emotional and behavioral changes we can make when we know how.) Neuroplasticity allows a child to stop being a worrier and start being a Positive Thinker, even if that youngster was *born* with a tendency to engage in worrying.

Here's more good news: Schwartz and Gladding point out that the same focused attention (the quantum Zeno effect) and repetition (the principle of Attention Density) that lead to building a worried brain can be used to build a calm and positive brain—that is, to create a brain filled with strong *positive* brain circuits. What this means is that little Amy can focus her attention, over and over again, on something that makes her feel good when she thinks about camp. She will then be able to create a happy-camp circuit. The more that Amy practices paying attention to positive, good-feeling thoughts, feelings and images, the happier and more positive she will become, because she will have many more positive brain circuits running. Being a Positive Thinker is the result of the *habit* of matching problems with positive images and then paying frequent attention to those good-feeling images.

Note that helping your child to become a Positive Thinker is not just a matter of telling her to "think happy thoughts" or "stop worrying" or "use affirmations"—all of which are extremely vague instructions that are hard for a child to apply in practice. Rather, this is a practical step-by-step process that you can teach to your child to enable her to literally rewire her own brain. Remember: *the more one focuses attention on positive thoughts, the more positive thoughts permeate one's thinking and the more positive one becomes.* As a bonus, we can note that the more one pays attention to good-feeling thoughts and images, the better one will *feel* physically and emotionally. A happy person even functions better mentally and intellectually, having greater capacity for problem-solving and creativity. Positive thoughts and images have a health-enhancing effect on body and mind; your child will thrive on every level through the process of changing her brain.

HELPING YOUR CHILD BUILD A CALMER, WORRY-FREE BRAIN

Although some kids, teens and adults have a strong *habit* of paying attention to negative scenarios (i.e., they are worriers), they can change this habit. They can learn to direct their attention differently. Indeed, each person, both adult and child, has the ability to determine where to place attention.

Teaching Children to Choose Their Thoughts Using the Lego Model of the Brain

Understanding how the brain works is an important part of solving the worry problem. Kids need to work with their own brains, taking responsibility for reprogramming them in healthy ways. The brain science described earlier can be taught to older kids and teens simply by explaining it and giving examples. The same laws can be taught to that age group and also to young children using colored Lego (or a similar interlocking construction toy or even a suitable Lego-type program for the computer or tablet). Here's how you can go about it: Collect about thirty yellow, thirty blue and twelve green Lego pieces.

Call your child to come sit beside you. Tell the child that you are going to build a model of the brain. Each Lego piece will represent a thought. Green pieces represent the brain core. Blue pieces represent good-feeling, calm thoughts. Yellow pieces represent uncomfortable, anxious, scared thoughts. (Between you and me, it is not pure cognitions that we are referring to here but rather emotion-laden thoughts. The idea "I will have ice cream later" is a thought that *feels* good to an ice cream lover, for example.)

Attach four green Lego pieces together to form the brain core, and then join twenty yellow pieces and five blue pieces around the green center. Explain to your child that the brain starts off with a strong tendency to look for problems (hence the preponderance of yellow pieces).

Put a pile of yellow pieces and a pile of blue pieces in front of the child. Remind the child that the yellow pieces are anxious, worried thoughts and the blue pieces are calm, happy thoughts. For children old enough to handle slightly more sophisticated concepts, say that the yellow pieces are "thoughts that make you feel bad, stressed or uncomfortable" and the blue pieces are "thoughts that make you feel calm, confident or happy."

Explain that we have thoughts that are already in our brain and we also *add* thoughts to our brain. Attach two yellow pieces to the right side of the green Lego brain core, and two blue pieces to the left side of the brain core. Explain that the brain tells us what to think about by choosing a thought from the *biggest* (non-green) section of the brain. For instance, if there are more yellow pieces in the Lego brain, the brain tells us to think a worried thought next. If there are more blue pieces, the brain tells us to think a calm, happy thought next. If there are an equal number of worried thoughts and happy thoughts (yellow pieces and blue pieces), *the brain will tell us to think a worried thought.*

Pick a topic that your child has been worrying about lately. Let's say that your child has been worrying about the fact that you and your spouse are going away on your own for a few days. Ask him to say one thing that he is worried about. Let's say that your child says he is worried that he won't be able to fall asleep without you. Ask him if that is a worried thought or a happy thought (a thought that makes him feel stressed or a thought that makes him feel comfortable). When your child acknowledges that this is a worried thought, ask him to take a yellow Lego piece to represent that thought and attach it to the brain.

Now ask your child to think of a happy thought about your trip. If he has trouble, remind him that you're going to bring him back a gift. Ask him to say the happy thought out loud and then choose a blue Lego piece to attach anywhere on the brain.

Now ask your child to say all the thoughts he is thinking about your upcoming trip. After each thought he expresses, ask, "Is that a worried thought (a thought that makes you feel bad, stressed or uncomfortable) or a happy thought (a thought that makes you feel calm, confident or happy)?" Take the corresponding Lego piece and attach it to the brain that your child is building.

Your child may need help generating happy thoughts. You can suggest some more, just to get him started. For example, "Mommy and Daddy will be back very soon," "I get to have a special treat each day that you are gone," "I like staying with Grandma and Grandpa," "I get to watch a special movie each day," "I can have lots of fun" and so on.

Ask the child to notice which thoughts are easier to think. Ask him if the brain is getting more scared or more calm (are there more yellow Lego pieces or blue Lego pieces in this brain). Now dismantle the brain except for the green core.

Pick another topic the child has been worrying about lately. Ask the child to build his brain again—this time without your help. The child should say each thought out loud before choosing the appropriately colored piece.

Explain to your child that we have a new brain (a new arrangement of Lego blocks) for each subject that we think about. For instance, if a child thinks about curling up with a good book, his brain might be virtually covered with blue Lego pieces. But if he thinks about the bully in his class, his brain might look like a mass of yellow pieces. In computer terms, the *screen* changes for each subject that we're thinking about. When the starter screen (or starter Lego brain) is mostly yellow, it will take hard work to add in so many blue pieces that they begin to outnumber the yellow ones. But this is what we must do if we want to be able to think about that particular subject happily in the future. We can make the blue section bigger by thinking the same happy thoughts over and over, because each time we think a thought—even if it's exactly the same thought we thought before—we can add a blue piece.

If a youngster wants to start having happy, calm thoughts about going to school, he may have to really look for happy images at first: playing at recess, learning something interesting in science class, having fun with a good friend, enjoying time with a favorite teacher and so on. After generating these positive images, he will have to picture them over and over and over again. The more the youngster works at it, the easier it will become. Soon, school will be associated with good thoughts and feelings instead of anxious ones, despite the fact that there is a bully in the classroom. If the child wants to specifically stop worrying about the bully, he can generate some positive thoughts about his ability to deal with the bully: "I can call the teacher for help," "I can get my friends to help me if I need to," " I can tell the bully off," "I can ask my parents to get involved" and so on. Thinking these proactive thoughts will calm the mind, flooding it with "blue Lego pieces," so to speak. The worrying alternative is to generate distressing images of being overwhelmed by the bully—a process that would only lead to more worry and more upset.

Thoughts to Choose

Now that your child understands her own role in building brain circuits, it's time to explain the process of choosing calm, happy thoughts. This will be easiest to do if you do some brain work of your own *first*. So I'd like you to spend a moment right now thinking about something that is pleasant. It could be anything—what you are

SARAH CHANA RADCLIFFE

looking forward to eating for dinner tonight, a memory of a funny conversation you had with someone or a fond childhood memory—as long as it is pleasant. Pause now to select a pleasant subject, and continue reading only when you have done so.

Now think about the pleasant subject and add another positive, good-feeling thought to it. For instance, if your subject was tonight's dinner, you could start thinking about different wonderful aspects of tonight's dinner, or you could remember last night's equally pleasant dinner, or you could think about some other pleasant activity you'll be doing after dinner, or anything either related or completely unrelated to dinner—as long as it is pleasant.

Now add a couple more pleasant thoughts. Notice how you feel as you are adding the pleasant thoughts.

Okay. Now I'd like you to pause so that you can select a different subject altogether—one that makes you feel worried. It can be any topic relating to the past, present or future. It might be about money, someone's health, a disturbing episode in your life or a problem that requires solving. Stop reading until you've got a worried subject to think about.

Now really focus your attention on the worry for a couple of moments—get into it! Then stop worrying and choose one positive, good-feeling thought to think. Was this easy for you to do? Notice whether the worry seemed to be calling to you as you were trying to think the positive thought—was it in the way or were you completely free to change your focus to the good-feeling thought?

Now add a couple more pleasant thoughts. How is it going? Is this easy or challenging? Is the worry still calling out to you? Are you able to completely get into the positive feeling of the good-feeling thoughts?

Pivoting Away from the Worried Brain Circuits

Most people will find that it is far easier to shift into positive thoughts from a predominantly "blue" (calm, happy) brain than from a "yellow" (predominantly worried, anxious) brain. When we are thinking about something that results in a brain loaded with calm, happy thoughts (blue Lego pieces), we can easily add many more such thoughts. However, when we are thinking about something that results in a brain loaded with worried, troubled thoughts (yellow Lego pieces), it will feel awkward and unnatural to start reaching for blue pieces (calm, happy thoughts). In fact, it is as if the large body of yellow pieces calls out to us, "Pay attention here! This is the truth! We are here to help you! Don't go there—that's just distraction and empty fluff! Come back to us!"

We need to understand that calm, good-feeling thoughts will *not* feel comfortable and natural until we have added lots and lots of them and have paid high-quality attention to them over and over again. We have to *work* to build a predominantly blue brain. Moreover, distressed and worried thoughts will not readily cooperate with a person's decision to focus attention elsewhere. In fact, they will tend to keep calling for attention *until they receive it.* Therefore, the very first step in shifting attention away from negative, scary thoughts to positive, pleasant ones involves *acknowledging* the worried thoughts.

For example, suppose Tina is worrying that something bad will happen to her parents—an unpleasant, worry-flavored thought that is stressing her out. Wanting to feel better, Tina would like to move her attention away from the worried thought and put it elsewhere. Before she does this, however, it is crucial for her to acknowledge the worried thoughts and feelings. Tina should *listen* to the voice of her scared part as if it is whispering in her ear, "Tina, something bad is going to happen to your parents!" She should respond (silently), "That's a scary thought. Let's try to think a thought that will make us feel better!"

By taking the moment to acknowledge her scared part this way, Tina is accomplishing several things: *Acknowledging* the feeling allows it to calm down. *Naming* the feeling allows it to shrink in size and begin to unravel. *Accepting* the feeling without judgment allows it to either disappear or relax enough for it to permit an exploration of other, better-feeling thoughts.

SARAH CHANA RADCLIFFE

Acknowledging, naming and accepting feelings just as they are without trying to change them are professional therapeutic strategies long noted for their ability to soothe, regulate and heal disturbed emotions. By now, you will also recognize these actions as the steps involved in the process called emotional coaching. Your child is *emotionally coaching* herself!

Parents can teach their kids how to emotionally coach themselves in two ways: by routinely engaging in emotional coaching—acknowledging, naming and accepting the child's feelings—and by directly teaching the child what to say to her frightened feelings. For example, Tina's mom or dad might say, "I know you're worried that something bad might happen to us and that you are seeing scary pictures in your mind. I know that's very upsetting. Let's see if you can think some positive thoughts and make some happier pictures in your mind." As we saw before, the parent avoids using the word "but" in these instructions. It is important to acknowledge the anxious thoughts and feelings in their own, isolated sentence. Use a "period" and a pause *before* going on to suggest replacing scary thoughts with more positive ones.

Remember too, that it is important for parents to refrain from discounting a child's worries by saying things like, "Don't worry—nothing bad is going to happen to Mommy and Daddy." Although it is so tempting to offer this kind of reassurance, doing so ensures that the worry will persist rather than vanish. It is the *child*, not the parent, who must conclude that nothing bad will happen. By acknowledging and accepting the worried thought without trying to change it, parents help loosen the thought's hold on the brain, putting it in a position where the child herself will be able to release it and replace it.

When Worries Refuse to Budge

Although acknowledging, naming and accepting feelings is usually sufficient for them to step aside for a short time, some intense fears and worries will refuse to budge. It's as if they are saying, "NO! WE WILL NOT BE QUIET! WE WILL KEEP WARNING YOU ABOUT THIS PROBLEM ALL DAY LONG!" As we saw earlier, emotional regulation techniques can help keep anxious feelings "comfortable" while awaiting emotional release techniques. An especially useful emotional regulation technique for the chronic worrier, as well as for the child with a worry that just refuses to budge, is the Worry Chest strategy.

Tell your child that you have a temporary solution for his worry. It will give him a break from the worry until he has time to deal with it properly later in the day. Describe a small chest, somewhat like a treasure chest, that a worry can be placed into. For instance, Tina can imagine wrapping up her bad-things-will-happen-to-my-parents worry, putting it carefully in the Worry Chest and *locking* the chest. She can then imagine placing the chest on a high shelf, where it can wait for her. She can come back later in the day, at a time when it's convenient for her, to unlock the chest and attend to her worry for a few minutes (see page 144 for instructions on how to attend to a worry). If the worry still exists after she has attended to it, it can be put back into the chest for the night or until the next convenient time for attending to it.

Some kids will appreciate a more concrete exercise. Children can be instructed to write down the worry on a piece of paper and put the paper in a real box, such as a lockable jewelry chest, a taped shoe box, a decorated jar (not a clear glass jar—you don't want to see those worries peeking out through the glass!) or some other physical container. Put the container on a high shelf or in a drawer in the child's room. Instruct the child to only think about the thought when he removes the note from the box to work with it (see "Making Time for Worry" on page 144).

Meanwhile, the Worry Chest strategy creates a temporary space away from the worry, so that the child can have a break from worry and engage in positive brain exercises.

SARAH CHANA RADCLIFFE

Relax, and Focus on a New Thought

Now that Tina's worried thought is temporarily out of the way, she can engage in her brain exercises; she can begin to select new thoughts to program into her mind. A trick for helping new, better-feeling thoughts to enter deeply, take hold and have powerful effects is to calm the body and mind *before* starting to add thoughts. This can be accomplished easily by slowing down the breath. Breathe in and out slowly while counting silently—*in-two-three-four, out-two-three-four*—for a minute or two (see "Coherent Breath" in Chapter Four, page 90). Doing so will calm both body and mind. The child should be instructed to continue this way for a bit and then, while still breathing slowly, to focus attention on a positive memory, image, thought or feeling. I offer specific examples beginning on page 139.

Focusing strong attention *repeatedly* (i.e., off and on throughout the day for many days) on these new, good-feeling thoughts will help wire them permanently into the child's brain. How should the child focus her attention? Attention can be focused in many different ways. Following are some ideas to experiment with.

Translate Thoughts into Images

Some good-feeling thoughts are easy to translate into images; for a few moments, just picture the positive image. An example of this would be choosing the good-feeling thought "My parents are safe and healthy" and then picturing a positive image of smiling, healthy parents for a minute or so. Repeat this activity several times a day until the anxious thought is no longer present.

Picturing positive images is also called Visualization. In fact, making a mental picture is a strategy that is found in many different fear fixers. We have already seen that parents can generate positive images and offer them to their kids. Kids can also be taught and encouraged to create their own calming pictures, which can then be used to calm all sorts of frightened feelings. While some kids are just "naturals" at this, creating their own imaginary support team, others will never think of the idea unless someone (like you) introduces it to them. Sometimes an image can be created on the spot. For instance, a child may quickly invent a friendly puppy to sleep in bed with her at night or walk her to school in the morning. At other times, the image is best "installed," much like the Breathwork techniques. In this latter case, the child or teen should use a favorite form of Breathwork for several minutes and then, while feeling pleasantly relaxed, see a mental scene or watch a mental movie of events unfolding in a positive, safe, happy way. After enjoying the positive image for a couple of minutes, the youngster should take a deep breath in and out, and then very slowly open her eyes. The Visualization exercise will have an even more profound effect when it is repeated just before falling asleep each night and again just upon awakening in the morning. This is because the child's brain waves at those times tend to be at a frequency that is particularly suitable for deep reprogramming of the mind. It's therefore easiest to uproot fearful thoughts and feelings then and replace them with positive ones.

Tapping-In
Use Tapping-In (see page 109) to "install" a new thought or image deeper into the mind. Use this technique alone until the anxious thought is no longer an issue. Alternatively, include Tapping-In along with other ways of paying attention to the new thought until the anxious thought is gone.

Breathing In
The breath can carry the new concept deeper into the mind. Focus attention on the new good-feeling thought and "breathe" it in, sending it to every cell in the body. Repeat several times a day.

Send It to the Heart
This is an even more focused form of breathing in a thought. Think the new thought and breathe it directly into the heart. Notice the way it *feels.* Continue breathing this way for a minute or two. Repeat several times a day until the anxious thought is gone.

Thoughts to Think

Tina can select any good-feeling thought in the universe. In fact, being totally free to choose, she should be encouraged to choose the best-feeling thought she can, since this kind of thought will be more powerful and faster in drawing her attention away from the worried thoughts. One category of thoughts a person can choose to concentrate on is called *Antidote Thoughts*. These thoughts generate images that are the polar opposite of the distressing, worried thoughts that are currently plaguing the imagination. Here are a few examples that Tina might use:

- She can generate an image of her very healthy, very happy parents when they are ninety-five years of age.
- She can generate an image of a golden light that surrounds and protects her parents from harm.
- If she's old enough, she can think about the statistical chances that her young parents will be just fine for many decades to come, picturing something like an insurance company's statistical fact sheet.
- She can create a strong picture image of herself and her parents (a series of snapshots) having happy times together five, ten, fifteen and twenty years from now.
- She can imagine a fairy princess with a magic wand who sprinkles protection from harm all around her parents.

If a child complains that positive images aren't "real," feel free to point out that the negative, worried ones aren't real either. Both kinds of thoughts are pure imagination. However, a brain can easily fall into the habit of choosing only scary pictures to imagine. Your child has to help her brain get into the habit of choosing happy pictures to imagine. Remember to point out that the benefits of selecting positive imaginary pictures include:

- happier feelings
- less stress

- better health
- if you believe in the theory of like attracts like, a greater chance that all will go well

You can also mention that the worried thoughts are statistically far less likely to happen (making them far less realistic) than the positive thoughts. For example, statistical odds are much higher that Tina's parents will make it home alive rather than dead.

On the other hand, choosing scary thoughts results in:

- feelings of stress and anxiety
- lowered immunity to disease
- physical symptoms such as headaches, stomachaches, habit problems and so on
- chronic worry getting carved into one's facial features as one ages
- if you believe in the theory of like attracts like, a greater chance that what you are worrying about will happen

Still More Thoughts to Think

When pivoting away from worried thoughts to place attention on good-feeling thoughts, your child is free to think *any* kind of pleasant thought—not just Antidote Thoughts (i.e., she can think thoughts that aren't related to the worry at all). She can draw good-feeling thoughts from the infinite storehouse of thoughts, choosing any distracting good-feeling thought to be the subject of her attention. Whenever her brain suggests the scary thought that something bad will happen to her parents, she can briefly acknowledge the fear (and, if necessary, place it in the Worry Chest for later), let her brain know she would like to think some happier thoughts, breathe slowly for a couple of moments and then switch her attention to some distracting, funny, irrelevant, meaningful or otherwise good-feeling thought. For example:

- She can focus her attention on what she will be eating for supper or what she wants to wear tomorrow.

- She can think of a really funny story, movie, incident or joke.
- She can make plans to do an act of kindness for a family member or friend.
- She can daydream an adventure story.
- She can replay a happy incident from earlier in the day or week.
- She can try to memorize a poem, do a difficult math challenge, learn something new or otherwise actively engage her mind.

Choosing Good Chemistry Thoughts

There are certain kinds of thoughts that are particularly powerful at releasing good chemistry into the bloodstream. When a person thinks these thoughts, he can *feel* their effects almost immediately. Thinking a good-chemistry thought is akin to popping an antianxiety drug, in the sense that it does create an immediate physical change in the body and mind. To get some idea of how this works, do a little experiment yourself: First, silently repeat a bad-chemistry word like "no" over and over again for about one minute. Really concentrate on the word as you are saying it and pay close attention to how your body feels. Now pause for one minute and then start saying "yes" for another minute, again concentrating on the word as you are saying it. What differences did you notice in the way you felt both physically and emotionally? You can also try repeating the word "hate" for one minute, followed by the same amount of time repeating the word "love." How did your body and mind respond to these words?

There are many, many types of good-chemistry words. You can teach your child to turn his attention to the following kinds of words in order to get an immediate chemical lift. Again, keep in mind that if your child is in an intensely stressed or anxious state, he may not be willing or able to start experimenting with any of the positive word strategies. If that is the case, this technique can be introduced *after* other strategies have lifted some of the negativity.

Beautiful or Happy Words

Each child will have words that are beautiful or happy to him, including names of favorite people, places or things. It's a good idea to have your youngster record a page or two of happy words—like flower, sunlight, easy, laughter, sunset, beach, love, chocolate, toys, cellphones, serenity, pizza, puppy and so on—that he can pull out to read as needed, or he can simply start saying those kinds of words over and over when a worry circuit is initiated.

Words of Gratitude

These words can be expressed in two ways: If your child relates to God, the thought can be expressed as "Thank you, God, for the cereal; thank you for my neat shoes; thank you for my cat; thank you for my home; thank you for my friends" and so on. Another way to express gratitude without reference to God is "I'm grateful for my neat shoes; I'm grateful for my cat; I'm grateful for my home; I'm grateful for my friends" and so on.

Positive Attitude Words

These are good-chemistry words that point to a needed state of mind or shift in emotional feeling. For instance, if the child is feeling worried about his ability to succeed, he might focus on the word "confident." If he's afraid that bad things will happen, he might focus on the word "faith." If he's worried that everything will go wrong, he can focus on the phrase "let whatever happens happen." If he's overwhelmed and panicked, he can focus on "one thing at a time" or "calm and focused." In other words, he can select the *opposite* of the current type of anxious feeling.

Funny Words

A collection of jokes (funny knock-knock jokes or other short-line jokes) that is always handy (i.e., in a small book or bookmarked on one's phone) can provide an immediate boost through smiles and laughter.

Building Positive Action-Circuits

In addition, your child can interrupt her worry practice by switching activities. Instead of *thinking*, she can *do* something satisfying and absorbing. For instance, when Tina notices that she is thinking about bad things happening to her parents, she can "say hello" to the worry and then *immediately* engage in an absorbing and satisfying activity. The worried feeling is the cue to begin the activity. Here are some activities your child can try when the worry process begins:

- Solving a puzzle. She might want to keep a key-chain puzzle (e.g., Rubik's Cube, Tangle, a number game, etc.) on her person at all times.
- Immediately stretching the body. If possible, she should do full body stretches (arms, legs, bends), but if sitting at a school desk, the child can stretch her fingers, toes, legs, stomach muscles, back muscles and so on by doing subtle, invisible isometric stretches (show your child how this is done).
- Playing a game on a device. If the child is in school, she can draw (doodle) or Zentangle* while the teacher talks, if possible. If it's not possible, the child can pay very close attention to what the teacher is saying and try to memorize it, take very good notes, if note-taking is permitted, and start participating actively in the classroom discussion.

---

* Zentangle is a calming, meditative doodling technique developed by Rick Roberts and Maria Thomas. It involves drawing repetitive patterns, like circles, squiggles, triangles, ovals, lines and so on, until they form an intricate, eye-pleasing pattern. Children, teens and adults can all use this beautiful and simple art form to help calm their nerves, focus their attention and relax body and mind. The "Zentangled" state of mind can reduce stress, improve mood and facilitate learning and creativity. See, for example, *Zentangle for Kidz!* by Sandy Steen Bartholomew.

- Cleaning a bedroom, working on a hobby or contacting a friend.
- Beginning a focused breathing technique such as the Coherent Breath (breathing in-two-three-four, out-two-three-four) or any other breathing pattern described in Chapter Four.

Although there are so many different things your child can do instead of focusing attention on an anxious thought, she can draw on the same *one* strategy over and over again. There is no need to diversify and, in fact, it may be preferable from the brain's point of view to establish a new habit with one single repetitive activity. For instance, every time your child starts to obsess about a fear, she might switch her attention to thinking about the needed state of mind (e.g., "courage"). Doing so time and time again will slowly but surely help to install a new first response to uncertain situations. Or, each time the child is aware of worrying, she could focus his attention on the Coherent Breath pattern for a minute or so, breathing steadily in and out, bringing her mind and body into a positive state of balanced calm. Over time, the brain will choose the healthier state of mind as its default. The only reason that I've included so many options for thinking and doing is to give you an overview of the different kinds of activities to choose from. The bottom line is to move attention off a worry and put it onto something else. The only criteria is that the new object of attention should elicit some sort of pleasant emotional state, whether that be calm, happy, confident or any other good-feeling emotional and bodily experience.

MAKING TIME FOR WORRY

Choosing positive thoughts and activities and applying oneself to them repetitively with deep concentration can help calm anxious feelings in the moment. Most important, however, this strategy can help build a calmer brain over time. However, the brain will only permit its owner to do all this if the owner also remembers *to attend to the frightened thoughts and feelings* at the right time. Remember the Worry Chest? It's time to go back now and pull out the worry. Failure to pull out a worry that has been waiting inside the chest results in an inability to use the Worry Chest in the future. The mind will simply not allow it, correctly claiming that the person is not trustworthy to return to help the worry. *As a result, worries will become chronic and unrelenting; there will be no relief.* Therefore, it is essential to help your child go back to the Worry Chest in order to get the worry and pay attention to it for a short time (three to ten minutes) each day.

Ways to Attend to Worry

Once the worry has been brought out of its chest, the child can use various kinds of emotional release techniques in order to process and heal the anxious feelings. One such technique is the Mindfulness-Yes exercise that was introduced in Chapter Four. When Tina uses the process for her worry about her parents, she might let her frightened thoughts "speak" as follows:

Mommy and Daddy will die when they are away.
Y-e-s.
I'll be left all alone. I'll be an orphan.
Y-e-s.
I'll miss them so much and I'll cry every day forever.
Y-e-s.
I don't want them to go; I want them to stay home with me.
Y-e-s.
They might not die, but I still don't want them to go.
Y-e-s.
I'm really mad at them.
Y-e-s.

They better bring me back a really good gift.
Y-e-s.

As we saw earlier, the Mindfulness-Yes technique can help unblock and release worries and fears by allowing negative emotions to be fully processed. Like all emotional release techniques, this strategy goes straight *to* the negative feelings. Whereas emotional regulation strategies give the child a new focus, diverting attention *away* from fear, emotional release strategies deal with the fear head-on in order to transform it.

Mindfulness-Yes is only one way to spend time with a worry that's been pulled out of the Worry Chest. A child can also use the Tapping method (EFT) described in Chapter Four. Tapping provides a double whammy of worry relief. First, worried thoughts and feelings are welcomed, named, accepted and released. Second, Tapping techniques facilitate cognitive restructuring. In other words, a child's worries are replaced with more rational, healthy thoughts (and feelings) as a natural outcome of the technique (see Chapter Four, page 115, and Appendix A, page 298, for instructions on and examples of Tapping).

Another emotional release technique is *Speed Journaling.* In this strategy, the child writes or types all his thoughts and feelings about a stressful issue just as he might when recording notes in a diary or journal. However, Speed Journaling differs from journaling in several significant ways. The first is the fact that a journal entry is meant to be a written record—legible and accessible after it is created. The Speed Journal is purely for emotional release: the child writes and writes as quickly as possible, without regard to legibility, grammar or style. In this way, the youngster invites everything to "tumble out" without censorship. Rapid writing facilitates a flow of emotion and allows for the release of pent-up or unarticulated stress. The journal should *not* be saved—rather, it should be shredded or erased at the end of each writing session. The shredding or erasing adds one more dimension of healing; it's a visual and tactile representation of releasing negative emotion. Poof—it's gone!

There are many other ways to release worries. Here are a few more to experiment with:

- Name a worry and put it inside an imaginary balloon. Continue naming all related worries and concerns and stuffing them inside the imaginary balloon. Tie the end of the balloon and release it into the sky. Watch it float away. (If you like, you can do this exercise with a real balloon, either with worries written on small pieces of paper stuffed inside or with imaginary worries stuffed inside.)
- Name a worry and all related concerns, dropping them one at a time into an imaginary burlap bag. Add a heavy stone to the bag and seal it firmly. Imagine taking the bag onto a boat, going out to the deep part of the ocean and dumping the bag to the bottom. (Again, this exercise can be made more concrete by stuffing paper or imaginary worries into a real bag and burying the bag in the garden or dropping it in a garbage bin on garbage pickup day.)
- Tell the worry to God. Pour out your heart, naming your deepest fears and crying heartfelt tears. Then sit quietly for a bit and listen for guidance. (Those whose faith allows them to take advantage of this practice have a research-validated overall reduction in stress and anxiety.)
- Tell the worry and all related concerns to a favorite doll, stuffed animal or live pet. The simple act of expressing the fears to a "listener" helps to melt the feelings away. (Interestingly, research with adults confirms that just expressing the fear to a perceived "other"—even to a computer or robot—significantly reduces it.)

Solving Worry Problems

Sometimes the most useful way to work with a worry is to take a problem-solving approach. Some worries are more suitable for this strategy than others. For example, if a teenager is worried about how she'll cope with her heavy exam schedule, she can—during her worry time—create a study schedule for herself. Once he's done that, her worry will most likely shrink considerably. A child who is worried about how she looks (a common adolescent concern) can take several steps to address her worry, using her first worry time to make a list of practical things she can do to address her problem. Afterward, she can use her worry time to work on the ideas on her list, turning the list into a practical self-improvement program. For instance, the youngster's to-do list can include tasks such as the following:

- Learn more about the subject of appearance by reading relevant books, magazines and online resources (all of which should be available at the local public library). Sometimes healthy information about appearance will help the child accept her appearance as it is, causing the worry to stop dead in its tracks; sometimes the child will come across helpful tips that can actually help her improve her appearance, leading to an increase in confidence and a decrease in worry.
- Consult a makeup specialist or hairstylist to learn how to emphasize her best features for an overall best look.
- Window-shop, study classmates, look through magazines and so on, in order to study the current "look" and how people achieve it, thereby increasing feelings of competence and confidence in the area of personal appearance.
- Share questions and concerns with a parent, sibling, cousin or trusted friends who may be able to offer help or advice.

The Two-Chair Technique

Sometimes a child is feeling so worried that he can't even begin to look at the practical side of the problem. An outsider might easily see that there are things the child could do to help calm the worry, but the child is so overtaken by anxious thoughts and feelings that he just can't see a way out. In this case, a parent can help a child begin to problem-solve despite the strong emotions by employing the Two-Chair technique. Set up two chairs facing each other; designate one the "Worry Chair" and the other the "Helper Chair." Instruct the child as follows:

Sit in the Worry Chair and imagine that another part of you is sitting in the Helper Chair. Tell this other part your worries. Now move to the Helper Chair and ask the imaginary part of you sitting in the Worry Chair what it needs—what would help make the worry feel better? Go back to the Worry Chair to answer this question. Finally, go back to the Helper Chair to offer help.

Here is how this technique sounds in action:

In the Worry Chair: *I've got so much studying to do that I'll never finish. But if I don't finish, I'll fail my exams for sure. I'm really worried.*
In the Helper Chair: *What would make you feel better?*
In the Worry Chair: *If I had no exams!*
In the Helper Chair: *I know. But since you do have exams, what would make you feel better?*
In the Worry Chair: *I need more time!*
In the Helper Chair: *I know, but since you don't have more time, what would make you feel better?*
In the Worry Chair: *Maybe I should just study.*
In the Helper Chair: *I'll help you do that. Let's get started right now.*

Here is another example of the Two-Chair technique for worries:

In the Worry Chair: *I'm worried that Melissa will be mad*

at me if I don't invite her to come skating with Nadya and me on Sunday.

In the Helper Chair: *What would make you feel better?*

In the Worry Chair: *If I knew that Melissa wouldn't be mad at me.*

In the Helper Chair: *I know, but since you don't know that, what would make you feel better?*

In the Worry Chair: *I don't know.*

In the Helper Chair: *Think about it.*

In the Worry Chair: *I can't think of anything.*

In the Helper Chair: *Okay. If you think of something, let me know.*

(After a few minutes:)

In the Worry Chair: *I thought of something that would make me feel better. If I show Melissa that I still like her, I will feel less worried about her being upset. I can invite her over on Saturday night to have popcorn and play some games.*

In the Helper Chair: *That's a great idea. I can help you with that. Let's call her right now.*

Here is one last example:

In the Worry Chair: *What if I forget something important? I've packed everything I can think of, but I have a feeling there's still more stuff I need.*

In the Helper Chair: *What would make you feel better?*

In the Worry Chair: *I need to make sure I have everything I'll need on the trip.*

In the Helper Chair: *I can help you with that. Let's make a written list and check off all the items you have already packed. We can see if there is anything left that still needs to be packed.*

The Two-Chair technique helps the child find a calm part inside himself. In most people, anxious parts are so loud and persistent that they effectively drown out the calmer, more rational parts that are still there. Indeed, a worried person can feel so distressed that he literally can't think. Cortical inhibition (the inability to problem-solve effectively) occurs when emotions are strongly agitated. Interestingly, it is possible, and even easy, to separate the emotional part of the brain from the thinking part by giving each part its own voice in separate chairs. Once separated, the thinking part can facilitate the problem-solving process, allowing the worry to be addressed in a truly practical way. The worried part then calms down. In this two-chair exercise, the main job of the thinking part is to ask the distressed part, "What would make you feel better?"

PROBLEM-SOLVING

The decision whether to use worry time to *release* a worry or to *address it practically* through problem-solving depends on the nature of the worry. There are three categories of worries that children and teens experience: (1) those that they can do something about (like the two we looked at on page 148), (2) those that they cannot do much or anything about (like terrorist attacks, war, school shootings and other sorts of random acts of violence, or their parents' marital or financial situation) and (3) those that have elements of both categories, with some features that are in the child's realm of control and some features that are outside the child's realm of control.

Parents can help children identify which kind of worry they are dealing with. If twelve-year-old Casey is worried about being popular, for example, is she dealing with something that she can or can't do something about? It's a little of both. Her parents can help her to identify the nature of the problem and the appropriate interventions for this kind of worry. For instance, they can guide her to use worry time to do Mindfulness-Yes or some other emotional release exercise to deal with the out-of-control elements of the problem. That might sound something like this:

They don't like me no matter what I do.
Y-e-s.
I wish I was part of that group.
Y-e-s.
I feel like a reject.
Y-e-s.
Only losers want to be my friend.
Y-e-s.
I like my friends, though.
Y-e-s.
But maybe I'm a loser.
Y-e-s.
I just want to be popular so badly.
Y-e-s.
It isn't fair!
Y-e-s.
I'm so miserable, I can't take it.
Y-e-s.
I want to get a new sweater.
Y-e-s.
I don't care anymore.
Y-e-s.

Casey's parents can also show her how to use her worry time to draw up a plan of action. For example, if she *really* wants to be friends with the "in-crowd" for some reason, she doesn't have to wait for them to call her. She can:

- Study their style, habits and interests and see what she can do to align with them and fit in better.
- Pick one member of that group who seems approachable and start to make some contact with that person (through social networking or in person).
- Make herself available to help a member of the in-crowd (e.g., help the person study, give her notes or assignments

that she missed, offer her assistance or provide some other small service that is easy to do and brings her into some sort of relationship with a member of the group).

- Develop a friendship with someone who is friends with members of the in-crowd, in order to move closer to that circle.

Alternatively, Casey can use her worry time to develop a strategy for enjoying her life and her friends *without* being included in the in-crowd. For instance, she can:

- Get busier with her own hobbies and activities or pursue new ones.
- Get busier with her own friends and strengthen those relationships.
- Make efforts to make more friends, even if they are not members of the in-crowd.
- Make her life more satisfying by improving family relationships, pursuing sports or exercise programs, developing talents and skills, joining social, political or religious groups and so on.

Whichever way Casey wants to go, her parents can help her learn to use a few minutes a day of worry time to plan a strategy that can be carried out during school and after-school hours. Worry time then becomes problem-solving time—a few minutes that can simultaneously calm and empower the child.

Here is a list of some strategies that will often be helpful for solvable problems, or the solvable *part* of problems:

- Set aside a time to look at a worry practically, to see if there is anything that can be done about it.
- Use the Two-Chair technique to help sort out what needs to be done to make things better.
- Chunk the problem down into smaller bits and work on it one bit at a time.

- Do research in books, magazines and Internet resources to learn more about the problem and its solutions.
- Speak to others who have experienced or solved a similar problem in order to get ideas and advice.
- Speak to others who have good listening skills and use them as a sounding board so that you can think your problem through out loud.
- Study how others have dealt with this issue.
- Take one practical step a day (or week—whichever is appropriate) to work on the solution.

Similar interventions can be used during worry time even for those problems that are largely out of a child's realm of control. Here too, the child can be guided to address sad, scared and upset feelings using the emotional release strategies described earlier (Mindfulness-Yes, Tapping, Speed Journaling, etc.). However, parents can also teach the child to address helpless worry in practical, problem-solving ways. Let's see how:

Nine-year-old Alex is worried that his parents might divorce. Alex has heard a lot of fighting and arguing going on between his parents, and he's heard the word "divorce" bantered about liberally. Alex has many friends whose parents have already separated or divorced, and he's very worried that the same thing will happen to his family. The worry nags at him constantly, interrupting his schoolwork, his sleep and his leisure activities. Mom has recently taught Alex how to put the worry away in his Worry Chest until he is ready to look at it at some point each day after school.

The problem-solving approach to working with worries of all kinds requires that a child ask himself the question: What can I do about this problem? There is always something a child can do about a problem (if you count prayer), and doing it always brings some relief from worry. Here is the menu of activities we've looked at for problem-solving worries. Note how they can be applied even to problems that are not within the child's ability to solve.

- Gather more information about the nature of the problem. In Alex's case, this might involve asking his parents directly about what is happening in their marriage. In the case of an ill relative, it might involve asking the name of the illness and for information regarding treatment and prognosis. In the case of worries about the world situation, it can involve learning more about what's happening and what governments are doing about it. Information itself—even negative information—reduces feelings of helplessness and overwhelm. Even if, Heaven forbid, a child knew he was dying and there was nothing more that could medically be done for him, learning about the death process and models of life after death could help reduce anxious feelings.
- Talk to friends who have dealt with a similar problem. In Alex's case, this might mean interviewing some of his friends who have experienced separation or divorce, or friends whose parents are in high conflict even though they are still married. Support from others is a major tool for stress reduction, evidenced in the great popularity of in-person and online support groups and the research that substantiates their positive effects.
- Pray for a positive outcome or the strength to handle whatever happens. Those who can pray during uncontrollable life challenges suffer less stress and worry than those who do not have this option available.
- Talk to parents about worries and upset feelings. Talking it out can help when parents know how to listen (see "Listening to Fear" in Chapter Two, page 40).
- Use anti-worrying mental strategies to stay calm and positive in situations in which there is little control. In other words, steer attention to good thoughts and positive images and away from negative thoughts and scary images

(remember the Lego brain). A person may have no control over a situation, but he always maintains control over his own thinking process. This is the main strategy we have examined in this chapter for the effective reduction of worry tendencies and the building of a positively inclined, calm, happier brain.

The Worry Protocol in Action

Marlee is worrying about how she is going to deal with her food sensitivities when she is away at college in the fall. Up to this point, Mom has purchased and prepared a wide range of delicious foods to accommodate Marlee's special needs. Now, however, Marlee will have to cope on her own. She hasn't cooked much so far and, in any event, she won't have access to a real kitchen; she'll have a small fridge, a hot plate and a microwave and will probably have to eat out a fair bit. Here is a sample of her typical conversation with Mom in the months before school starts:

> Marlee: *I'm going to starve! I can't eat the regular food in a restaurant! I won't have enough time to make special meals for myself—I'll be hungry all day. Am I supposed to live on celery sticks? This will never work!*

In the olden days, Mom would have responded with facts and logic ("Marlee, don't be silly—you can find gluten-free, soy-free, dairy-free products everywhere these days, and you can ask the cook in a restaurant to make you customized meals"). Now Mom starts off with emotional coaching:

> Mom: *I hear you, honey. You're really worried you won't have the food you need and you also think you won't have the time or facilities for making it at home. That would make anyone feel anxious.*

While Mom's emotional coaching is supportive, it isn't doing the trick for Marlee—she's still very stressed about the whole thing. Every day, she brings up the subject, whining about how awful it will be and how there is absolutely no solution. Mom doesn't want to give Marlee too much attention for this negative thinking process, so she moves to problem-solving:

> Mom: *Sweetheart, why don't you schedule a bit of time each day to actually work on this problem? Can I make a few suggestions? (Marlee responds in the affirmative, so Mom continues.) Instead of thinking about this all day, why don't you set aside a short period each day to deal with this issue—say, fifteen or twenty minutes. During that time, you can do a little research about the stores around the school and also the school cafeteria and local restaurants. Talk to people—find out if they've dealt with this issue before. Also, maybe go online and start looking at recipes that you can put together quickly and easily using just the hot plate and microwave. In fact, maybe you can also think of a bunch of other steps you could begin to take in order to get a handle on this so you don't go off to school in a panic about your food.*

Marlee agrees to put in some constructive worry time (in this case, problem-solving time) and, in fact, comes up with a seven-day menu plan that covers all her food needs! Although she feels a bit better after this, she still remains unsettled and still roams around the house complaining that things might not work out and she'll have to quit school to come home to eat. Hearing these irrational fears, Mom makes another suggestion:

> Mom: *Marlee, I think you've got a plan, but I can see you're still worrying. Would you like me to teach you a couple of techniques that can help stop your brain from working overtime on this?*

Marlee, desperate for relief, agrees to take some tips from Mom. Mom teaches Marlee to use thought-replacement strategies during the day. Marlee now employs the following steps each time she catches herself worrying about the food issue:

- She acknowledges the agitated feeling that always accompanies her thoughts about food.
- She removes her focus from the worry and practices the Coherent Breath for a minute.
- She begins breathing in the word "calm."

Marlee also learns an emotional release technique to use during her designated Worry Time. She now uses Tapping, working on the statement "I'm afraid I won't have the food I need." Marlee taps nightly now instead of whining and, after a week or so, stops talking about the food issue altogether. Thank goodness!

In the next chapter, we'll be looking in depth at emotional healing techniques that work on the biological level. One such technique is called Bach flower therapy. As you will see, this modality can often help ease or even resolve children's fear, panic, stress, worry and rumination. In the Bach system, there are thirty-eight different remedies, each addressing a particular shade of emotion, including all types of frightened feelings. As you read the next chapter, you might keep in mind that the Bach flower remedy called White Chestnut is used to calm and quiet a "noisy" brain—the kind of brain that tends to worry, obsess, ruminate and keep its owner awake at night.

PROFESSIONAL HELP

Self-help techniques for soothing worry are often highly effective. However, if you find that your child is still worrying excessively despite at-home treatment, do seek the help of a mental-health professional. Excessive worry is any amount of worry that causes your

SARAH CHANA RADCLIFFE

child significant distress (e.g., "Mommy, I can't turn my brain off and I can't stand it!" or "Mommy, I can never go to sleep because my brain won't turn off") or that interferes with your child's ability to function at home or school (e.g., the child can't go to school because he's worried that something bad will happen to his mom when he isn't home). Rumination—the chronic replaying of anxiety-provoking thoughts—is a characteristic of several different anxiety disorders. It may be found, for instance, in post-traumatic stress disorder, some types of OCD and in the mental-health disorder called General Anxiety Disorder (GAD). GAD is characterized by intense and illogical worries about a lot of things—seemingly *everything*. A child with GAD may worry about health, social problems, schoolwork, parents, safety, the world situation and anything else that can be worried about. The worry takes its toll on sufferers, causing physical symptoms like headaches and stomachaches, trembling and twitching, an excessive need to urinate, excessive sweating or difficulty swallowing. It can also interfere with sleep and the ability to concentrate on schoolwork, and it is sometimes associated with a depressed or irritable mood. Doctors and mental-health professionals can rule out other causes for such symptoms and provide a diagnosis where appropriate. Children and teens often experience significant relief from stressful worrying, particularly from GAD, with short, targeted professional therapies.

FAST TRACKS FOR WORRY

Fastest Fast Track

Ask the child to take action whenever a worried thought or feeling appears, immediately focusing full attention on a happy, good-feeling thought, image, object or memory, or engaging in an absorbing pleasurable activity.

Teach the child how to release worries during a daily designated "worry time" by writing or talking them out, doing Mindfulness-Yes or a Tapping technique or problem-solving.

Offer the Bach flower remedy White Chestnut (see Chapter Six, page 168) several times a day whenever the child is in a period of obsessive worrying.

Fuller Program Fast Track

Ask the child to take action whenever a worried thought or feeling appears, immediately focusing full attention on a happy, good-feeling thought, image, object or memory, or engaging in an absorbing pleasurable activity.

Teach the child how to release worries during a daily designated "worry time" by writing or talking them out, doing Mindfulness-Yes or a Tapping technique or problem-solving.

Offer the Bach flower remedy White Chestnut (see Chapter Six, page 168) several times a day whenever the child is in a period of obsessive worrying.

CHAPTER SIX

Outside Helpers

Fear is both a state of mind and a state of the body. Calming the mind helps to calm the body and, as we've seen, calming the body helps to calm the mind. In this chapter, we'll look at more ways to calm the body, this time using *Outside Helpers*.

ADULT SOLUTIONS

Adults don't like feeling stressed, anxious, worried or fearful any more than kids do. Unlike kids, however, adults have access to a wide range of calming substances. A panicky adult flyer, for instance, can bring along a pharmacy of anxiety busters prescribed by his doctor before a flight. Similarly, a claustrophobic woman undergoing an MRI can be calmed down with an antianxiety drug, as can a reluctant public speaker. Those suffering through a period of situational stress—an issue at work, a divorce, a death in the family—can be helped through it with the temporary use of benzodiazepines. Moreover, while the following practices certainly can't be recommended, some adults find other Outside Helpers to calm anxious feelings, such as wine and other types of alcohol, marijuana and other types of drugs, cigarettes, binge eating and many other unhealthy ways of altering mood and stress levels. In other words, grown-ups sometimes find life so stressful or so frightening that they reach for help to "calm their nerves"—some sort of temporary, quick-acting relief to get them through particularly uncomfortable moments in time. We all appreciate the value of a "quick fix" when we don't feel physically or emotionally well; perhaps you yourself have reached for a pain reliever (like aspirin or Tylenol) for a headache instead of relying on your own ability to address the buildup of your negative emotions and to relax the muscles of your head and neck using Breathwork or progressive relaxation. If so, you know the appeal of fast relief, particularly when it is safe, readily available, effective, affordable and socially acceptable.

But what is available for the younger set? They have the same kinds of stressed feelings without having access to the same kinds of endorsed or "unendorsed" mood-altering substances. What is a terrified eight-year-old flyer supposed to do? What can a child do when her intense fear makes the class outing, the sleepover at Grandma's or the drive through the underground tunnel an unbearable event for everyone involved? Video goggles are now replacing sedation for frightened pediatric MRI patients, but what can a terrified child outpatient do when the doctor *will* have to cause some pain? What can a teenager do to calm his nerves during an important date or interview? As we've seen, kids who have installed effective relaxation strategies can calm themselves down in many kinds of tense situations. But sometimes even these "pros" can't call upon their tools when they are most needed. For instance, a child may be too overwhelmed before a high-stakes performance to concentrate on her breathing technique or even remember to use the Soft Eyes approach. Alternatively, it could be that a child is able to use her tools but does not find sufficient relief in a particularly stressful situation. And, of course, for many young people, no relaxation strategy was ever installed in the first place. Indeed, the younger the child, the more likely it is that there are no ready-to-go self-management techniques in place.

SARAH CHANA RADCLIFFE

While psychotropic medication—the same kind of Outside Helper that an adult might take—is an option for a child with an anxiety *disorder*, it is not an option for a child who is simply experiencing normal fear. The difference between the frightened feelings found in anxiety disorders and those found in "normal" fear is in both intensity and frequency. Children with anxiety disorders tend to have unremitting, overwhelming types of fear that interfere with their overall sense of well-being or their ability to function well. Other kids may have intense fear on occasion or low-grade fear often, but neither type interferes with their functioning or basic peace of mind. As I previously mentioned, if your child has a lot of fear, it's best to get a professional opinion. An assessment by a child psychologist or psychiatrist can determine whether the child's fear is best treated by professional therapy or psychotropic medication, or whether at-home management is all that is needed.

At-home management includes all of the techniques in this book— ways that parents can talk to frightened children, interventions that parents can use, tools that children can employ on their own to help regulate their emotions, and Outside Helpers that can effectively calm body and mind. Fortunately, there *are* safe, healthy Outside Helpers for children's feelings of fear, three of which we will explore in this section: Bach flower remedies, essential oils and herbal medicine. Although there are many other forms of child-friendly treatment for anxious, fearful and stressed feelings, we will examine these particular natural remedies in some detail.

Of course, you may choose never to offer any Outside Helpers to your child. They are simply options that many people aren't even aware of. Once parents learn that there are safe remedies they can give their child to help relieve the youngster's fear, they can then decide whether or not they want to offer this help. When considering whether Outside Helpers might be appropriate for your child, you might think of them as:

- an option to consider when your child's fear seems overwhelming in a given situation and both you and the child are at a loss as to how to restore balance in a timely fashion (i.e., as an intervention to use during a moment of panic)

- a way to deal with moderate levels of fear in order to improve performance in very important situations (i.e., when anxious feelings would negatively affect an important performance or examination)
- a first step that helps a child calm down enough to focus on other cognitive and behavioral strategies that she can use in a frightening situation (i.e., to help the child calm down enough to remember how to use the Coherent Breath or any other fear-fixer strategy)
- an option to try when all else has failed (e.g., for a toddler who needs to be fully toilet trained by the time school starts in two weeks but who is absolutely terrified to have a bowel movement in the toilet)
- a safe and healthy alternative to "self-medication" (teens who know to reach for a healthy Outside Helper when experiencing high levels of stress are far less likely to ever reach for unhealthy stress and anxiety "helpers" like drugs; alcohol; excessive, insufficient or inappropriate foods; or other addictive, compulsive, unhealthy mood-regulating substances or activities. This protective effect can last a lifetime.)

DEPENDENCE ON OUTSIDE HELPERS

Outside Helpers are physical substances that can alter emotions. Some parents worry that offering a child any physical substance to calm anxious thoughts and feelings can lead to dependence on that substance. While this is an understandable concern, it should be noted that the Outside Helpers described here do not lead to any kind of physical dependence or addiction. One reason for this is that none create an intensely positive (high) feeling; they simply help balance the child's agitated state, helping to bring the youngster back to feeling normal. Normal mood never leads to addiction, whereas the internal chemical characteristics of a "high" mood certainly can. Besides failing to create euphoric feelings, the Outside Helpers described in this chapter have no more glamour or appeal than a cup of hot cocoa. Nonetheless, it is certainly possible for the child to develop a touch of *psychological* dependence on them—an emotional rather than physical attachment to the substance. Still, even when a child does become temporarily psychologically dependent on a fear-reducing substance (I say "temporarily" because I've never seen a permanent attachment to any of these substances), there is no harm in it at all: a youngster who gets "hooked" on chamomile tea is no worse off than a mother who likes a cup of coffee daily or a father who carries a water bottle wherever he goes. We all get attached to our comforts and, providing that the comfort we are attached to is healthy and safe, there is no problem with that at all. Mildly soothing and gently calming, these interventions can be considered as relevant to the maintenance and support of emotional well-being as regular exercise, sufficient sleep and a healthy diet.

EFFECTIVENESS OF OUTSIDE HELPERS

A final issue that some people have regarding these kinds of fear-fighting interventions is doubt about their effectiveness. In fact, that concern is—for some people at least—certainly valid. Indeed, *no* medication or treatment intervention invented so far for any illness of any kind works for all people all the time. However, many people *have* benefited from these interventions, some of which have been around for hundreds of years. This latter claim is unimpressive to staunch skeptics who feel that any therapeutic effect of natural remedies is only due to the *placebo effect* (an effect that is due to something other than the therapeutic properties of the remedies themselves, such as the power of suggestion). And they could be right. I have seen, however, time and time again, that people who are highly skeptical about the remedies can also experience positive results for themselves and their children. Of course, placebos also work well on people who don't believe in them, because of all kinds of subconscious associations.* (For instance, simply taking a "potion" or visiting a "healer" can trigger a healing response in the body.) Nonetheless, even babies and animals respond to these interventions, though infants, cows, cats and dogs tend to be less affected by placebos than the rest of us. Still, even if the remedies only work because of the placebo effect, that wouldn't bother *me*. As Dr. Herbert Benson points out in his book *Relaxation Revolution*, the placebo effect itself is a powerful healing tool. Why would we care if our cancer went into remission just because of a placebo effect? The important thing would be that we were healthy again. And if your child's fear completely diminishes or even partially improves just because of a placebo effect, would that bother *you*?

Indeed, if you'd like to empower the placebo effect and supercharge it with the power of suggestion and the power of belief when giving natural remedies to children and teens, go ahead! There is no one in a better position to influence a child's belief, and thereby enhance the placebo effect, than a parent. Indeed, a parent is a master hypnotist to his child, having far greater influence than any other person will ever have on the child's subconscious and conscious mind. In fact, many parents unintentionally enhance the placebo effect when offering remedies to their child, by saying something like, "This will help you feel calmer." But if the child feels better—more relaxed, more confident, more calm—only because he believes his parent, so be it. By the way, doctors also say something like this to their patients when prescribing treatments: "This will help your condition." Similarly, parents say it to their children about pain-relief medicine, other medicines and other treatments—which enhances the effects of all interventions. Interestingly, a meta-analysis of statistical research conducted

---

* See the article "Cure in the Mind" by Dr. Maj-Britt Niemi (a psychologist and researcher at the Institute of Behavioral Sciences at the Swiss Federal Institute of Technology in Zurich), in *Scientific American Mind*, February 2009.

SARAH CHANA RADCLIFFE

by Jay Fournier and his team in 2010 (reported in *The Journal of the American Medical Association*), has found that, in cases of moderate clinical depression, antidepressant medication is no more effective than a placebo. In other words, antidepressants might also be triggering the healing response only through the power of suggestion. The unfortunate thing is that these medicines can cause very real negative side effects. If parents can trigger emotional healing through the placebo effect using a placebo that has no negative side effects, their children are obviously better off.

THE SCIENTIFIC APPROACH TO AT-HOME TREATMENTS

I have no idea whether the Outside Helpers described in this chapter work because of the placebo effect or whether they work because of their vibrational effects, chemical properties, physical properties or something else—I just know that they often seem to effectively relieve a child's anxious thoughts and feelings. Fortunately, there is no need for you to believe in these remedies. Rather, take the scientific approach: do your own experiments. Offer your child one of the following interventions. Observe the child's behavior over the next days and weeks. Note whether it has worsened, stayed the same or improved. If it has improved, you can either continue giving the Outside Helper or, to be more scientific about it, remove the Outside Helper for a few weeks to allow the child's system to revert to her baseline. Observe the child's behavior at that baseline. Now, give the Outside Helper again for a number of weeks and record the child's behavior. Again, if you are seeing positive results, you can either continue with it or continue the experiment by withdrawing the intervention again in order to return to baseline for further trials. If the baseline itself is higher after the third round of treatment (i.e., the child's anxiety is lower than it was before you first started giving remedies), it could be that the remedy has triggered a lasting positive effect (or it could be that the weather is nicer outside—you'll never really know). While these steps do not constitute a proper scientific method, they might at least give you some impression of whether or not the remedy is useful for your child.

Now let's turn our attention to the remedies themselves.

BACH FLOWER REMEDIES

Bach flower remedies were developed by Dr. Edward Bach in the 1930s. They are currently used worldwide and, in European countries, are frequently employed within traditional medical settings. They are water-based tinctures that bring emotions into healthy balance. They can take the edge off irritability, stress, rage, moodiness, grief, homesickness, hysteria, worry, fear and panic. In fact, they can help settle any negative emotional state. The only problem is that it's really hard to believe that anything made only of water can do all that!* Therefore, even though I knew about the Bach remedies for twenty-five years before I ever used one, I thought they were weird and probably useless. Here's what made me change my mind:

When one of my children was very young, he developed a strong fear of robbers. The fear would surface right at bedtime and I would have to sit with him nightly, helping him in every way that I knew how to calm down and go to sleep. Unfortunately, as is so often the way, his fear grew over time rather than diminishing. He started worrying about the robbers at dinnertime, and then he started worrying about them as soon as he got home from school. Eventually, it became an all-day concern. As a psycho-

---

* The water in Bach flower remedies was heated for a period of time while the head of a particular flower was in the water dish. The flower was then removed. The remedy is the water itself, now altered vibrationally due to the method of preparation. See Dr. Richard Gerber's *Vibrational Medicine* for a discussion of the scientific principles involved.

SARAH CHANA RADCLIFFE

logical practitioner, I had a lot of tools in my tool kit, but nothing was working with this child. I put him on a waiting list to be seen by a specialist, but meanwhile we still had to deal with the fear that had already been affecting the whole family for about two years. I cannot remember now why I decided to try a Bach flower remedy with my little boy, but I am guessing that pure desperation was at play, as I was willing at that point to try anything. What I do remember is that I gave him the Bach remedy called Mimulus one evening, and the next morning, the fear of robbers was gone. Completely gone. And it never came back. I could not believe it! That's when I decided to look more deeply into this system of emotional healing, eventually becoming a professional Bach practitioner myself. Since that time, I have had the pleasure of helping many other people help themselves and their children in an equally successful manner.

There are thirty-eight different remedies in the Bach flower system, each one addressing a different emotional state. They are available worldwide online, at health-food stores and at some pharmacies. On page 170, I list the remedies that are most often used to help children through their anxious moments. Note that each remedy is suited for a particular type of panic, worry or fear. Several remedies can be mixed together in one treatment bottle if the child has more than one type of fear. A few drops from the treatment bottle are then taken a few times a day until the fear is gone. Many parents find that their child makes quicker and easier progress with behavioral interventions (such as the use of positive reinforcement, positive feedback, negative consequences, etc.) when the child is taking Bach flower remedies. For instance, a child who is normally afraid to sleep in his own bed may respond positively to a reward chart once the fear has been brought down a few notches with some days on Bach flower remedies. See Appendix B (page 310) for complete details on how to prepare and use Bach flower remedies in the home treatment of panic, worry and fear. The following table lists the remedies most often used to help relieve anxious moments.

Bach Flower Remedy	Type of Frightened Feeling
Aspen	For vague fears like fear of the dark, fear of "something bad" happening, fear of monsters, etc.
Cerato	For fear of trusting one's own judgment—always needing someone else's opinion or validation
Crab Apple	For the child who worries about his appearance or who worries about germs or contamination
Larch	For fear of failure
Mimulus	For fear of specific things like dogs, lightning, dying, being separated from parents, etc.
Red Chestnut	For the child who worries about the health, safety or well-being of loved ones
Rescue Remedy	All-purpose turn-off-the-fight-or-flight-response remedy (see complete description on page 171)
Rescue Sleep	For the child or teen who is having trouble sleeping because his mind is too active or full of worry
Rock Rose	For feelings of panic

Bach Flower Remedy	Type of Frightened Feeling
Scleranthus	For fear of making the wrong choice—going back and forth endlessly on the pros and cons
Walnut	For discomfort and fear of change, for transitions and for new beginnings
White Chestnut	For the child with a noisy brain—who is always thinking and worrying about something

One needn't worry too much about selecting the exact correct remedy. In fact, there is never any harm in choosing the *wrong* Bach flower remedy, apart from the fact that there may be no response. When someone uses a remedy that she doesn't need, it simply has no effect. The remedies are wide-acting and can have positive effects on many aspects of fear. However, sometimes the best treatment results are obtained after consulting a professional Bach practitioner; if your own use of the remedies fails to yield the desired results, do consider this option.

Rescue Remedy

Manford had been break-dancing for several years and was actually really good at it. He was so good, in fact, that his classmates began asking him to perform at parties. Manford always agreed good-heartedly, but then he'd suffer terribly in the days and, particularly, the hours before a scheduled performance. He was essentially a very shy fellow, not the kind who enjoyed being in the spotlight. Break-dancing put him right there—the lights shining on him as everyone formed a circle around him, clapping and cheering him on. Fortunately, Manford generally managed to pull off an excellent performance, but then he'd come home completely drained from the strain of the whole affair. One night, after the usual "torture," Manford mentioned his problem to his mother. "I don't think I can do this anymore," he said, describing the stress he experienced each time he performed. "It's too hard on me. I'm not accepting any more invitations to dance."

Mom did some emotional coaching, sympathizing with his distress and even sharing her similar experiences when she used to play the violin in the school orchestra. Then she asked Manford if he wanted to try taking some Rescue Remedy in the days before a performance to see if that would take the anxiety down a few notches. Manford didn't really want to give up dancing publicly, so he agreed to try the remedy on the next occasion. That opportunity arrived just a couple of weeks later. As instructed, Manford squirted a couple of sprays of Rescue Remedy into his mouth several times a day, starting as soon as he began to feel the stress. On the day of the performance, he took it a few extra times, even though he wasn't feeling particularly stressed anymore; he was afraid that he would feel stress if he didn't take it, so he took it preemptively. He was feeling surprisingly well by the time it was his turn to perform, but he took a couple more sprays just before he went onto the floor. Afterward, Mom asked Manford how it all went. "AMAZING!" Manford responded enthusiastically. "I can't believe how good I felt—especially right before the performance. I actually enjoyed myself for the first time!"

Rescue Remedy is a mixture of five different Bach flower remedies. It is an "adrenaline-buster"—a remedy that helps calm the fight-or-flight response. It is available in many forms: liquid, spray, candies, chewing gum and even skin cream. Many moms around the world carry a small spray bottle or vial of Rescue Remedy in their purse "just in case" (i.e., for those times when a child has a sudden fall or other injury, or some emergency occurs while they are out and about. In true emergencies, the parent should also take Rescue Remedy before giving it to her child, in order to be able to function better). Rescue Remedy is used for high-stress circumstances in which the effects of adrenaline can be felt—circumstances that make the heart beat faster, the mind feel dizzy and confused, and the emotions feel panicky or overwhelmed. It is meant to be taken before, during and after intensely stressful situations such as:

- surgery or medical or dental procedures
- tests and examinations
- public performances
- high-stakes circumstances (job interviews, dates)
- competitive sports events
- witnessing or experiencing shocking, life-threatening or otherwise terrifying events
- being in a car accident or other dangerous situation
- first-time experiences (first day of school, first haircut, first time off to overnight camp, getting married)
- being exposed to anything that one is normally very afraid of (such as animals, flights, heights, etc.)

Rescue Remedy is always worth using in such situations, but intense states of fear will require further intervention as well. It is the ideal first step, a perfect emotional "first-aid" remedy. It can pave the way for effective use of other techniques, and in many cases, it can prevent overwhelming anxiety from occurring in the first place. When a child is feeling any kind of fear and all you have handy in the cupboard is Rescue Remedy, then definitely use it. Even though it may not necessarily be the best fit for the fear that is occurring, it can still help bring about a level of stability and calm. Rescue Remedy can be used along with any emotional regulation tool in this book. If Rescue Remedy doesn't help, either try a more appropriate Bach flower remedy for the specific type of fear or worry that your child is experiencing (see the table on pages 170–171) or use a completely different calming strategy such as Breathwork, Heart Hold, essential oils and so on. Once the child's immediate fear has subsided, use other strategies found in *The Fear Fix* to help prevent reoccurrence of the fear in the future.

Finally, keep in mind that, although Rescue Remedy can also be used for vague anxious feelings that occur "for no reason," it should only be used that way for occasional, quickly passing feelings. Although it may feel like the disturbed feeling happens "for no reason," anxious feelings always have roots *somewhere*. Whether it's from too much unmanaged stress, a food intolerance, physical disorders within the body, unrecognized emotional trauma, mental-health disorders or some other source, frequent stressed and anxious feelings are *signals* that should be heeded. A visit to a doctor and a mental-health professional can help shed light on the source of and appropriate treatment for the problem.

ESSENTIAL OILS

Our second Outside Helper is aromatherapy—the use of essential oils for calming tension and fear. These highly concentrated aromatic essences of plant extracts are applied *externally* (as opposed to Bach flower remedies, which are normally taken internally). There are many ways to use them: mix them in a bit of carrier oil and apply them directly on the skin, sniff them straight from the bottle or on a cotton ball or tissue, or fill a room with their aroma using various dispensers and diffusers. (See specific instructions for preparing and using essential oils in Appendix C, page 317 .) Aroma acts directly on the brain through nerve receptors in the nose that send impulses to the emotional centers within the hypothalamus and limbic areas. In this way, aroma rapidly influences physical and emotional functioning. There are many stress-reducing and calming oils that can help children recover from frightening experiences or cope with worry and nervous anticipation. Essential oils like lavender, rose, orange and chamomile are often recommended for young people, and there are many others as well (see Appendix C for specific recommendations).

Unlike Rescue Remedy and other Bach flower remedies, essential oils *are* medicinal. This means that they *do* sometimes (not always) interact with personal health conditions, medicines and other types of remedies. Because of this, it is important to speak to a qualified aromatherapist (someone who has completed professional study in this discipline) at least once. You'll want to be sure that the particular oils you wish to use have no contraindications, and you'll also want to know the proper dose for the age and weight of the child you are treating—particularly when you plan to use them for a toddler or preschooler. A certified aromatherapist will also be able to recommend the most suitable essential oils for the type of fears or worries you are hoping to address, and can often sell or prepare the oils for you as well. After one consultation, you should be good to go with an essential oil tool kit that will suffice for your decades of child-rearing.

Despite the medical sound of all this, the kind of essential oils found in health-food stores around the world tend to be safe, "over-the-counter" products that are meant for home use. Moreover, there are plenty of self-help aromatherapy books that can provide information and guidance. However, pain relievers are also sold over the counter at drugstores but taken incorrectly can be fatal. Dosage, timing and other factors must be adhered to in order to experience health benefits safely. It's the same with essential oils: be sure to keep these substances away from children's curious hands—they require adult administration and supervision. A teenager should ideally have his own meeting with the aromatherapist in order to learn how to safely use the oils for emotional regulation and self-help.

Now, you might be wondering what it is that essential oils can do for your child or teen that would make them worth the time and trouble of learning about them and making an appointment with an aromatherapist. I'll tell you: These little sweet-smelling potions can calm a rapidly beating heart, quiet a racing mind, relax tight and tense muscles, lift mood and otherwise make your child feel *wonderful*. Essential oils can help your worried child fall asleep at night. They can help your stressed child feel calmer and happier. They can help your anxious teen stop "sweating the small stuff."

Whereas Bach flower remedies act behind the scenes, helping your child feel his normal self, essential oils are definitely an up-front intervention. Your youngster will *feel* the direct effects of the oil. That's why it's important to know the right dose for the oil and the child. Too much of this substance can give your youngster unpleasant side effects like unwanted drowsiness, spaciness or even a headache or nausea. The right amount, however, can rapidly calm your youngster's nerves and gently relax his body. A few drops of the right essential oil in a warm bath can help a child forget his worries and settle down to a good night's sleep. A couple of sniffs of oil from a tissue can help restore the child's emotional balance after watching a scary movie or experiencing a frightening incident. A bit of oil mixed in a carrier oil and rubbed onto pulse points can help a child negotiate travel more peacefully and comfortably. In fact, essential oils are useful anytime you want to help your child deal with stress, pressure, overwhelm or panic.

HERBAL MEDICINE

Herbs have been used for millennia to help heal both mental and physical distress. Currently, herbs are regulated and prescribed as medicines in many European countries, including Switzerland, France and Germany. However, in North America, herbs are not yet considered medicines by the FDA and so remain unregulated. Complementary or alternative medicine (CAM) is gaining in popularity nonetheless, to the point that at least two-thirds of medical schools in the United States now include some form of alternative medicine in their curricula, and at least a third of Americans use some form of CAM (and this number is constantly increasing).

Herbs have a special role in the relief of stressed and nervous

SARAH CHANA RADCLIFFE

feelings. Like essential oils, they can help lift mood and calm the body and mind. Herbs are much less concentrated than essential oils, however, and they can provide a very gentle, soothing effect on the nervous system. Whereas essential oils are so powerful that they can almost feel like a drug (a desired characteristic under conditions of acute stress and anxiety), herbs are often so mild that their immediate effects are barely discernible. With regular use, however, a herb can slowly "nourish" the nervous system, leading to a state of greater resistance to stress and anxiety. For this reason, herbs are well-suited to children and teens who have regular bouts of anxious and stressed feelings—those who worry a lot, have trouble sleeping due to anxious rumination or agitation, or tend to be overly fearful.

A parent can certainly offer children herbs for relief of chronic stressful emotions, but if the herbs and other self-help interventions do not provide significant relief, it is important to get a proper medical evaluation to determine if an actual anxiety disorder or some other condition is present. If it is discovered that the child is suffering from an anxiety disorder, it is possible that herbs can still be used as part of her program of recovery, as long as other interventions (like appropriate therapy for anxiety disorders) are also employed. On the other hand, your doctor may recommend a psychotropic medication for anxiety. Be aware that, like essential oils, herbs are *medicinal,* meaning that *they can interact with the child's health conditions, medications and other types of alternative treatments.* It is important to consult with a professional herbalist or naturopath (N.D.) in order to learn which herbs are safe and appropriate for the particular child being treated—especially when a child is on other medication of any kind—and to always inform the child's medical doctor when your child is taking herbal products.

An herbalist can also prepare herbs in a child-friendly way: herbal lollipops are more popular with the younger set than herbal teas, for example. Herbalists can also offer herbal tinctures to be dropped in liquid. In addition, some herbs can be stuffed into little "herb pillows" (homemade three-by-three-inch cotton squares) and placed beneath a pillow to help a youngster ease into sleep. Teens may enjoy preparing their own herbal potions in tea form as a comforting nighttime ritual or as a daytime beverage that helps keep stress levels in check. Like essential oils, a warm cup of herbal tea can quickly and gently calm a worried mind or settle one's "nerves" after a frightening incident or before a big event.

Herbs that are currently used in Europe to treat anxious feelings and sleep disturbances include St. John's wort, chamomile, valerian, hops and passionflower—all of which are commonly available in health-food stores around the world. See Appendix D (page 321) to learn how to prepare and use specific herbs in the home treatment of children's stressed and anxious feelings.

OTHER OUTSIDE HELPERS

An Outside Helper can be anything—a food, drink, natural product, toy or activity. Anything that helps a child calm down, turn off the internal alarm sirens and feel better can be considered an Outside Helper. Keeping this perspective in mind, go ahead and be creative: enlist whatever help you can for your child. The following are a few suggestions to get you started.

Comfort Symbols

A comfort symbol is any object that becomes associated with feelings of calm and security. Little children often carry comfort symbols around with them to help them negotiate the often overwhelming new world they find themselves in. Security blankets, bears and other soft toys can help a toddler hold himself together in strange or stressful circumstances. These kinds of objects can also help older kids and teens—at least, more age-appropriate, socially acceptable versions of them. Mind you, people of all ages keep stuffed animals in the privacy of their bedrooms, and there is certainly no harm in that practice. If a favorite bear helps an adolescent fall asleep more easily, go for it!

SARAH CHANA RADCLIFFE

Children (and teenage girls) can get away with carrying "key-chain friends"—cute animals or other figures that attach to school bags, belts and purses. In fact, at one time, it was common practice for a whole generation of people to carry a "lucky" rabbit's foot on their key chain—a soft, furry thing that brought a measure of peace of mind to the owner. (Many people are still using them.) These little comfort toys can help bring an extra measure of security in difficult situations by the process of association—that is, the toy becomes linked to feelings of security and then is able to actually trigger those feelings when it is touched, looked at or even thought about. Through habit and repetition, the child or teen creates a neural pathway in his brain linking a particular object or symbol to feelings of comfort. Many kids spontaneously make associations between feelings of comfort and an object, thereby creating their own supply of comfort symbols. For instance, a child may have a happy memory attached to a particular object (like a prize pen that he won in an important competition or a gift received from a special friend). Looking at the object elicits the good feelings of the happy memory and elicits positive chemistry that soothes and comforts the nervous system.

It's great when kids make their own associative chains of comforts and symbols, but parents can help this process along as well. A parent can actually teach a youngster how to make associations. For instance, a parent can say something like, "When you notice you're worrying about something, just squeeze your prize pen and remember the day you won the contest—it will help you feel calm again." Even if an object is not connected to a good memory, it can be used to elicit comfort. In this case, it helps if the object is attractive or interesting to the child. A parent can give a child a piece of jewelry, a postcard, a worry stone, a small toy, a photo or anything else, saying something like, "When you are feeling stressed or worried, just look at or touch or hold this object and feel my love pouring out of it to hug and comfort you," or "Whenever you are feeling stressed, just look at or touch or hold this object and notice how beautiful it is." The comfort symbol both distracts the child from his worry and also triggers specific feelings of security.

Lifestyle Factors

When a child has lots of fears or worries, it is important to consider lifestyle factors. Certain substances and activities can increase and decrease anxious thoughts and feelings in vulnerable children. For example, some medications can increase the tendency to be fearful. If your child has suddenly become fearful and is taking a new medication, speak to the prescribing doctor. Some illnesses can also trigger sudden fearfulness—any out-of-character anxious tendencies should be assessed by the child's doctor.

In some kids, food intolerances increase anxious thoughts and feelings; dietary adjustments can bring the child to a state of greater emotional balance.* Eliminating some foods can actually put an end to scary nightmares or other types of frightened feelings for some kids. In other kids, poor eating habits—skipping meals, failing to drink enough liquids, eating too many sweets and refined foods, and engaging in other poor eating habits—can increase panicky and unsettled feelings. It's amazing how fear can sometimes be reduced by simply engaging in better "food hygiene," like eating five or six small meals a day, drinking plenty of water, eating wholesome food instead of junk food and chewing slowly enough to digest it all.

Some children are sleep deprived even though they're in bed on time, and the sleep deprivation can lead to an increase in worried and anxious feelings. Sleep apnea or other conditions can be hidden culprits. Some kids are sleep deprived because they stay up too late. Let them know that they may be experiencing more frightened feelings because of this bad habit, and do what you can to help them settle down for the night earlier.

Even when the child is otherwise healthy, it is sometimes possible to decrease fears simply by increasing exercise. Research has shown that exercise can have powerful positive effects on mood and emotion, effects comparable to those of psychotropic medication

---

* See *The Anti-Anxiety Food Solution* by Trudy Scott.

SARAH CHANA RADCLIFFE

(without the negative side effects). It is certainly worth an experiment to see if *your* child will respond positively to the effects of exercise, since exercise is healthy and beneficial in any event. Therapeutic effects require regular exercise, however—running around the schoolyard may not be enough to make a consistent change in brain processes. However, three or four periods a week of scheduled exercise may be just right for calming a worrying brain. Depending on your child's age, stage, fitness level and interests (and your availability and budget), you might consider signing her up for karate lessons, swimming lessons, trampoline, dance, yoga or other sports. Teens might appreciate a program of weight training and aerobic activity that can be performed in the comfort of home with minimal cost and equipment. Today, there are personal trainers who specialize in working with children and teens, setting up safe and enjoyable programs that not only improve emotional balance but help build strength, confidence, endurance and overall health at the same time.

Leading a more balanced, healthier lifestyle can help some kids feel calmer more of the time—especially children with biologically sensitive systems. Nonetheless, there is no need to *add* stress to a child's life by making radical or unpleasant changes in routines. If your child is interested in and cooperative toward modifications in lifestyle, then go ahead and make any adjustment you think might be helpful. With older kids and teens, talk about your concerns and your ideas and see how they respond. With younger children who don't like change, make only the most minute and gradual adjustments to diet and other routines, allowing them to make painless changes over time. If possible, seek guidance from health professionals concerning diet and exercise recommendations. Lifestyle changes can take some stress off a child's body and mind, helping the youngster to be calmer, happier and more resilient in general. It's just one more way that parents can help their kids cope well with the normal pressures of life.

Outside Helpers can be used on an "as needed" basis for many children and can be used on a daily basis for kids who routinely experience anxious, worried, frightened and stressed feelings. While they certainly will not completely erase a child's chronic, overwhelming or disabling feelings of anxiety or fear (professional intervention will be necessary for that), they are valuable helpers in any fear fighter's tool kit. Let's picture a sobbing child who has just witnessed a screaming match between her parents. She's terrified that her parents will get a divorce and her home will fall apart. It's way past her bedtime, but there's no way she can go to sleep now—her mind and heart are in turmoil. Though there is nothing that can completely remove her emotional pain, there's *much* her parents can do to help soothe and support her in these anxious moments: assuming that at least one of the parents has calmed down enough to turn attention to the upset youngster, he can provide presence (sit beside the child quietly), listen gently with emotional coaching (welcoming and accepting her feelings without trying to change them), rub a mixture of calming essential oils on the child's chest around the heart center (to calm her racing and aching heart) and prepare her a warm cup of herbal tea (to help her sleep restfully) laced with Rescue Remedy (to help reduce trauma). Finally, the parent can kiss the child good night and tuck her in bed with a favorite plush animal (for added comfort and security).

Steps like these can get a distressed and anxious child through the night and her day at school. They can help minimize or even prevent the negative impact of frightening and disturbing life experiences. Parents needn't stand by helplessly while their children struggle with stress and fear; they can come to the rescue with a full array of stabilizing and calming interventions, pulling out all the fear fixers they have at their disposal.

CHAPTER SEVEN

Helping Your Child through Fears
of People, Places and Things

Fear of bugs, animals, thunder, strangers,
blood, needles, circuses, heights

Anyone can have a fear of anything, but the things that people tend to have fears of generally have *potential* danger linked to them. It's just that the danger is being overrated. For instance, having a fear of lightning does make some sense, because lightning can strike and even kill someone. Similarly, having a fear of dogs makes some sense, because dogs can chase and bite a person. Fear of bridges isn't totally crazy either, since someone could fall off a bridge and die. However, people don't tend to have fears of pencils, because pencils have no reputation for causing pain or harm—unless, of course, a pencil is used as a weapon. In that case, a victim of a pencil-induced wound might develop a fear, but the fear is not the ordinary kind of fear we are talking about in this section. It would be an example of a *traumatic* fear—the fear of something that was associated with a traumatic event. We will be looking at traumatic fears in a later chapter. For now, we will just note that neither children nor teens tend to have fears of cups, chairs, telephones, socks or other inherently harmless items.

So let's get back to the types of things kids *do* have fears of and look at how parents might help them cope. The following is a very brief list of commonly feared people, places and things. Some, like the fear of clowns and strangers, are most likely to occur in very young children, while others, like the fear of needles, are equally likely to be found in older kids and teens:

- clowns, masks and dressed-up characters (e.g., amusement park characters)
- strangers
- noisy and crowded places like party halls or amusement parks
- loud noises
- blood
- elevators
- dogs, cats or other animals
- spiders or other creepy crawly bugs
- bees and wasps
- lightning and thunder
- snakes
- needles
- heights

Although none of these commonly feared people, places or things might seem terrifying to adults, the majority of children have felt afraid of at least one of them at some point in time. If a child or teen is really fearful of these or other similar triggers, the whole family can be impacted. For instance, dealing with a child with a serious fear of dogs can turn routine family visits into a major challenge. Everything begins to revolve around the youngster's fear. Does Uncle Ted have a dog? How will the family attend the surprise birthday party he is having for Aunt Sally? How can the family spend the weekend at their best friends' cottage when the friends own a big white poodle? How can Mom drop in on her neighbor for a quick chat when little Tyler won't go near the house because of the yapping terrier who lives there? Other fears have a similarly disruptive impact. A child who has a fear of clowns may sadly miss out on classmates' birthday parties. It's impossible to leave a child who becomes hysterical during thunderstorms with a babysitter even though Mom and Dad *have* to go out to an important business function. Traveling with a young lady who refuses to go on an elevator restricts the family to visits in hotel rooms and tourist sites that are on lower levels. Or, if parents choose not to make accommodations for their child's fear, then the family is forced to listen to the unpleasant wails of distress from terrified youngsters.

Some kids experience fear that is intense enough to be considered a phobia. Phobias tend to be accompanied by more symptoms of the fight-or-flight response than regular fears, including reactions such as a pounding heart, shortness of breath, emotional overwhelm, feelings of panic, dizziness, chest pain, nausea, choking sensations, upset stomach, sweaty palms, feeling an intense need to escape, fear of dying or going crazy and so on. Moreover, as we saw in Chapter One, phobic fear has a greater negative impact on a child's life, often leading to extreme efforts to avoid the trigger, and extreme reactions when avoidance is impossible. Teens will tend to have more clearly articulated symptoms of phobia than younger children. The latter typically express their phobic response as a simple, total meltdown.

Parents who live with a child's fear must address it in some fashion. Fortunately, home treatment of these kinds of fears is usually quite effective and often completely sufficient. When it isn't—when fear persists in intensity and frequency despite the use of home-based interventions—take your child to a mental-health professional. Phobias often respond quickly and completely to a short course of therapy.

In this chapter, we will see how the practical tools and strategies we have explored in earlier sections can be used to address specific fears.

HELPING DANNY DEAL WITH HIS FEAR OF DOGS

Let's take a look at how the Millers help their seven-year-old son Danny overcome his intense fear of dogs. Danny doesn't want to play in his backyard with his visiting cousins because the neighbors have allowed their spaniel, Pepper, to play in their own yard next door. Even though a wire fence separates the two yards, Danny can see and hear Pepper. He therefore absolutely refuses to go outside with the other kids. Ruth and Bob Miller are upset and frustrated. They want their son to be a good host to his cousins, they want him to actually have fun and they want him to be able to carry on with his life normally despite the presence of dogs in the world. Below we'll see how they use a mix of fear fixers to accomplish these goals.

Step One: Emotional Coaching

Dealing with a child's fear always starts with emotional coaching. You might recall that most parents either don't know the technique of emotional coaching or they forget to use it in the heat of the moment. A very common response to Danny's refusal to go outside might be "Go on, Danny. All the other kids are going outside. There's a fence that's keeping Pepper in his own yard. There's nothing to be afraid of!"

The Millers, however, choose emotional coaching as their starting point and respond to their son's adamant refusal to play as follows:

Parent: *I know you're afraid. You don't like Pepper running around barking like that. It's scary.*

This comment does not solve the problem; it simply establishes that the parent understands and is sympathetic to the child's fear. It increases the parent's power to educate in subsequent steps. At this point, Danny agrees with his parent that it's scary and continues to balk: "I'm staying inside." Now the parent proceeds to the next intervention: problem-solving.

Step Two: Problem-Solving

Parent: *I understand that you don't want to go outside, and
I know that this issue is going to come up all summer long.
Pepper likes to play in his yard. The problem is that you are
going to be stuck inside the house the whole summer while
your brother and all the kids go out to play in the backyard! I guess we'll just have to deal with that for now, but
I'd like to show you a way to feel more comfortable around
Pepper and other dogs too so that next summer you can go
outside if you want to. I know a method that we can work
on this summer that will make you feel a whole lot calmer
and more comfortable around Pepper by the time school
starts again. You won't have to feel so scared anymore.
Would you like to try it?*
Danny: *Okay.*

Note: If Danny did not agree, the Millers would have had to take
a firmer approach, making some sort of treatment plan—either with
them or their doctor or mental-health professional—*non-negotiable.*
A child cannot be left to live with his fear any more than he can
be left to live with a physical health condition. Note also that the
parents do not pressure Danny to recover from his fear today, this
week or even this month. They are respectful of the intensity of the
fear and realize that it might take several weeks of real work before
it will go away for good. In fact, as you will see below, when they
create their plan of attack, they give themselves eight full weeks to
work on the fear. This is a fair amount of time to address a serious,
persistent childhood fear. It might turn out that the child's fear eases
more quickly, or it might take a bit longer than the anticipated eight
weeks. However, creating a realistic, non-pressured time frame for
getting over fear will always help create the relaxed state of mind
that contributes to a successful outcome.

Step Three: Gradual Exposure

The Millers now work out a program of Gradual Exposure to help Danny become more comfortable with dogs. Although the protocol looks lengthy on paper, keep in mind that Gradual Exposure is really one simple process: break a target behavior (like fear of dogs or fear of sirens) down into a series of baby steps. Help your child move through each small step, one at a time, until he can face the target fear comfortably.

Here are the steps that the Millers have outlined to help Danny learn to be comfortable in his yard when Pepper is in his:

Week One
Every night at bedtime, read Danny some children's books about dogs, books that have realistic photos and good information about how dogs grow, how they play and behave, what they eat, etc.

Week Two
Make three separate visits to a local pet store that keeps dogs behind a glass window and just look at the dogs playing. Talk about their behavior, using words like "playful," "frisky," "curious," "sleepy," etc., to help Danny learn to read a dog's body language. Ask Danny to describe the dogs' behaviors and what they might mean about how the dog is feeling (e.g., "He's drinking water, so I guess he's thirsty" and "He's barking, so I guess he wants to play, or maybe he is hungry").

Week Three
Arrange two or three home visits with Pepper's owner. The owner is asked to keep Pepper on a leash while Danny visits with his Mom or Dad for just a few minutes. Show Danny that Pepper can't get off the leash.

Week Four
Two or three times during the week, arrange with Pepper's owner to let Pepper run freely in the backyard while Danny watches him

SARAH CHANA RADCLIFFE

from behind a window inside their house (or his own house if he has a good view of their yard). Ask Danny to describe Pepper's moment-by-moment behavior and what it might mean (e.g., "He's barking at a squirrel—maybe he wants it to go away," "He's lying down—he likes the sun" and "He's sniffing the grass—maybe he's looking for something").

Week Five
Two or more times, arrange for Danny to watch Pepper play Frisbee or catch with someone. Ask Danny to describe Pepper's behavior and what it might mean.

Week Six
On two or three occasions, have Danny sit in his own backyard while a parent goes into Pepper's yard (having arranged this with Pepper's owner, of course). Danny watches while one parent plays with Pepper. The other parent stays in their own yard with Danny, asking him to verbally describe what Pepper is doing every moment or two.

Week Seven
On two or three occasions, both Danny and a parent go into Pepper's yard to play ball with him.

Week Eight
Have Danny play in his own yard several times a week or even daily, shouting a big warm, friendly "Hi" to Pepper whenever the dog is out in his yard too.

Step Four: Carrying out the Plan of Gradual Exposure

Everything can look great on paper, but you know how things work in real life: not always so great! Danny's parents had to make several adjustments in their program in order for it to work successfully. You will see as their story unfolds that I make a couple more recommendations about fear fixers they might have employed along the way to help make the Gradual Exposure easier on their child. When you are designing a program of Gradual Exposure for a child's relatively minor fear, you may not need additional fear fixers. However, when a child has a very strong fear, and certainly when he has a phobia, he will benefit from any fear fixer that helps him manage fear during the steps of Gradual Exposure. Let's see how the program actually unfolded for the Miller family.

Mom explained the first step of the program to Danny. He complained a bit about having to look at dog pictures but agreed to at least cooperate with the story time. The reading went well that first week and so his parents moved on optimistically to the second step, explaining that they would now visit a pet store. Danny got quite upset at the idea of being close to real, moving dogs even though they were going to be securely behind glass. Mom added a step to the program: they would watch moving dogs on the computer screen before going to an actual pet store. Even this was hard for Danny at first, but he did calm down after a few trial runs and sat through quite a few video clips of playful puppies and active dogs. (Note: using the Tapping protocol while watching the video clips might have made the exercise easier and more comfortable for Danny.) Now the Millers moved on to the next step: they scheduled a visit to the pet store.

Unfortunately, Danny just couldn't do it. As soon as Dad tried to get him to go near the glass window at the pet store, Danny started to whine and run the other way, yelling, "NOOOOOOO." He took off out of the store. Dad ran after him and, when he caught up with his son, acknowledged the boy's terror: "You're too scared to come into the pet store. That's okay. I have something that will help you for next time. Let's go home now."

Danny's fear was too intense to make more progress at that point on the Gradual Exposure program. The Millers decided to see if Bach flower remedies might help take the fear down a few notches so that Danny could better tolerate the stress of the more challenging levels of the Gradual Exposure protocol. On the way home from the pet store, they stopped into the health-food store to pick up Rescue Remedy, Mimulus, Rock Rose and an empty Bach mixing bottle.

At home, Mrs. Miller filled the mixing bottle with water and added 2 drops of Mimulus, for fear of dogs, and 2 drops of Rock Rose, for feelings of panic (see Appendix B for complete instructions for selecting and preparing Bach flower remedies). She explained to Danny that taking the remedy daily for a while would help him feel more calm when he encountered a real dog, and she gave him the regular dose: 4 drops in a little liquid, four times a day. The Millers temporarily interrupted the Gradual Exposure program to allow the Bach treatment to settle into his system. After two weeks on the Bach flower regime, they went back to Gradual Exposure, beginning at the visit to the pet store. This time, however, Dad gave Danny 4 drops of Rescue Remedy before leaving their home and—having put 4 more drops of Rescue Remedy in a small water bottle for the excursion—gave him a drink of the flower-water as they approached the store. Dad explained to Danny that it was important for him to be able to look at the dogs in their cages through the glass window, that doing so would help free him from his fear of dogs. This time, Danny agreed to go into the store and take a look at the puppies. (During the two-week hiatus from the Gradual Exposure protocol, I might have taught Danny how to regulate his emotions using Breathwork or some other emotional regulation tool. This would have helped him take charge of his physiology—calming his feelings through calming his body—when his fear was rising, an important skill to have whenever confronting fear directly. However, the Miller's approach of using a combination of Bach flower therapy *before* exposure and Rescue Remedy *at the time of* exposure also worked brilliantly to make the exposure itself much more tolerable.)

The Bach flower remedies did their work, easing enough fear out of Danny's system to allow him to complete the remainder of the Gradual Exposure protocol. As Danny accomplished each step successfully, his parents employed the CLeaR Method (see my book *Raise Your Kids without Raising Your Voice* for a detailed description of this tool) to gently reinforce his courage in confronting his fear.

The three steps of the CLeaR Method—Comment, Label, Reward—were used as Danny successfully completed a step in the Gradual Exposure program. For example, upon leaving the pet store, Mom Commented to Danny, "You looked at those puppies even though it was really scary!" She Labeled: "That was very *courageous* of you." And she Rewarded: "I think you deserve a trip to the ice cream store [or a big hug, or an extra story at bedtime tonight, or fifteen more minutes of computer time, etc.] for working so hard today." The acknowledgment and reward made it much easier, and more pleasant, for Danny to do the work of confronting his fear.

Now Danny is able to play in his own yard whether or not Pepper is out in his. He feels much more comfortable around dogs altogether, no longer reacting with panic whenever he sees one. Danny's fear of dogs is satisfactorily resolved.

HELPING OLIVER LEARN TO USE THE POTTY

At three and a half years of age, little Oliver should be physiologically and psychologically ready to use the toilet. However, while he is willing to urinate in a toilet or potty, he absolutely refuses to have a bowel movement there. Wearing regular "big boy" underwear, Oliver knows better than to soil his pants; he insists on being diapered whenever he wants to defecate. Mom has had enough of this routine and, in fact, the matter has become urgent: Oliver will not be accepted into the preschool program closest to home unless he is fully toilet trained within the next six weeks. Unfortunately, there is no "reasoning" with Oliver. He neither understands nor cares about the six-week deadline; he simply has a meltdown whenever someone drags him to a toilet. Amazingly, Oliver has learned to "hold it in" for extended periods of time—days on end—until his parents have become concerned for his health and the doctor is ordering laxatives.

Oliver's parents understand that, for reasons unbeknownst to them, Oliver is terrified of having a bowel movement in the toilet.

Mom has a colleague at work who had a similar issue with her own toddler and who successfully resolved it using Bach flower remedies. Mom suggests to Dad that they give the Bach approach a try. Dad is horrified. "We're not doing weirdo voodoo treatments on our kid," he tells her. Mom protests: "Listen," she says, "from what I understand, the Bach flower remedies aren't going to hurt him at all and while they may not help him, there *is* a chance they *will* help him. Shouldn't we at least try them?" Dad says, "Absolutely not." Mom understands his reaction. She can't cite the science on this one and she must admit that the whole concept sounds pretty weird. They go back to the pediatrician.

The doctor tells them not to worry—Oliver is perfectly healthy; he will grow out of this phase and eventually learn to use the toilet like everyone else. On the way home from the doctor's visit, Oliver's parents stop by a health-food store to purchase some Bach flower remedies. "What have we got to lose?" they're thinking now. "He's got to go to school in a couple of weeks and no one has any better ideas of how to make him use the toilet." (There was one idea, actually, from Oliver's uncle, who suggested holding Oliver forcefully over a potty for as many hours or days as necessary until he finally defecated. The uncle said that this treatment would definitely cure Oliver's fear, but Oliver's parents weren't convinced about that; in fact, they thought that he might develop a few new ones. I think they were right about that one!)

Bach Flower Remedies for Oliver

At home, Mom mixes a bottle of the following remedies for Oliver:

- Mimulus for fear (of having a bowel movement in the toilet)
- Rock Rose for feelings of panic
- Cherry Plum for fear of losing control (and for the wild, out-of-control behavior that accompanies Oliver's feelings of panic)

- Vine for powerfully strong will and emotionally intense meltdowns

All efforts at toilet training are put on temporary hold. Oliver is given his Bach flower potion four times a day for about a week and a half. Then his parents explain to him that he will no longer be given diapers and he should use the toilet like "the big people" in the family. On the first day of toilet training, both parents take a bit of Rescue Remedy to help calm their own nerves: they want to be as relaxed as possible in their dealings with Oliver. Fortunately, Oliver is unusually cooperative. In fact, when Dad tells him "no diaper" in response to Oliver's request for one, Oliver doesn't say a word. He just takes Dad's hand as Dad silently leads him to the bathroom. Nor does he fuss when Dad helps him undress and places him on the toilet. He just goes about his business! From then on, Oliver just asks Mom or Dad for help going to the toilet when he needs to use the facilities. Toilet training is finally completed, and Oliver is accepted into school. Oliver's folks say, "It was a miracle!"

Note: Although this "potty-training cure" is a common phenomenon in Bach flower treatment, it is not a guaranteed outcome. There are times when the "cure" happens but much more slowly, and there are times when no "cure" happens at all. However, the treatment is definitely worth trying, because, as Oliver's mom noted, it won't cause any harm and it *might* help. In fact, many, many parents report fantastic results when using Bach remedies for toileting fears and other fears, and quite a number make liberal use of the word "miracle" in describing their child's response to Bach flower treatment. Hopefully, you will be able to count yourself in that group when you try this approach with your own child's fear.

CINDY DEALS WITH HER FEAR OF NEEDLES

Fifteen-year-old Cindy has a fear of needles. Although she's never had a full-blown panic attack, she's certainly experienced a lot of distress every time she has to get a shot or endure a blood test. Her schoolmates mock her whenever they must receive mandatory inoculations together, failing to understand what "the big deal" is. Cindy can't help her reaction; her body shakes, her heart beats, her palms sweat, and she feels intensely nervous as she waits in line for her turn.

Knowing that Cindy was due for a shot this school year along with her classmates, her mom, Kathryn, decided to offer some help. "Sweetie, would you like to learn a technique to help you deal better with getting a needle?" she asked Cindy about three months before the needle was due. "Sure!" Cindy replied. That very night, Kathryn taught Cindy about the power of the breath and mind to calm anxious feelings. "There are two parts to this technique," Kathryn explained. "I'm going to teach you the first one now. It's just a simple breathing technique to help your body relax deeply. Use it every night as you are getting ready to sleep." Kathryn taught Cindy how to perform Herbert Benson's Relaxation Response (see Chapter Four, page 90).

Cindy found herself enjoying the few minutes of pleasant relaxation she experienced with the technique as she drifted off to sleep. "I like that breathing thing," she mentioned to Mom when she was a few weeks into it. "It stops my mind from thinking and helps me fall asleep." Mom was very pleased to hear this and proceeded to give Cindy further instructions for using the technique specifically for her fear of needles. "Okay. Here's how to use the Relaxation Response to help you deal directly with your fear. At least once a day, do the breathing for five or even ten minutes and, when you feel very relaxed, start watching a movie of yourself on an imaginary movie screen. See yourself getting that needle: see yourself waiting in line, then sitting down with the nurse, rolling up your sleeve, looking away while the nurse gives you the needle, feeling a quick, little stinging pinch, waiting for a moment until the nurse removes the needle from your arm, then rolling down your sleeve, feeling perfectly fine, getting up and leaving the room feeling completely normal, going back to class with your friends, laughing and chatting, and coming home after school. Make sure you watch *all* of it just like you're watching a movie."

Cindy agreed to do the Visualization exercise daily for the next two weeks. On the day of the inoculations, Mom asked Cindy how she was feeling about getting the needle. "Oh—I completely forgot to tell you, Mom—they gave them to us one day early, yesterday. I used my breathing and visualizing and everything went so well that I didn't even think about it when it was over. I'm sorry I forgot to tell you!" Mom didn't mind at all. She was thrilled at the success that Cindy had experienced.

RON'S FEAR OF ESCALATORS

At seventeen, Ron was embarrassed to admit he was afraid to go on escalators. However, his fear was greater than his embarrassment, so he asked for some help with this problem. His mom called me to set up an appointment for him but asked if I could help him over the phone, as he was currently staying with relatives during a school break. I told his mom that I could teach him a self-help tool on the phone—something that would take just one session. If the self-help tool didn't work, he should really visit the counseling service at the school he was attending. Mom spoke to Ron, who wanted to give it a try, and we scheduled a time for the lesson the following week.

During the session, I taught Ron how to do Tapping. I asked him to draw a picture of a face and upper body, and I told him to mark an X on the top of the head, the eyebrows near the nose, the outer edge of the eyes, under the eyes, under the nose (over the top lip), under the bottom lip, under the collarbone and on the side of the body (a few inches below the underarm). I couldn't see Ron's picture, of course, so I didn't know how accurate his drawing was, but I wasn't worried. In my experience of Tapping, the effect of intention is far greater than that of the physical technique itself. I was pretty sure it would work even if he tapped in all the wrong places. I instructed Ron to tap on the Karate Chop location on the side of his hand (see diagram in Chapter Four, page 120) for about twenty seconds and then to imagine going up and down escalators while tapping the designated points on his body. I also asked him, following the Tapping protocols, to rate, from zero to ten, before each round of tapping, the amount of fear he was feeling while doing the exercise. He started at ten on the first round. As we tapped the eight points over and over again, his fear rating fell lower and lower until, after twelve minutes of Tapping, he said he just couldn't think about the escalator anymore. This inability to think about the target is a common Tapping outcome of a successful resolution of fear, so I told him that he could practice the same exercise a couple more times later in the week if he wanted to and then go to a real escalator and see how it felt to ride it up and down. I asked him to let me know how it went. About two weeks later, I got a call from Ron apologizing for the delay in getting back to me but letting me know that even though he hadn't practiced the Tapping after our session, it obviously had worked. He was ecstatic about his escalator experience! The fear was completely gone and he felt confident it wouldn't come back.

Ron's experience illustrates some of the strengths of the Tapping approach. For one thing, it is so easy and so powerful that it can routinely end a stubborn fear even after just one short session. Although it doesn't always happen that way, it is certainly a common outcome for uncomplicated fears like the ones we are talking about in this chapter. Sometimes, a few extra practice sessions are needed to put the finishing touches on the treatment, but that's okay too, because each session really only requires a couple of minutes of time and attention. As I stated earlier, Tapping does not require tremendous precision or skill and so lends itself nicely to self-help situations. This technique can also be done "invisibly" (see Appendix A for details) so that it can be performed in public situations—a bonus for those suffering fears that occur in the classroom, on airplanes and so on. Remember, too, that many therapists around the world are currently trained in Tapping protocols and they can both treat your youngster and teach him how to use the technique independently.

TAMING CAT TERROR WITH A LITTLE TAPPING

Here's another example of how Tapping can be useful. Mikey, who is seven years old, is deathly afraid of cats. When visiting some relatives with Mom and Dad, Mikey spots a cat sleeping on a sofa in the family's living room. The child screams and begs to go home. Mom and Dad have just spent an hour traveling for this occasion and they're not about to leave. The child is so distraught, however, that the visit is going to be miserable for everyone unless something is done. Removing the cat is not an option, because Mikey wants it out of the house altogether—putting it in another room is not good enough for him. Unfortunately, the creature is an indoor cat and cannot be allowed outside. Moreover, the parents realize that avoiding the problem will only make matters worse in the long run. Dad tells Mikey that the cat is staying put and they are staying put too. He tells the youngster that he is going to help him calm down using a special Tapping technique. Dad works with the youngster for four or five minutes (see Appendix A, page 298 for exact protocol)—not enough to cure him totally of his cat phobia but quite enough to get the child to stay in the house and behave, if not happily, at least normally, for the duration of the visit. The Tapping intervention turned off the adrenaline and its attendant hysteria, leaving Mikey sane enough to control himself for the next while. After the visit, Mom called a therapist to arrange for a few sessions of professional Tapping treatment for Mikey. After four sessions, Mikey's fear of cats was completely neutralized. He no longer reacts with fear or even discomfort in the presence of these common pets.

HOW TO CHOOSE A FEAR FIXER

With so many tools available for calming anxious and frightened feelings, how does one know which one to use in a particular situation? Here are some guidelines for choosing:

- Start with the one that is most appealing to you and to the child who is using it.
- Try an easier one before trying one that requires more time and effort to learn and apply.
- Try another one if the first one doesn't work.
- Try using more than one at the same time.
- Try every single one of them if necessary.
- Seek professional help if nothing you've tried has worked and if the fear is either significantly bothering your child or getting in the child's way of functioning well at home, school or elsewhere.

FAST TRACKS FOR FEARS OF PEOPLE, PLACES AND THINGS

Fastest Fast Track

When anticipating an encounter with a feared person, place or thing, give the child Rescue Remedy (see instructions in Appendix B, page 310) before, during and after exposure (e.g., for fear of crowds, when going to a crowded place, take Rescue Remedy before arriving, as often as needed during the experience, and once or twice afterward).

If the exposure was unanticipated, simply offer the child Rescue Remedy as soon as possible, as many times as needed.

Fuller Program Fast Track

Offer Rescue Remedy as described in Fastest Fast Track above.

To prevent the fear from occurring in the future, offer a mixture of Mimulus and Rock Rose several times a day until the fear is no longer an issue (see Appendix B, page 310, for full instructions).

When the child is confronted by the person, place or thing he fears, instruct him to look at his feet (if possible)* and blow air out of pursed lips slowly—as if blowing up a balloon or making a whistling sound—until exposure to the feared person, place or thing has ended or until he is feeling calmer.

---

* Looking down at one's feet is a "grounding" activity that helps transform scattered, panicky feelings into more stable and settled ones. The effect is even stronger if the child imagines that there is a sack of potatoes or a small pile of bricks sitting on top of each foot.

SARAH CHANA RADCLIFFE

CHAPTER EIGHT

Helping Your Child through Fears Fueled by Imagination

Fear of monsters, illness, germs, death,
kidnapping, disasters, bad things happening

People of all ages worry about "bad things" happening. Some, however, worry about vague dangers more than others. Preschoolers, for instance, are notorious for worrying about monsters under the bed and dangers that lurk in the dark. While older kids and teens usually stop thinking about monsters, many persist in their discomfort with a darkened bedroom. Parents want their kids to be afraid of dark alleyways and take the necessary precautions, but they prefer that their kids not be afraid of their own bedrooms. The main difference between an alleyway and a bedroom is the element of real danger. In fact, there *is* a risk in walking down an isolated, dark alley late at night, whereas there is very little risk involved in sleeping in one's own bed (in safe countries). If there is little actual risk, why do older kids persist in feeling uncomfortable in the dark?

The answer lies in the realm of imagination. A child's mind can conjure up danger using only a few cues. For example, note how each of the following cues can contribute to a sense of foreboding:

- darkness
- sounds and noises with unknown sources
- broken, deformed or malformed objects
- isolation, aloneness
- lack of control, perceived helplessness

Imagine being in a situation that contained all of those cues. Wouldn't *you* feel scared? Unfortunately, it's easy to have all of those cues in one's room at night: darkness as the lights are turned off, noises emitting from the heating or cooling systems and appliances such as the refrigerator, creaking floors, strange-looking objects (that seem misshapen in the darkness), lying alone in one's bed and the reality (in young childhood) of being small and helpless. It's a perfect mix for fueling feelings of terror. Indeed, if you ask most kids what they are afraid of in their bedroom, they will have only the vaguest of answers: the dark, something or someone lurking, something bad happening and so on. Some fear that a robber might burst into their room or that kidnappers might enter through the window. The right conditions are there—all that is needed is "the bad guy." It's all vague and murky, a potential problem arising out of the unknown, unclear shadows of the night. These youngsters take the real seed of the fear—the true fact that bad people can and do hide in dark corners—and they water it until it harvests a full stalk of pure negative imagination.

There are many other vague disasters that children are prone to imagining. For instance, kids aged four through eight often have an intense fear of their parents dying—despite the fact that their parents are young, healthy and living in safety. As the fear does not stem from real-world considerations, it is also a fear fueled by imagination—a fear of bad things happening.

Older kids and teens often imagine, and then dread, bad happenings of a different kind. Catastrophic illness is a favorite of many; fear of cancer is popular, as is fear of AIDS or just fear of "something serious" being wrong. The fear of dying from a disease that one does not have is essentially a fear fueled again by imagination. In this case, the child takes the seed of the fear—typically a minor physical symptom stemming from a minor physical condition—and waters it until it has blossomed into a full-fledged drama of epic proportions: "I'm going to die!" The tendency to develop a fear of illness is thought to have biological roots. When the fear is intense enough to have negative consequences for the child's emotional well-being or functioning, it is considered to be a mental illness (hypochondriasis). Many adults also suffer from hypochondriasis. While their family members may mock them as being overly anxious hypochondriacs, these people are truly suffering from a painful condition of chronic, debilitating anxiety. The human body is prone to lots of harmless symptoms—bumps, marks, pains, odd sensations. However, these same symptoms can also underlie deadly disease. The person suffering from hypochondriasis does not *imagine* symptoms, but rather imagines a disastrous outcome of real symptoms, misinterpreting all unaccounted for bodily quirks, aches and sensations as having potentially lethal consequences. In so doing, the child or adult rarely has a moment's peace of mind. Left untreated, the disorder tends to persevere throughout the lifetime, causing unnecessary stress and discomfort.

Sometimes kids grow up to project the fear onto their own children or loved ones, worrying about the health of those people instead of (or in addition to) their own. Like many other types of stress and worry, this particular type of anxious feeling can sometimes respond very well to some of the home treatments we will examine in this chapter. However, if self-help doesn't provide adequate relief of worry about deathly illness, do take your child for professional treatment to relieve this fear.

BASELESS FEAR

Vague fears are considered to be the most irrational fears of all, since they are less connected to the facts of a situation than most other fears. Parents often react to these kinds of fears with exasperation. "There is *nothing* to be afraid of!" they'll tell their youngsters. "Bad people aren't going to climb into your window, and that little girl who was kidnapped last July lived on the other side of the country, so please stop thinking about it and go to bed already!" "Honestly, you're not going to die from using a public toilet! Just use it, because we're not turning around and going home right now!" "I don't care if you're afraid of the basement—I've told you there's *nothing* down there for you to be afraid of, so please run down and get me the sugar from the pantry, because I need it right now and I can't leave the kitchen!" Anybody who's read the earlier chapters of this book knows that these heartfelt reassurances are going to do exactly *nothing* for the child's fear. The child's own power of imagination is far stronger than any facts that Mom or Dad might offer in the moment of terror.

When there is no real reason to believe that something bad will happen, fear is generated and fed by one's own imagination. When the doctor has given a bill of clean health, for instance, continued fear of serious disease is unwarranted and only fueled by the negative thought process. Here are some common fears that are fueled by imagination in children and teens:

- the dark
- being kidnapped (in safe localities)
- being robbed (in safe localities)
- parents dying (when they are healthy)
- bad things happening in the world (e.g., war, terrorist attacks or violent weather conditions in locations where there have never been any)
- natural disasters (in locations where there haven't been any)
- superstitions (e.g., fear of stepping on cracks)
- monsters, ghosts, demons
- deathly illness (when the person is basically healthy)
- separation from significant others (e.g., when parents go out for the evening)

SARAH CHANA RADCLIFFE

- contamination (of the type found in obsessive-compulsive disorders)
- something bad happening to loved ones (when everything is stable and safe)
- something bad happening to oneself

Fears fueled by imagination can be treated using most of the techniques in *The Fear Fix*. However, kids who are prone to fears of this kind are also particularly good candidates for interventions that specifically employ the imaginative process. In other words, an imaginative child's imagination can both create and *cure* a fear.

HELPING ABIGAIL GO TO THE SECOND FLOOR HERSELF

Five-year-old Abigail will *not* go upstairs by herself. "I'm AFRAID!" she wails when Mom asks her to go to the second floor of their two-story home. Mom is getting annoyed. "She's five years old already and I can't always go up with her anymore. The bathroom is on the second floor and so is her bedroom. I'm busy with the toddler and the baby, and I can't just drop everything every time Abigail has to get ready for bed, use the toilet or get a piece of clothing. She needs to learn to go upstairs by herself!" Mom develops a plan to help Abigail conquer her fear.

Her first strategy is to use Gradual Exposure. Mom creates a step-by-step protocol (pun intended!) that she figures will take a week or so to carry out. On the next occasion that Abigail needs to use the bathroom, Mom walks up the stairs with her but stops on the top step. "I'll wait right here, Abigail," Mom says. "You can see me from the bathroom doorway." Abigail really has to rush to the bathroom. so she doesn't linger to argue with Mom. She runs in, keeping her eye on her mother the whole time. Mom does the "top step" routine for a number of days, walking up the stairs with Abigail but waiting for her on the step instead of accompanying her along the second floor hallway. Abigail starts to relax with the process, barely bothering to look at Mom. After a number of days, Mom moves down a couple of steps, sitting so that only her head is in sight when Abigail is running down the hallway. Abigail is okay with this, as she can still see Mom from the bathroom and from her bedroom doorway as well. A few days later, Mom moves down two more steps so that it's hard for Abigail to see her when she's on the second floor. However, Mom keeps talking loudly so that Abigail can feel her presence, and this seems to provide sufficient comfort. Some days later, Mom stays in the same spot but stops the constant chatter. Now Abigail gets anxious, calling out every few moments, "Mommy? Mommy?" On the next occasion, Abigail absolutely refuses to go up the stairs unless Mommy comes all the way with her.

Mom realizes that she has to add some features to her Gradual Exposure protocol, since she has hit a wall with Abigail. For the next week, Mom sits on the top step again, while giving her daughter the Bach flower remedy Mimulus (for fears of separation and bad people) and Aspen (for fears of monsters and other undefined negative forces). After a week, Mom continues giving the remedies but starts the Gradual Exposure again, slowly moving down the stairway, step by step. Again, she gets to the point where Abigail can no longer see or hear her, but this time, Abigail can tolerate the discomfort. Mom continues to move down the stairs until she is sitting on the bottom step. Abigail is okay with that.

Now Mom is hoping that Abigail can manage going upstairs *without* anyone needing to sit on the bottom step. Mom is busy in the kitchen when Abigail starts to call for help: "Mommy, come sit on the stairs—I need to go to the bathroom." Mom replies that she's busy and Abigail should just run quickly upstairs by herself. Abigail gets frantic, screaming, "COME RIGHT NOW! I CAN'T WAIT—YOU HAVE TO COME RIGHT NOW!" Mom gives in.

Mom realizes she must add one more intervention to the mix. Abigail's fear is a fear of imagination, so Mom figures that Positive Imagination might help. Later that day, Mom explains to Abigail: "Sweetie, Mommy can't always sit on the stair when you need to go upstairs, but do you want to know about a little trick that can help

SARAH CHANA RADCLIFFE

just as much as having Mommy sit on the step?" Abigail is curious, so Mom continues: "You can take my magic wand with you." And she hands Abigail her new pastry brush with the pretty pink flowers on it. "I'll leave it at the bottom of the stairs for you and you can take it up with you anytime you need to go to your room or the bathroom. If you wave it around a bit, it will scare away all the bad things and fill the air with flowers and fairies. You'll love it!" Abigail looked delighted as she stroked the bristles of the small brush in her hand. She turned and ran toward the stairs, waving the pastry brush up and down as she made her way to the bathroom. Mom was right: Abigail's vivid imagination could be enlisted to help her feel calm just as surely as it could be used to scare her silly. The pastry brush was an excellent tool for stimulating Positive Imagination.

Some of you may be wondering whether it is right to encourage a child to use "magical thinking." Perhaps you are concerned that the flight into fantasy distances the child from healthier, reality-based thinking. If so, keep in mind that children with these kinds of fears are already taking a flight into (negative) fantasy, doing so in a way that produces pain, suffering and a slew of depleting chemicals. There are other techniques like journaling, Tapping, Mindfulness-Yes and others that can help the child directly face her fears, and these can be used instead if desired. However, the act of practicing Positive Imagination for fears fueled by imagination has the benefit of training the brain to be creative in a healthier direction. All feelings of comfort and security are fueled by imagining a benign and safe world. Since anyone whose illusions of safety have been shattered by traumatic events can testify that such an image is also out of touch with reality, we can simply ask ourselves which fantasies serve us better in day-to-day life. There is both beauty and tragedy in human existence, but focusing endlessly on what might go wrong can only destroy the quality of one's living experience. Teaching a child to look for, and even create, symbols of safety will help her to enjoy greater peace of mind.

HELPING JAMIE THROUGH HIS FEAR OF WAKING UP DEAD IN THE MORNING

Jamie is seven years old. Lately, he has become very worried that when he goes to sleep at night, he won't wake up in the morning. "I'm going to die in my sleep," he tells Dad. "I'm afraid to go to bed." Dad greets Jamie's fear with emotional coaching. "That's a really scary thought," Dad tells him. "You must feel awful when you think about that." Jamie agrees wholeheartedly. Dad wonders if he can move Jamie's fear with facts (see Chapter Three). He's tempted to tell Jamie that little boys almost never die in their sleep but quickly realizes that this sort of fact isn't likely to help calm Jamie's fear. Instead, the technique calls for a fact that *directly addresses* the fear. In this case, the fact would have to concern what Jamie would do if he did indeed die in his sleep! Although this exploration might be fruitful for an adult with a similar fear, Dad realizes that the Move Fear with Facts technique is not the most appropriate intervention for his son.

Dad switches tactics. He reasons that Jamie's fear derives from an overactive imagination. He wonders what Jamie might have been reading or watching that could have stimulated the idea that someone might die in the night. He asks Jamie about his activities, and Jamie tells him that he first started thinking about dying in his sleep when he heard that his friend's baby sister died of sudden infant death syndrome (SIDS) in her sleep. At last Dad understands how the fear started—it isn't from books or movies but rather a real-life event. No wonder the little guy is terrified! Jamie doesn't know that SIDS generally affects babies six months old and under, not big boys. Now Dad is sure he can make the fear go away by providing education. "Jamie, seven-year-olds don't die from SIDS—that's something that just happens to babies," Dad tells his son. Jamie replies, "I know that, but I'm still scared."

Jamie isn't suffering from a lack of information after all. He is suffering from an anxious brain. His mind clings to the idea of dying even though there is no reason whatsoever for this fear. Dad thinks

SARAH CHANA RADCLIFFE

about this a bit and then remembers that he read about a technique that helps move information from the logical, left side of the brain across to the emotional, right side of the brain: Tapping-In. He asks, "Jamie, would you like to help your whole brain to know that you'll wake up alive in the morning?" Of course, Jamie says he would. Dad proceeds to do Tapping-In with Jamie. To do this, Dad asks Jamie to draw on the positive memory of successfully waking up every day of his life so far. He does this by asking his son, "Is it true that you wake up every morning and have woken up every morning every day of your life so far?" Jamie acknowledges that this is true but expresses the worry that things could change at any time. Dad says he understands the worry. He then instructs Jamie to tap left, right, left, right three times on his thighs while saying the true statement, "I always wake up in the morning." (See Chapter Four for instructions on Tapping-In.) Tapping-In this way allows the fact that lives in the left brain ("I wake up every morning") to move to a feeling location in the right brain so that Jamie can both *know* and *feel* the truth of the statement. (Although Dad knows that there are very rare situations in which children die in the night, he feels that this is not an important fact to share with Jamie at this time, since Jamie's concern is really fueled by an imaginative reaction to SIDS.) After a few rounds of Tapping-In, Jamie is thinking normally again. He feels confident that he'll wake up alive tomorrow morning just as he has done on all the previous mornings. His fear that he'll wake up dead disappears and doesn't return.

Tapping techniques such as EFT or Tapping-In can often fix a fear in just one quick session, as with Jamie. Indeed, this may be the most commonly successful tehnique for simple fears (i.e., a child's single, specific fear when that child does not have a trauma history, a history of multiple fears and anxieties, previous mood issues, other mental health diagnoses or other complicating factors). However, even when a Tapping exercise needs to be completed a few times, it is still a very quick fear fixer. When Tapping fails to relieve a simple fear after several occasions of using it, it's best to switch to another home-based treatment or take the child to a professional who is trained in Tapping techniques and can resolve the simple fear quickly. Of course, if a child has many fears or intense fears that cause distress or get in the child's way of living a normal or comfortable life, it's important to see a mental-health professional who has specialized training in the treatment of children's anxieties.

HELPING TANNER DEAL WITH HIS FEAR OF THINGS THAT GO BUMP IN THE NIGHT

Five-year-old Tanner was being impossible! Ever since he saw that scary movie, he would not go to bed at night. Tanner was suddenly afraid of being in his own room. "I want to sleep with YOU," he told Mom. Mom already had enough problems with one-year-old Max's constant interruptions in the night—she certainly did not want a big boy tossing and turning in her bed. "No way," she told Tanner. "You'll just have to sleep in your own bed!" "But I'm afraid of the monsters," Tanner responded pitifully. Mom understood. That movie was scary stuff and it was definitely a mistake to have let Tanner see it. But all the cousins were watching it together and Mom hadn't realized at the time how frightened Tanner was feeling. "I should have known better," she lamented later. "Tanner is very easily influenced by things. If he hears a disturbing story or watches a sad movie, he's bothered for weeks. Even his sleep is affected." She felt guilty for subjecting Tanner to the frightening images, but most of all, she felt anxious to help him recover.

Mom knew from past experience that nothing she could say would make Tanner feel better. "Once Tanner gets freaked out, there's no talking to him. His brain won't budge," she noted. It was Dad who offered a solution. "I think we should make a mixture of Bach flower remedies for Tanner," he suggested. Gazing down a list of remedies he found in an appendix of *The Fear Fix*, he read, "We can give him Walnut for being so easily affected by things he sees and hears, Aspen for being afraid of the dark, and Rock Rose for feelings of panic." Mom agreed that this might be the best approach, or at least the easiest one to begin with, since the remedies might help Tanner's fear diminish without him having to work hard. Meanwhile, Mom was firm in her insistence that Tanner continue to sleep in his own room. She knew that if he avoided the problem, the fear would only intensify and persist. Avoidance, as we know by now, makes fears worse. Moreover, knowing that she was helping her son with the Bach flower mixture, Mom didn't feel too bad about making him tough it out. "He'll be okay," she said. "Hopefully, the remedy will help take the edge off his fear." In fact, that's exactly what happened. Tanner continued taking the flower remedy mixture for a couple of weeks and the fear melted away. During that time, he put up a small fuss each night but was easily persuaded to stay in his own room. Mom decided to keep Tanner on the remedy regime a bit longer, even though this particular episode of fear cleared up nicely; she wanted to see if the remedies might reduce his overall sensitivity to images and his general tendency to get easily frightened.

PATTY ADDRESSES HER FEAR OF SERIOUS ILLNESS

Nineteen-year-old Patty was very fearful of illness. She was one of those people who felt that every unusual physical sensation portended a death sentence, or at least a major health crisis. Recently, she had become aware of yet another unexplained symptom in her body: a rapid heartbeat. "I've never noticed that before," Patty thought. "What could it mean?" Of course, Patty suspected it meant serious trouble. Normally, she would have immediately made a doctor's appointment to check it out, but this time she hesitated. She had been there only four days before to investigate a suspicious cough (which turned out to be caused by a cold). She felt embarrassed. She knew that she visited the doctor way too often and felt self-conscious about making yet another appointment. "I will make an appointment if I can't get rid of this fear," she decided. But how was she going to get rid of her fear?

Patty went online, searching for techniques to calm fear. She came across a lot of information, but something that really piqued her interest was Tapping. The technique was described as being "rapid" and "easy to do" and most important, "highly effective." She decided to give it a try. Patty studied the instructions and then jumped right in. She rated the intensity of her fear as a nine on a ten-point scale and then commenced with simple Tapping—just tapping the eight points on her body (see Chapter Four, page 115, and Appendix A, page 298 for Tapping instructions) while naming her fear out loud at each point: "I've got a heart problem. I'm probably going to die. I've got a serious heart problem. I've got heart disease. Something is very wrong with my heart," and so on. By the time Patty had finished her eighth Tapping point, she felt a little less sure that she had a serious heart condition but still rated her fear at five on a ten-point scale. She now used something called the Choices Method (see Appendix A, page 303, for complete instructions for this technique).

The Choices Method involves three full rounds of tapping the eight treatment points instead of just one round, as in regular EFT. While tapping on the Karate Chop spot (or rubbing on the Tender Spot), the person makes a statement that sounds like this: "Even though I have this fear [name the fear], I choose this [make a choice]." For example, "Even though I am afraid I'll fail the test, I choose to study hard and let whatever happens happen." Next, the person taps the eight points three times. On the first round, the person names her fear. On the second round, the person names her choice. On the final round, the person alternates naming the fear and the choice.

Patty begins the Choices Method by tapping on the Karate Chop point while saying, "Even though I still think I've got a serious heart condition, I choose to recognize that most people my age have very healthy hearts." She repeats that statement three times. Then she begins to tap on the eight points, naming her fear at each point as she previously did ("I'm probably going to die. I have a heart disorder. I have a heart defect. I might die . . ."). Then she begins the second round of the Choices Method, tapping the eight points again, this time naming her choice as she taps: "I know that people my age have healthy hearts. I know that, statistically speaking, I probably have a healthy heart. I know that young people normally have very healthy hearts . . ." On the third and last round of Choices Tapping, Patty alternates what she says at each Tapping point, starting at the top of her head with the frightened thought "I'm probably dying" and moving to the eyebrow near the nose, saying, "Young people have healthy hearts," naming the worry at the outer edge of the eye— "My heart is defective"—and the choice statement at the under-eye point—"People my age tend to have strong hearts"—and continuing to alternate her fear and her choice statements at the remaining points.

When Patty finishes tapping all three rounds, she rates the intensity of her fear concerning her heart one more time. Now she feels that the idea of having heart disease is highly unlikely. "Nah, I don't think there's anything wrong with my heart." Tapping has helped tame Patty's overactive imagination by opening the previously blocked pathways to the perfectly good, logical information that was already in her brain.

HELPING HANNAH THROUGH HER FEAR OF TERRORISM

Hannah is the youngest of the four Hanson children. Her parents and the three teenagers enjoy reading current events magazines and have a couple of subscriptions to weekly tabloids. The magazines end up lying on the bathroom floor and the kitchen table, where ten-year-old Hannah can easily see the cover pages. Sometimes Hannah picks up a magazine and leafs through the pages, just out of curiosity. Of course, world news being what it is, Hannah often sees gruesome pictures and articles with alarming titles. This is probably the reason that she has begun to worry about something bad happening where she lives.

"Daddy, are the terrorists going to come here?" Hannah asks. Dad acknowledges the fear in Hannah's voice. But then, falling into his old parenting patterns, Dad tries to offer reassurance: "I don't think we have anything to worry about here, Hannah. Everything seems to be fine where we live." Unfortunately (and predictably), these kinds of facts do little to soothe Hannah's fear. Like all imaginative worriers, Hannah knows that there are exceptions to the rule and generalities don't always apply. She retorts, "But, Daddy, there can always be a first time, can't there? Maybe nothing has happened in our city yet, but the terrorists can go anywhere, can't they?"

Realizing his strategic error, Dad switches tactics. "You're right, Hannah. No one really knows what will happen from day to day. So we have a choice: we can think about all the bad things that *might* happen, or we can think about all the good things that we hope will happen." Dad then pulls out the old Lego box from the toy cupboard and teaches Hannah about her role in building her brain (see Chapter Five, page 129). "So when you start to imagine all sorts of bad things happening, you can just say hello to your scary thoughts and then say good-bye to them. Just let them sit there while you put your attention on something else. Try thinking about how beautiful our city is, how safe and happy we all feel here and how blessed you are to be able to live in this place. Keep adding more and more good pictures—see the flowers growing, the people smiling, the city flourishing. In this way, you will build yourself a happy brain that thinks good thoughts instead of dark and scary ones."

Seeing the Lego model didn't immediately cure Hannah's fear. However, the image of growing a frightened brain yellow brick by yellow brick stuck in her mind whenever she entertained a thought about terrorists in the next few weeks. She took Dad's advice to heart and forced herself to focus her attention on happier images. However, she found that Dad's suggestion of thinking about the city itself really didn't work for her. Every time she thought of the city, pictures of bombs popped into her mind. After some experimentation, Hannah found that she could stop thinking about terrorists if she focused really hard on thinking about her cat. Hannah's love for her pet immediately flooded every cell of her body with warm, happy chemistry that provided a strong antidote to the disturbing feelings of fear. After a while, Hannah forgot to think about terrorists (or cats) and just got on with her life.

HELPING BRIAN AT BEDTIME

Six-year-old Brian cannot fall asleep at night. He tosses and turns and thinks about things. His thoughts roam all over the place, focusing on nothing in particular. He just can't settle down. Brian's parents describe him as "wired" and "anxious," an eager-to-please youngster who is happy but stressed. They suspect that his sleeping problems are fueled by feelings of overwhelm and insecurity.

Knowing that Brian is an imaginative youngster, his parents decide to tell him imaginative stories just before bed. They call them Brian-the-Brave stories. These stories center around the experiences of a little boy whose name just happens to be Brian too. Brian has many adventures—disturbing, frightening, overwhelming adventures. Each time, however, he rises to the occasion and masters the challenge before him. Brian-the-Brave stories feature feelings of fear followed by mastery; the details of each story don't really matter. Telling stories such as these to kids, particularly in the pre-bedtime moments, is an almost hypnotic exercise in that the stories contain a therapeutic subtext: life is challenging, but a person can use his tools to face and master those challenges. This message would help anyone sleep better at night. With just a little creativity, Brian's parents are able to make up a new story every night for months on end (or years on end if they want to). Brian loves listening to the empowering stories and asks for them every night. Here are the features of a Brian-the-Brave story:

- Brian starts a pleasant adventure (e.g., visiting a jungle, a new planet, a new country, a mountain, a cave or any other new environment).
- Brian encounters a threat to his safety (e.g., dangerous environmental conditions, enemies, ferocious animals, dangerous sea creatures, fire and so on).
- Brian pulls out a magic solution and successfully eliminates the danger (e.g., a magic potion that shrinks or vanquishes a human or animal threat, a special spray that calms environmental threats, a pill, a magic word, a special tool or weapon).

- Brian continues on his adventure, enjoying beautiful and interesting experiences until he encounters another threat. He successfully subdues this threat as well. Brian continues encountering one or two more threats until the story ends very happily with him achieving his goal (e.g., finding the treasure, meeting new friends, learning a new skill, enjoying a fun experience, etc.).

A Brian-the-Brave story can be as brief or as long as desired, anywhere from three to ten minutes, and can contain two or more successfully subdued threats before the inevitable happy ending. Children don't care very much about the content of these stories. They simply thrive on the feeling of competence and safety that they impart. The fact that they are completely nonsensical doesn't seem to matter at all. When telling a Brian-the-Brave story, simply use your own child's name and your imagination to come up with fantastical stories. Here is an excerpt from a Brian-the-Brave story:

> One day, a little boy named Brian-the-Brave decided to go on a trip in the jungle. He was hoping to find a precious jewel that was in the care of a wise man who lived there. Brian-the-Brave took five of his strongest men with him, and they packed their bags and their boat. The men carried the boat on their backs as they trudged through the thick jungle. There were big trees, strange insects and so many brightly colored birds everywhere. Suddenly, from out of nowhere, a large Bengal tiger leaped toward them. Quickly, Brian-the-Brave threw himself on the ground, reaching for his magic key chain, which was dangling from his pants. The other men leaped out of the way as Brian-the-Brave pulled the special lever on the key chain, causing a huge net to puff up and capture the tiger. "That wasn't nice," Brian-the-Brave said to the tiger. "You should warn people when you are coming. You scared us! You will have to stay in this net until tomorrow, when it will melt away. Please walk quietly through the jun-

gle next time." The tiger was ashamed of himself for scaring everyone and lay down and went to sleep. Brian-the-Brave and his men continued onward. Soon they came to a deep river. "Put the boat in the water," Brian-the-Brave ordered his men. They did so, and then everyone got in the boat and started to paddle down the stream. There was a beautiful warm breeze and everyone felt so happy and relaxed in the boat. Suddenly, one of the men called out: "Look out! There's a sea serpent coming toward us!" Sure enough, a large, scaly, fire-breathing sea serpent was heading toward their boat. Brian-the-Brave was ready. He reached into his backpack and pulled out a spray gun. "Don't worry," he told the men, "I'll take care of this." Sure enough, as soon as the sea serpent was close to their boat, Brian-the-Brave aimed the spray gun right at him. The sea serpent immediately shrank into a tiny lizard. The little creature was very surprised. He turned around and started swimming away from the boat. "Bye-bye, little serpent," waved Brian-the-Brave. The men were relieved. They started singing happy songs as they continued paddling down the river. By this time, the sun was setting. The men were getting hungry and decided that they should pull to shore to make a campfire and cook some dinner . . .

I bet you want to know how the story ends. Well, finish it off for yourself and your child, and you'll find out. Brian-the-Brave stories are one of the more fun fear fighters in a parent's tool kit.

HELPING JACOB THROUGH HIS FEAR OF SOMETHING TERRIBLE HAPPENING

Jacob, age eight, has always been a neat and orderly child. However, in recent months, he seems to have become obsessed with orderliness. His older brother, Jonathan, can't stand it. He's complaining bitterly to Mom and Dad that Jacob keeps lining up all the pillows on the sofa in the family room, needing to have them balanced just so. If Jonathan accidentally moves a pillow when he sits on the sofa, Jacob has a fit, screaming at him for messing up the pillow arrangement and complaining, "Now I have to do it all over again!"

Jacob's behavior is of concern, both because of the distress it causes Jacob himself and because of the distress it causes the family. It is possible that Jacob is beginning to manifest symptoms of obsessive-compulsive disorder (OCD). This disorder is characterized by fear and dread that something terrible will happen. The fear is calmed by some sort of behavior that "magically" makes everything okay. In Jacob's case, he happens to be terrified that something bad will happen to a family member, but he feels that everything will be okay as long as he keeps the pillows lined up properly.

OCD manifests in endless varieties, although there are many common themes. In general, there is always some sort of named or unnamed fear and a physical or mental behavior that temporarily calms the fear. (Kids can't always say what they're afraid of; they may simply feel very anxious.) Once they feel that fear, however, youngsters suffering from OCD worry that something terrible will happen to themselves or others if they don't perform the necessary physical or mental behavior. In order to avoid having to do the work involved in the behavior (such as constantly straightening pillows), the child starts to avoid those situations that require the behavior. For instance, Jacob might start avoiding going into the family room so that he won't have to arrange the pillows. Similarly, a child who must wash her hands fifty times if she comes into contact with germs, dirt or other perceived forms of "contamination," may start trying to avoid having to do all that washing by refusing to touch doorknobs with her hands. Instead, she might hold a tissue in her hand while turning the knob, she might get someone else to open the door for her or she might just push the door open with her elbow or leg. In cases of untreated OCD, it is possible for fear to expand and expand until it seriously interferes with the child's peace of mind and ability to function well.

The kinds of "magical" mental and physical behaviors that OCD sufferers discover usually fall into one or more of the following types:

- repeating an action a certain number of times
- saying or writing words a certain way, counting to a certain number or saying a "magic undoing" word or phrase
- repeatedly correcting and redoing things (so as not to forget to do something or so as not to do something imperfectly)
- performing numerous checks to make sure everything is as it should be (e.g., checking over and over again to see if the stove has been turned off)
- engaging in excessive religious practices (including abnormally lengthy prayer sessions)
- making sure things are lined up correctly, in a certain order or precisely even
- washing and cleaning excessively in order to prevent contamination

Because of all the work involved in doing these rituals, the child or teen inevitably develops ways of avoiding having to do them by avoiding being triggered in the first place (as we saw in the case of a child who refuses to touch a doorknob in order to avoid the contaminated feeling that requires endless washing). Avoidance includes not seeing, doing, hearing, writing or saying the thing or things that might trigger a need to do a ritual.

Some OCD-type behaviors can occur without a child having an actual diagnosis of OCD. In fact, except in the case of the Pediatric Autoimmune Neuropsychiatric Disorders Associated with Streptococcal Infections (PANDAS) version of OCD (i.e., OCD symptoms that have been suddenly triggered by a streptococcal infection), the behaviors are often hard to detect at first. They just look like the normal but weird things that kids do. For example, five-year-old Jennifer insists that her Mom give her four kisses at bedtime. That's a normal request for a five-year-old to make. But soon, Jennifer starts insisting on having exactly ten kisses and claims that she can't go to sleep without them. Mom thinks the request is just "typical Jenny." The demands keep increasing, however, until Jennifer refuses to go to sleep until she has had exactly thirty-six kisses—eighteen on each cheek. Mom, losing patience, decides to ask the pediatrician for advice. The pediatrician tells Mom to go back to four kisses and leave it there. That night when Mom tells Jennifer the plan, Jennifer becomes hysterical; she screams, cries, yells and throws herself around until, after some hours, she falls asleep on the floor in utter exhaustion. The intensity of Jennifer's response is typical for withdrawal from rituals that are rooted in OCD-type feelings.

The good news is that Jennifer was cured that night: she found that she *could* fall asleep after four kisses after all. However, the "treatment" was rather rough for both her and her Mom. It would have been better if Mom had refused to engage in the odd behavior in the first place. The truth is, however, that Mom hadn't really noticed that the increasing need for kisses was rather strange. After this episode, Mom's radar was more finely attuned to unusual requests. From that time onward, Mom carefully refused to cooperate when Jennifer asked for any behavior that wouldn't look quite right to an outsider. She realized that strange requests had anxious feelings at their source and that giving in to the behavior would cause those anxious feelings to become more intense over time.

It can take parents a really long time to recognize that their child's worries and behaviors are out of the normal range and actually require professional attention. However, knowing what to look for can help. In the case of OCD worries, there are ways to recognize some of the early symptoms of unmanageable anxiety. A clue that all is not well, for instance, is that the child doesn't just *want* to do a particular behavior, he seems to *have* to do it. If the child is prevented from doing the behavior, some sort of adrenaline-driven meltdown will ensue. Another clue for further investigation is the parent's own fear of the child's reaction to the word "no." Specifically, if the parent becomes afraid of what will happen if the child is prevented from doing a somewhat odd behavior (e.g., erasing schoolwork for the tenth time for no observable reason), it is time to ask the doctor for advice. Moreover, when OCD worries and behaviors are causing a child distress or interfering with him functioning at home, school or elsewhere (for example, causing him to be unable to get to school on time or complete assignments or behave normally within the classroom), it is time to seek professional help. A clinical psychologist or child psychiatrist can assess your youngster to determine if OCD is present. The same professional can also offer effective treatment. Fortunately, OCD responds very well to cognitive-behavioral therapy (CBT), a treatment that helps a child correct unhealthy and unhelpful thought patterns *and* prescribes and monitors necessary changes in behavior. CBT is best conducted by professionals who specialize in the treatment of obsessive-compulsive disorder. Occasionally, medication may also be indicated—most often as a temporary measure that facilitates behavioral treatment by reducing overwhelming feelings of anxiety.

As I stated earlier, many children have OCD-*type* worries and behaviors. They do not meet criteria for a diagnosis of OCD. Whether these youngsters are in the early stages of OCD or whether they are OCD-free kids who will soon outgrow their anxieties, parents can use strategies to help reduce their fears and worries. These strategies may also help prevent more symptoms from developing.

The techniques that can help OCD-type thoughts, feelings and actions are scattered throughout this book. Feel free to draw on any intervention you think might help your child's particular version of this fear. Keep in mind, however, that at its core, OCD-type fear is a fear that is fueled by imagination. The child both imagines that something bad will happen to himself or someone else and imagines that some ritualized behavior he performs will stop it from happening. The tendency to imagine in this way is considered to be both biologically and environmentally triggered (the result of vulnerable genes and various environmental stressors, including streptococcal infection, the PANDAS variety of OCD). Interestingly, successful interventions can both reduce the current thoughts, feelings and behaviors of OCD-type fear and also reduce future vulnerability to them. This is consistent with the new science of epigenetic healing, described by modern researchers like Dr. Herbert Benson and Dr. Dawson Church, which states that experience enables genes to be turned on and off. Thinking and behaving in certain ways not only rewires the brain, but it actually influences gene expression. This means that a child who is "naturally" fearful or "naturally" prone to OCD-type thinking, feeling and acting may eventually develop a calmer nature as a result of practicing *The Fear Fix* strategies.

Let's return our attention to young Jacob now, to see how certain strategies can be employed to help reduce OCD-type thoughts, feelings and actions.

Jacob's parents sit him down. They begin their intervention where all interventions begin: with emotional coaching. They tell him that they've been noticing how distressed he feels when the pillows are scattered about and how hard it is for him to just let them sit any old way on the sofa. They let him know that they can help him to feel less stressed about that and ask him if he is interested in learning how to make the uncomfortable feelings go away. Jacob is definitely interested, although he doesn't believe that his parents can really make the feelings go away. Jacob's parents bring out some Lego pieces and teach Jacob how he can build his brain by the thoughts he thinks (see Chapter Five, page 129). They show him that each time he moves the pillows, he is building a bigger section of the brain that must move pillows. Each time he worries about his family's safety and well-being, he is building a bigger section of the brain that worries about the family's safety and well-being. They also show him that when he notices that he is thinking a scary thought, he can *choose* a pleasant, happy thought instead. For instance, he can think, "My family is healthy and safe," and then look around to see everybody looking healthy and fine, or he can close his eyes and imagine everyone looking just fine. Or he can think, "Pillows don't keep my family safe—God does" and then he can picture his home being filled with a loving, healing energy, or he can picture his family members all smiling and happy. Alternatively, he can just think a silly or funny thought that has nothing to do with the family but that makes him feel happy. (By the way, Jacob didn't have a logical reason to be worrying about his family's safety or well-being in the first place; nothing bad was going on inside the house or in the world that Jacob occupied. However, it's always important to ask any fearful child if there is anything on his mind, anything that he has been upset about or disturbed by. Remember that many kids develop their fears when they are not able to express their real stress in words. For instance, children often develop all kinds of symptoms when their parents are divorcing or when abuse or bullying is occurring at home or school).

Jacob's parents also explain that some people have "sticky" brains that really want to go their own way. In other words, some kids can just easily think the new thoughts when encouraged to do so, but some kids will find it harder to choose new thoughts because their brain really *wants* to think the old thoughts. They can offer Jacob Bach flower remedies to help his brain become less sticky if he has any trouble choosing and concentrating on new, better thoughts. If Jacob wants that help right away or finds that he is having trouble working on his thoughts and actions, then his parents can give him a mixture of the following Bach flower remedies (see Appendix B, page 314, for mixing instructions):

- Aspen for fear and dread of something bad happening
- White Chestnut for worry and rumination
- Red Chestnut for worrying about the health or safety of family members
- Cherry Plum for fear of losing control (e.g., intense strain from not being able to arrange the pillows)
- Rock Rose for terror or panic

Besides changing thoughts, Jacob will need to change his *behavior* in order to turn off his OCD-type reactions. In fact, this is the most important part of rewiring the brain. Jacob's brain has to learn through *its own experience* that nothing bad happens when he doesn't rearrange pillows. Unless Jacob stops performing this magic ritual, his brain will stay in its same old OCD-type thinking. Therefore, Jacob will have to just leave the pillows as he finds them, without straightening them up. At first, doing this will make Jacob feel very uncomfortable, maybe even panicky, because in his current way of thinking, putting those pillows right is somehow saving his family. Mom and Dad explain that Jacob is tricking his brain into thinking the wrong thought. Since the family has been healthy and safe ever since Jacob has been arranging the pillows, his brain thinks that arranging the pillows is keeping them healthy and safe. Now Jacob's brain needs to learn that the family will stay healthy and safe even when the pillows are lying all over the place. In order for the brain to learn this, Jacob needs to be in the room when the pillows are in disarray, leave the pillows alone and see how his family is doing. His parents know that it is essential for Jacob to avoid avoidance—the only way he can get over his fear is by facing it and feeling it.

At first, Jacob is bound to be scared to try the experiment, but after seeing for himself that nothing bad happens to anyone, he will soon learn that things can be out of order and his family will be fine. In order to help him conduct the necessary experiment without undue fear, Jacob's parents could give him the Bach mixture four times a day for two weeks *before* they ask him to leave the pillows as he finds them on the couch. The remedy can help settle his emotions and balance his thoughts. They can continue giving him the remedy for as long as he wants it—after a while, Jacob will feel comfortable without taking it. There are other things that Jacob's parents can offer him if he is very distressed about sitting in the room with messy pillows: a bit of calming essential oil on his chest or pulse points can help relax his body and mind and make it easier for him to get through the stressful moments. Calming music might help as well. They can give Jacob calming herbs for a couple of weeks before his "work" begins as well, because the right herbs can help calm and relax both body and mind. How much Outside Help is necessary depends on how frightened Jacob feels about leaving the pillows as he finds them. If he's only a tiny bit anxious, he can probably conduct his experiments without any Outside Helpers at all.

Interestingly, Jacob's eighteen-year-old cousin Jeffrey has also manifested OCD-type worries and behaviors off and on for many years (it's not unusual to find similar tendencies running through family trees). Jeffrey overhears Jacob's mom talking to his mom (her older sister) about Jacob's pillow issue. Later, he tells his mom that he does things like that too. Jeffrey's mom asks him what he is referring to. Jeffrey explains that he worries about things he shouldn't worry about and does things he probably shouldn't do. For example, he always places a fresh towel in the washroom every time he needs a towel—he acts as if a towel can only be used once. If any other family member has used a towel to dry their (clean) hands or body, he feels that he can't use that towel. He ends up creating a lot of unnecessary laundry.

Jeffrey's anxious feelings and behaviors are so mild that no one has really taken note of them. However, Jeffrey knows that he is experiencing unnecessary stress and worry and would like to stop having to deal with these feelings. Now that Mom knows what is going on, she teaches Jeffrey about the nature of obsessive-compulsive thinking, feeling and acting. She tells him about the mental-health disorder called OCD and lets him know that he can get professional help if he would like it. Jeffrey says he wants to try working on it himself, and if that doesn't solve it for him, then he would like to get some professional assistance. To get him started, Mom orders a book for teens about OCD. Even though Jeffrey probably doesn't have the disorder, he certainly has some OCD-type feelings and behaviors. Jeffrey reads the book cover to cover and, with his increased awareness, starts pushing himself through uncomfortable feelings without trying to relieve them in any way. Sometimes he takes a little Rescue Remedy. Sometimes he just watches the feeling happen and waits for it to pass. Sometimes he focuses his attention on his breath. Jeffrey has learned from his reading that just accepting the frightened feelings and letting them ride their wave *without trying to relieve them by taking action of any kind* is the best way to get rid of them over time. And, in fact, a number of months later, Jeffrey reports to Mom that he isn't bothered by his feelings or habits anymore!

FAST TRACKS FOR FEARS FUELED BY IMAGINATION

Fastest Fast Track
Give the child the Bach flower remedy Aspen (See Appendix B, page

311, for instructions on preparation and use of Bach flower remedies). Or, if your child is engaged in rituals, use the Bach flower OCD-type mixture that Jacob's parents gave him (see page 223). Be sure to get professional help if symptoms are intense.

In moments when the child is overwhelmed by fear, offer Rescue Remedy.

Fuller Program Fast Track

Do the steps outlined in the Fastest Fast Track above.

Ask the child to create a happy and safe imaginary antidote or positive thought to combat the frightening stimulus. Here are some examples:

- The monsters in the cupboard are very friendly and shy (as in the movie *Monsters, Inc.*)
- The people lurking outside the house aren't thieves and murderers but rather private police and army soldiers whose job it is to protect the property from harm.
- The sudden noise upstairs isn't a ghost—it's a good angel coming to protect the home.
- Daddy will not die when he is away because he will be too busy laughing with Grandma, shopping for gifts and having a good time.
- The rain isn't going to flood the houses, because the grass is too thirsty and is drinking it all up. (Can you hear the *shlurp shlurp* noise outside? That's the sound of grass drinking the rainwater.)
- The bad forces in the world will shrink as you fill the world with more and more good forces by making happy, positive pictures in your mind and sending them out into the world as you breathe your out breath.

SARAH CHANA RADCLIFFE

CHAPTER NINE

Helping Your Child through Fears of Doing Things

Fear of flying, swimming, using the potty,
having surgery, getting a haircut, driving a car,
skiing or skating, riding a roller coaster,
vomiting, first-time experiences

Kids can be afraid of doing things for a lot of reasons. In upcoming chapters, we will examine fears of doing things that stem from previous bad experiences or from fear of painful emotional consequences like failing or being embarrassed. In this section, however, we will look at fears of doing things that stem from a sense of threat to physical survival. We all have fears like this; many of us are afraid of riding in a helicopter, driving a motorcycle or going scuba diving, for example. In fact, most people are probably afraid of engaging in extreme sports or taking solo hikes through treacherous mountain terrain. It all makes sense: no one wants to risk his life! The difference comes in our opinions of what constitutes life-threatening activities. What one person considers fun, another might consider life-threatening. As you may know from your own experience, if an activity feels life-threatening to *you*, then it doesn't matter at all what anyone else thinks about it. Your own body and brain take over, sending out warning waves of panic that you can't argue with: you are caught in the grip of fear.

HELPING KIDS THROUGH PANIC

Interestingly, people tend to consider themselves experts on the definition of *dangerous*. If Jon tells Bob that he's scared of flying, Bob usually has no trouble telling Jon, "There's nothing to be afraid of—planes are safer than cars!" Similarly, if Kaitlyn tells Mom she's afraid riding on the underground subway train, Mom may say, "There's nothing to be afraid of—the subway is totally safe!" As we saw in earlier chapters, however, these cheery reassurances tend to fall on deaf ears. Particularly when a child or teen is experiencing something that feels life-threatening, help needs to be aimed at the emergency centers of the brain, not at the frontal lobes of the cortex. The former is the section that pumps out adrenaline to fuel the fight-or-flight response, while the latter is the rational, thinking part of the brain. Parents who are dealing with a terrified youngster need techniques that turn off the terror and panic—reading insurance statistics isn't one of them.

In previous chapters, we've seen many interventions that will help turn off the panic response. We'll put these and more into action in the following scenarios, illustrating how they can be used to help a child cope with her fear of doing things.

HELPING JOSEPH THROUGH HIS FEAR OF DRIVING

Joseph is already nineteen years old. Always a timid child, Joseph is now characteristically reluctant to learn to drive a car. All his friends have been driving for years, and Joseph knows he can't put off his driving lessons much longer if he still wants to be considered "normal" by his peers. He approaches his parents for help.

SARAH CHANA RADCLIFFE

"Every time I think of getting behind the wheel, I just freeze," he tells Dad. "I don't think I can do it." Dad explains the fight-or-flight response to Joseph, adding that it is often called the "fight-flight-or-freeze response" because adrenaline can give a person strength to fight or run, but it can also cause a person to freeze in his tracks when fighting or running are not possible options. "Your freeze reaction tells us that the idea of driving a car floods your brain with adrenaline," Dad says. "You'll be fine once you learn how to create some calm chemistry. Here are a couple of ways to do that. Practice with each one for a bit, pick the one you like best and then spend more time practicing with that one. Keep at it until you no longer feel like freezing when you think of driving." Then Dad goes on to give Joseph a few strategies that he thinks might help. Here's how he describes each strategy to Joseph:

Visualization
At night and again just before getting out of bed in the morning, do this exercise. Begin with the Relaxation Response: breathe in normally and think the number "one" on the out breath. Continue for a few minutes until you start to feel a little relaxed. Then continue breathing slowly while you watch a mental movie of yourself driving a car, looking and feeling relaxed, confident and happy. See yourself driving all over the neighborhood, really enjoying yourself. Watch the movie for a few minutes, then take a deep breath in and out to finish the exercise. Repeat the visualization every morning and evening for a week or two, and then book your driving lessons.

Tapping
Tap on the side of your hand while saying, "Even though I am afraid to drive, I choose to help myself through this fear." Do this three times. Now tap the eight Tapping points (top of the head, eyebrow near the nose, outer edge of the eye, under the eye, under the nose, under the lip, under the

collarbone, a few inches under the arm) while feeling your fear and saying, "I can't drive, I'm afraid to drive, there's no way I'm going to drive, I can't do it," and so on. At the end of the round of tapping, take a deep breath in and out. Think about driving and notice your fear. If it's gone, you're finished. If it's still there but somewhat less, do another round of tapping, the same as before. If it's more, start again, but instead of tapping on the side of the hand while making the "Even though . . ." statement, rub the Tender Spot on the chest (see complete Tapping instructions in Chapter Four, page 115, and Appendix A, page 298) and then continue tapping the eight points as before. Continue Tapping rounds until you no longer feel afraid. Go book your driving lessons.

Heart Hold

Think of being in the driver's seat with your hands on the wheel and your foot on the gas pedal. Feel the fear in your body. With two fingers, press firmly in the center of your chest, above the rib cage. Hold your hand there and breathe nice and slowly, in and out, in and out, really slowly. Continue this slow breathing for a minute or two, and then, while you're still breathing slowly, picture yourself being in the driver's seat. Continue pressing and breathing for another couple of minutes. Do this exercise nightly for two weeks. Book your driving lessons.

Joseph does as Dad suggests: he tries each technique for a few days and then decides to give the Heart Hold his full attention. After using it for a couple of weeks, he no longer puts his hand on his chest; he simply focuses his attention on his chest and breathes slowly in and out. Now he can maintain a calm feeling when thinking about being behind a wheel. He also feels confident that he can help himself calm down using this strategy *when he is actually taking his lessons.* Joseph books his driving lessons and is ready to learn.

HELPING CHLOE THROUGH HER FEAR OF PUTTING HER FACE IN WATER

Six-year-old Chloe is learning to swim. She likes the teacher. She likes the children. She likes the water. And she particularly likes her new polka-dot swimsuit. However, she *hates* the idea of having to put her face in the water; she is terrified to immerse herself completely. Chloe's mom, Nicole, understands that Chloe needs to learn to turn off her panic response and just relax. In a relaxed state, Chloe will be able to close her eyes and her mouth and just dunk in the water for a moment. It should be easy.

Of course, the tricky part is not the dunking—it's helping Chloe learn how to relax! Nicole uses the following strategies:

Bach Flower Remedies: Because Chloe is really panicky about immersing in the water, Nicole decides to offer an adrenaline-calming Outside Helper. She gives Chloe two Bach flower remedies: Mimulus (for specific fears—in this case, for fear of drowning and fear of dunking) and Rock Rose (for panic and adrenaline rush). Chloe receives these two remedies four times a day for a week and then has her next swimming lesson. She'll stay on the remedies until she no longer has any swimming-related fear. Nicole also gives Chloe a couple of doses of Rescue Remedy right before each swimming lesson. Rescue Remedy helps calm the fight-or-flight response.

Bonus Breath: Nicole explains to Chloe that she needs to feel relaxed in order to be able to dunk under the water. She teaches her the Bonus Anti-Panic Breath (breathe in slowly and breathe out through pursed lips, as if blowing up a balloon—see Chapter Four, page 93). Nicole tells Chloe that she can use this breath to calm down before dunking under the water.

Parental Presence: Nicole asks the swimming teacher if she can join Chloe in the pool while the child learns to get her face wet. The swimming teacher is fine with that, knowing that kids feel more secure when they are physically close to their parents. Mom tells Chloe that she's coming into the water to be right there with her when she dunks underneath the water.

Gradual Exposure: Chloe has been standing in water for a long time already. Now, in order for her to get used to having her hair and face wet, the swimming teacher and Mom play some splashing games with her, inviting her to splash water at them and also splashing some water gently toward her.

Modeling: Both Mom and the teacher take little dunks under the water so that Chloe can see what the dunking looks like. Chloe can also see that the grown-ups are surviving the experience with big happy grins on their faces.

Moving Fear with Facts: This technique involves offering facts that provide practical help in dealing with whatever negative outcome the child fears. Since Chloe is afraid that she will swallow water, choke, drown or otherwise be overwhelmed by water, Nicole teaches her that if she keeps her mouth shut when dunking, the water won't harm her. The swimming teacher adds that humming a little tune is a good way to keep the mouth shut during the dunk. Chloe agrees to hum "Happy Birthday to You" while she dunks, because she likes that tune—it reminds her that her birthday is coming soon and she'll be getting some presents. The happy thought helps her relax a bit more, while it simultaneously puts her mouth in the right position. As an extra aid, the swimming teacher suggests that Nicole hold a finger to her mouth as if saying, "Shhhh," to help her mouth remember to stay shut.

Facing the Fear: Nicole asks Chloe to use her Bonus Breath for a few moments, start humming and then quickly dunk down and up. Chloe does it! She survives and is thrilled.

SARAH CHANA RADCLIFFE

HELPING BENJAMIN THROUGH A FIRST-TIME EXPERIENCE

Doing something for the first time is challenging for most people, no matter what their age. Many kids are terrified on the occasion of their first haircut or first day at school. Something about first-time experiences can leave a child feeling as if he is in a life-threatening situation—the emotional overwhelm of feeling unable to cope is very similar. Adults can be nervous, stressed or even panicky about their first day at work, about going into labor for a first birth, about their wedding and so on. All of these jitters stem from a culprit we've met before: negative imagination. When human beings don't know what's ahead, they tend to fill in the gaps with frightening scenarios. (*What if something goes wrong during labor? What if I need a caesarean? What if the doctor doesn't get here in time? What if the baby dies? What if I hemorrhage? What if I die?*) Even when a child can't articulate what he is worried about, the vague sense that something bad might happen is close to consciousness. (*I don't know what I'm afraid of—I'm just afraid!*)

Children run into first-time experiences more often than adults, for obvious reasons: as newcomers to the planet, they just have to do a lot more things for the first time. Entering the world of the strange and unknown is stressful. Nonetheless, some children seem rather impervious to their first-time experiences, seeming to take everything in their stride. Some are a little unsettled but come around when parents offer some preparation and fear-management strategies. And, due to their inherited nature, some kids are completely overwhelmed by their first-time experiences, requiring additional levels of support to negotiate them without trauma.

Benjamin falls into the latter category. He is temperamentally very similar to his older sister, who also had trouble with most of her first-time experiences—the first visit to the dentist, the first time at the hairdresser's, the first time she went to camp and the first time she went to the hospital were all horrible experiences for both her and her parents. Now Mom can see that Benjamin is falling into the same pattern. Mom is not pleased. "I've had enough of this stuff with

Sophie," she complains. "We're not going through all this again!"

Fortunately, Mom has a few more tricks up her sleeve than she had when Sophie was younger. Benjamin is due for a trip to the barber. Mom has put it off for as long as possible because she knows what is likely to happen there: the toddler will have a meltdown that will leave the barber begging her to take her child home and let his locks grow down to his knees. Mom is ready to help rewire Benjamin's brain so that he will handle his first haircut better and hopefully handle all his first-time experiences more comfortably. Here's what she does:

Bibliotherapy: Picture books and stories can be used to help prepare children for frightening experiences. Such books and stories can also provide new ways to think about frightening situations, and they can offer strategies to help calm the fear and change the situation. Mom reads *Sammy's First Trip to the Barber* to Benjamin a million times—okay, not quite a million times, but at least once a day before bedtime.

Dry Run: One of the best calming tools for first-time experiences is the dry run, or dress rehearsal. Using dolls, puppets or role-playing, parents can take the child through what's going to happen in the first-time experience. A few different scenarios can be enacted so as to increase flexibility and make allowance for the "unexpected" to be expected. Wanting to make sure that Benjamin is prepared for what is really going to occur at the barber's, Mom goes to a local secondhand store and picks up a broken but long-haired doll for a dollar. She then puts this doll in a chair, puts a bib around its neck and asks it what kind of haircut it wants. Mom then proceeds to actually cut the doll's hair nice and short. Mom offers Benjamin the scissors so he can take a couple of snips of hair as well. The doll comes away with a new look and Mommy-Barber takes a broom and sweeps up the hair that is lying on the floor. Mom asks the doll if it hurt when she cut the hair and the doll says she didn't feel a thing.

Reducing Unknowns: Fear of first-time experiences shrinks in direct proportion to the reduction of unknown factors. Taking the child to the barbershop where he'll be getting his hair cut reduces the unknown physical factors: what the place looks like, who will be there, what they will be doing and what will happen there. If it's possible to introduce the child to the particular barber who will be giving him the haircut, go ahead and do that too. The second time the child meets the fellow, he'll automatically be more comfortable with him. Just sit with the child and watch people coming in for their haircuts and leaving normally—no one is screaming or crying or looking like they're suffering. If you have the time and energy, this step can be repeated a couple of times before the day of the actual haircut.

Bach Flower Remedies: Mom starts Benjamin on a mixture of three Bach flower remedies (see Appendix B, page 314 for instructions):

- Walnut for those who have trouble with first-time experiences and other changes
- Rock Rose for those whose fear reaches the level of panic
- Cherry Plum for those who lose control when they feel strong emotions
- Rescue Remedy to calm the fight-or-flight response on the day of the haircut—Mom gives it to Benjamin the morning of the haircut and on the way to the barber

In some situations, it is not possible to reduce the unknowns. For instance, let's look at the case of a child or teen who is afraid of flying. While it *is* possible to go to the airport and watch the planes taking off and landing—and this is a great thing to do to reduce at least some unknown factors and offer reassurance that planes can actually do this sort of thing—it may *not* be possible to watch what happens during turbulence and how passengers cope with it. However, do not be dismayed: this information can be garnered from YouTube. In fact, on YouTube, you can find video clips showing the inside of a plane, the pilot's cockpit, the passenger's section and other features of a plane; you can find clips of takeoffs and landings, emergency procedures, turbulence and every other aspect of air travel. If various flight-related video clips cause your youngster to feel intense fear, have him watch the clips over and over again while performing the Tapping procedure (see Chapter Four, page 115, and Appendix A, page 298, for instructions). Tapping will usually rapidly reduce the fear that is being triggered and help rewire the brain for calmness in the face of various flying challenges.

The protocol for fighting fears of doing things has been used successfully for decades to help women feel calmer during their first labor. Their improved mental attitude has been correlated with fewer complications during the birthing process. The women attend classes that provide important information about birthing and may read books and handouts about that process—similar to the Bibliotherapy step described earlier. A dry run for labor involves all sorts of breathing exercises to be practiced repeatedly in preparation for the actual birth. Reducing unknowns is accomplished through the hospital tour that is given to all new mothers-to-be, showing them the emergency entrances, the check-in desks, the birthing floor in the hospital, the birthing room and equipment. Meeting the staff or learning more about who might be on call or rotation is also part of it. Although most North American hospital programs don't know about, and so don't recommend Bach flower remedies, any mother who is terrified of the birthing process might benefit from a mixture of Mimulus, Rock Rose and Cherry Plum as well (in general, Bach flower remedies are safe and beneficial for pregnant and laboring women, but it's always a good idea to check with your doctor).

HELPING STEPHANIE LEAVE HOME FOR COLLEGE

Leaving home is a first-time experience that is often exciting and frightening at the same time. Kids moving from adolescence into adulthood are eager to spread their wings, but many also feel vulnerable after two decades of being supported and nurtured by their parents in every way. Even when kids have had a less than ideal relationship with their parents, they may have reservations about leaving the family home. It's one of those first-time things—in this case, the first time being fully responsible for oneself (although many will still remain financially dependent for a long time). It's also a separation issue—something that frequently affects younger children but can actually affect people of all ages who must endure separation from their loved ones under various circumstances. In addition, leaving one's house is difficult for most people. The elderly, for example, often have serious reservations when it comes time to downsizing from their family home into a smaller apartment or an old-age facility of some kind. Familiarity brings comfort, while strange surroundings bring uncertainty and disorientation. It is scary for all of us to make big life changes and transitions, even when they are positive ones.

Stephanie has always been a homebody. She's maintained a very small circle of close girlfriends and has never had a boyfriend. Stephanie is a family girl: she loves helping Mom in the kitchen, regularly babysits her little niece and nephew, and has plenty of hobbies and interests that can be maintained right out of her own quiet, quilted corner of the universe that she calls her room. Now that high school graduation has passed, it is time for Stephanie to pursue her studies at college. Her small town does not offer the academic program she is looking for, so she is moving halfway across the country at the end of the summer—and she's scared.

Stephanie can articulate a lot of her fear. She knows she's really worried about missing her sister's kids. She knows she's afraid she'll be very homesick. She even knows that she's worried about her parents missing *her* too. Going from a very small town to a huge college campus, Stephanie recognizes that she's concerned about the social dynamics—will she feel lost and overwhelmed there? There are also fears that Stephanie can't quite articulate. It's just that the whole thing is so new and different, so alien and unknown. It makes her feel nervous during the day and agitated at night.

Dad asks Stephanie if she's looking forward to school in the fall, and Stephanie tells him honestly, "Yes and no," and then goes on to explain the way she feels and all the concerns she is having. Dad acknowledges how normal these feelings are, welcoming them without attempting to minimize them or correct her thinking process (he uses emotional coaching). He then asks her if she'd like some help to feel more calm and confident about the whole move, and Stephanie tells him that she's all ears. So Dad gives Stephanie the following tips:

Access Support: People handle fear and stress more successfully when they have access to a support system. This has been shown to be the case for people who have been diagnosed with cancer, for example. Cancer patients who access support actually have better survival rates because human support calms the nervous system significantly enough to reduce the harmful effects of fear chemistry. For someone like Stephanie, who doesn't naturally draw a social net around herself, it can be helpful to make a plan for acquiring emotional support. Dad suggests that Stephanie find out where the mental-health services are located on campus and recommends that she should make use of them if she feels stressed, painfully lonely, overwhelmed, depressed, anxious or otherwise distressed. He also urges her to look into the services that are provided for new students and make use of them (some schools actually organize new-student programs to help new students make smooth adjustments to school). Dad mentions that online support is equally helpful and easily available, so Stephanie might just do a search on "adjusting to college" to see what she can come up with. Finally, he suggests that she join a group or two on campus, whether to pursue a hobby, an interest, a skill or a cause. Working with others on a regular basis can lead to developing at least one friendship with a like-minded person.

Comfort Symbols: Security blankets aren't just for babies; people of all ages can be calmed by symbols of comfort and security (Outside Helpers), as we saw in Chapter Six. Stephanie can plan to take several comfort symbols with her to school, bringing a bit of home with her. Blankets, stuffed animals, photos and other special items associated with feelings of security can help her make a more comfortable transition.

Visualization: Dad recommends that Stephanie spend ten minutes or so each day doing the Relaxation Response followed by positive Visualization (as described in Chapter Five, page 137)—seeing a "movie" of herself having a great time in her new environment, loving the classes, making new friends and enjoying the feelings of freedom and independence.

Consider Outside Helpers: Stephanie might try a mixture of the following three Bach flower remedies: Walnut, for going through transitions (moving away from home and starting a new school), Honeysuckle, for feelings of homesickness, and Mimulus, for fear. With these remedies working quietly in the background, Stephanie might feel calmer in the daytime. If she still has trouble sleeping, Dad suggests she try "Rescue Sleep," a special type of Rescue Remedy that helps quiet a "noisy" brain at night so a person can relax into restful sleep. Relaxing herbs for a nighttime tea might be a nice ritual to put in place now and later, when she's actually at school. A few drops of an essential oil like chamomile can also help settle and relax both body and mind.

HELPING CAROLYN THROUGH HER FEAR OF VOMITING

Some kids (and adults) have a full-blown phobia of vomiting. This group not only fears the act of vomiting but may also obsess about it. For instance, they might worry when flu season starts, because there's a higher chance of having to vomit at some point or of being exposed to the vomiting of a family member. The very word *vomit* might be hard for these people to deal with. Every time that they or someone in their family feels a little sick, they may start to feel panicky. People like this will find their most successful treatment in the office of an anxiety disorders specialist.

Carolyn, like most people, hates vomit and vomiting but probably doesn't have a full-blown phobia. She never worries about vomiting; she never even thinks about it. It's just that when she has to vomit, she gets overwhelmed and scared. Dad doesn't want her to be so afraid, so he provides three interventions:

Moving Fear with Facts: After acknowledging Carolyn's fear with emotional coaching, Dad explains the mechanics of vomiting to his daughter, showing her clear diagrams of what happens during an episode. Although he does mention the health benefits of vomiting, he does not dwell on this aspect of education. Rather, he gives his daughter the kind of facts that will help her cope best during an episode of vomiting. He describes the sensations that precede vomiting and gives her a couple of practical scenarios to plan for: sudden vomiting in a classroom, and vomiting that occurs once she has reached a suitable location, like a toilet. He discusses with her ways to minimize a mess, ways to clean up quickly and thoroughly and ways to freshen up afterward.

Breathwork: Dad explains to Carolyn that steady, slow breathing can sometimes calm the nervous system and digestive tract so that nausea and the urge to vomit will settle down. He teaches her Herbert Benson's Relaxation Response (see Chapter Four, page 90) and encourages her to use it at night when preparing for sleep. This way, her brain will install the breath. If she needs to call upon it in the classroom setting, it will be ready and available to provide a strong antidote to anxious physical and emotional feelings.

Rescue Remedy: Dad suggests that Carolyn keep Rescue Remedy spray with her at home and school. If she starts to feel sensations that warn of the need to vomit, she can take a bit of Rescue spray internally or externally (on her wrists, for instance) to help calm her panic and relax her system. Even if she has to vomit, she will feel less stress and anxiety during the process, helping the vomiting episode to be more of a minor inconvenience than an overwhelming event.

SARAH CHANA RADCLIFFE

HELPING MICHAEL DEAL WITH HIS FEAR OF GOING ON AMUSEMENT PARK RIDES

As with fear of vomiting, overwhelming fear of *anything* is best dealt with by a mental-health professional. However, sometimes a person just needs a little help getting through an activity that he is very afraid of doing. In some cases of such fears, a dry run and other types of preparation will be very helpful. In some cases, as we have already seen, Moving Fear with Facts will help. Sometimes, just taking a little Rescue Remedy before doing the scary activity is all that is needed.

Knowing that eleven-year-old Michael hated and feared amusement park rides, Mom asked him what he was planning to do about his best friend's birthday party at an amusement park on the coming Sunday. Michael said he was definitely planning to go and also planning to go on at least some of the rides. He didn't want to "wimp out," as he put it, but he was unquestionably uncomfortable at the thought of having to go on any rides. Mom asked if he would like to practice with her—she was willing to take him to the park before the party and go on some rides with him. Michael thanked her but declined her offer. ("Going to an amusement park with my mother will make me look like a baby!") He said he was just going to force himself to go on the rides with everyone else. Mom said he could add a few drops of Rescue Remedy to his water bottle and take a couple of sips before going on each ride. No one would know what he was doing and the Rescue Remedy might help him feel calmer. That seemed to be something Michael could handle. When Sunday came, he went off to the park, taking a sun hat, a wallet and a small bottle of water. He handled the stress of going on rides surprisingly well and came home suntanned and pretty pleased with himself—he had gone on his first roller coaster!

HELPING NOAH DEAL WITH HIS FEAR OF GOING ON AMUSEMENT PARK RIDES

Sometimes, a child isn't so courageous. He can't "force" himself to conquer his fear. This is the case with twelve-year-old Noah. Noah's class is going on an outing to a local amusement park to celebrate their graduation. Noah is not excited in the least. In fact, he's quite troubled about it. He has a fear of things like roller coasters and rides, and he has an even bigger fear of his classmates finding out about his fear. He knows that they'll make fun of him, calling him a baby or worse. He asks his parents if he can skip the trip by feigning illness on the date it falls on. His parents are tempted to save Noah from the challenge of dealing with his fear, but they wisely decline his suggestion, deciding instead to help Noah face his anxiety in the following way: They ask Noah which fear he'd like to deal with—the fear of being ridiculed by his friends or the fear of riding on roller coasters. Noah decides that overcoming his fear of riding on roller coasters will also solve his concern about being ridiculed, so he goes for that one. His parents use three fear busters: avoid avoidance, Butterfly Tapping and Rescue Remedy.

Avoid Avoidance: By agreeing to go to the amusement park and working toward being able to get on a roller coaster, Noah has used the avoid avoidance strategy for overcoming fear and anxiety.

Butterfly Tapping: Noah's mom takes him through several rounds of Butterfly Tapping. Butterfly Tapping is yet another form of tapping on the body to help process and relieve feelings of stress and fear. It is a form of bilateral stimulation, stimulating the left and right side of the brain alternately in order to facilitate whole-brain integration. Unlike Tapping-In (described in Chapter Four), Butterfly Tapping is performed with fast taps (as opposed to slow ones) and constant tapping (as opposed to three short rounds of six taps each). The person using the technique taps the whole time he is imagining a single step in the series of steps involved in the activity. The scary activity is broken down into steps such as the beginning of the activity, middle of the activity and end of the activity (and each section can be similarly divided into smaller sections). The child or teen thinks of each section in order, tapping on one section at a time until feeling calm on that section. Butterfly Tapping is helpful for preparing to undertake a frightening or overwhelming activity, like having a medical or dental procedure, going on a long airplane flight, traveling through an underground tunnel and so on. (Warning: this technique should *not* be used for fears that stem from past bad experiences; use only with simple, anticipatory fears of doing things.) The tapping occurs on the shoulders or upper arms. The child places his arms in a sort of a hug, placing the right hand on the left shoulder and the left hand on the right shoulder. He taps the left shoulder, then the right shoulder, alternating left, right, left, right throughout the exercise.

Mom shows Noah the correct hand positions and tells him that he's to tap like this while imagining going on a roller coaster. She tells him that they're going to work through the whole experience while tapping left, right, left, right and picturing each step of the process from beginning to end, one section at a time. They start with imagining buying a ticket for the roller coaster ride. Noah pictures himself in the ticket line, tapping his shoulders lightly until he feels no anxious feelings while imagining the scene. Then Mom asks him to imagine standing on the platform with his friends, waiting for the next roller coaster to pick them up. Noah needs to tap on this scene over and over until he's not feeling scared while thinking about it. Next Mom asks Noah to imagine being in the train as it starts to roll down the track. This is fairly easy for Noah and takes only a few short taps. Then Mom asks him to imagine the roller coaster chugging slowly up the first tall hill. Again, Noah requires several rounds of imagining this before he feels completely calm all over his body. Now Mom asks Noah to imagine being right at the top of the hill, just before the steep dip down. Noah imagines this and taps. He has to work on this scene many times until he feels perfectly calm thinking about it. Mom asks him to imagine the roller coaster zooming down the steep hill and going around several curves and bends. Noah imagines and taps—again, this one takes many rounds of tapping. Finally, Mom asks Noah to see the roller coaster sliding into the station again and coming to a halt. Noah imagines and taps. Then Mom asks Noah to see himself getting off the train and heading back down the stairs. Noah taps while picturing himself being safely off the roller coaster. Noah feels really relaxed after the Butterfly Tapping session but decides it will be helpful to repeat the exercise before bedtime each night the week before the trip.

Rescue Remedy: On the morning of the outing, Noah takes Rescue Remedy with breakfast. He puts 8 drops in the 16-ounce water bottle that he is taking with him on the excursion. When he arrives at the amusement park, Noah takes a sip of his water. When he looks at the gigantic roller coaster that his friends are lining up to buy tickets for, he takes another sip and joins the line. Just before getting on the roller coaster train, he takes one more sip. After the ride is over and he is safely on the ground again, Noah takes another couple of sips. He's done it—he's taken a ride on the roller coaster! He is incredibly proud of himself. And, as it turns out, he *loved* the ride and is ready for more.

FAST TRACKS FOR FEAR OF DOING THINGS

Fastest Fast Track

Avoid avoidance. Help the child to face the fear.

Use Gradual Exposure with Rescue Remedy and Bonus Breath. If possible, break the task down into small steps. While working on each step, have the child use the Bonus Breath to further reduce any feelings of panic. Give the child Rescue Remedy to calm adrenaline.

Fuller Program Fast Track
Do the steps outlined in the Fastest Fast Track above. Add any other

intervention that might help, such as Parental Presence, Moving Fear with Facts (education), Tapping and Positive Imagination.

Add other Outside Helpers to further calm the sympathetic nervous system.

CHAPTER TEN

Helping Your Child through Fears Caused by Bad Experiences

Fear of going to camp after being bullied there in the past;
fear of flying on a plane after suffering a bad flight experience;
fear of going to a shopping mall after being mugged in that
location; fear of going to the doctor after having
had a painful procedure

Bad things happen. Once they do, our sense of safety and security can be shattered. Our nervous system expresses its reaction in no uncertain terms: "If you take me back to that place, I'll set off every alarm I have at my disposal! This means that if you drag me back on the subway train after I was stuck in that dark tunnel for six hours with no water, no bathroom, no air conditioning and no other comforts of life, I will send such a rush of adrenaline through the chambers of your heart, you will feel like you will explode from the inside! Am I making myself clear?" Yes. Very clear. We can try to talk to ourselves all we want, reminding ourselves that the bad experience was a one-time freak incident or just an experience in the past. But the body will have none of it. It protests, acting as if the problem is still happening right now or could recur at any moment. That's trauma.

Traumatic events come in big and small sizes and yet both are traumatic. Rape is called a *big-T trauma*—the kind of event that wreaks havoc with virtually every victim's psyche, sending out ripples of consequences for decades afterward. Examples of other big-T traumas include anything that feels like a threat to one's life: being held up at gunpoint, witnessing a terrorist attack, being assaulted (by a stranger or a family member), being in a catastrophic car accident and so on. Any event that brings one to the brink of death or to a feeling of complete helplessness, either as a witness or as a participant, can shock the mind to the extent that one suffers from the syndrome known as *post-traumatic stress disorder* (PTSD). This syndrome is characterized by a distinct pattern of three different kinds of symptoms (a person must have symptoms in each category to be diagnosed with PTSD):

- **Re-experiencing Symptoms:** flashbacks (sudden, intrusive mental replayings of the incident with all of its horror), nightmares (with content or emotions that are related to the traumatic incident), daytime feelings of fear and dread, unwarranted guilt
- **Avoidance Symptoms:** feeling numb, disconnected, uninterested in life; avoiding the people or objects or location of the trauma; blocking out the memory of the event or its details
- **Hyperarousal Symptoms:** a nervous system on "high alert" —chronic edginess, irritability, tension, distractibility, hypervigilance (super-sensitivity to potential danger), overactive startle response, insomnia

In children, PTSD symptoms may be expressed somewhat differently, although they still fall within the categories above. For instance, children may experience bed-wetting (in toilet-trained children), angry outbursts and poor emotional regulation, excessive clinginess and separation anxiety, forgetting how to talk or inability to talk, and acting out the traumatic event during play.

To the onlooker, a child's trauma symptoms can be very confusing, whether or not she has a full-blown case of PTSD. The youngster may suffer from panic attacks that seemingly come "out of nowhere." She can also have panic attacks that happen as a result of exposure to something similar to an aspect of the original trauma, something that she may or may not be able to recognize and explain. For instance, after watching her puppy get crushed under the tires of the family van, six-year-old Natalie developed a panic response to the sight of vans—something pretty understandable. However, she also panicked whenever she saw daffodils; although she didn't consciously recall the fact, Natalie had stopped a couple of minutes before the accident to speak to her neighbor, who had a small bunch of daffodils growing in a patch on the front lawn. Natalie's brain had made the connection between the daffodils and the horrific accident, without her conscious awareness.

Nightmares and bad dreams, unwanted visual and auditory memories (flashbacks), emotional numbness, spaciness, moodiness, hypersensitivity (overreacting to small things), hypervigilance (being jumpy, paranoid, overestimating signs of danger) and aggressive meltdowns are other symptoms that often occur in the wake of a traumatic incident. The entire mind and body are dysregulated by trauma.

Nonetheless, parents can't assume that a lack of apparent distress means that the child is not disturbed after being exposed to what anyone would consider to be a traumatic event. For example, when eleven-year-old Zachary discovered his father's act of suicide (his dad had shot himself in the head), he was horrified and hysterical. However, adults swooped in on the scene and did what had to be done. The funeral took place and life carried on. Zachary went back to school and seemed to be sad but otherwise normal. At home, Zachary asked some questions for the first couple of weeks but then stopped talking about the event. He slept like a log, behaved well, continued to get good grades and continued to spend time with his friends. All in all, it seemed that he was "adjusting." No one could see at the time how the trauma was worming its way deep inside of Zachary's young mind. No one could predict the many adult dysfunctions that Zachary would experience as a direct result of burying that event: alcoholism, severe anxiety, relationship problems, intimacy problems, career difficulties and more. Zachary suffered lifelong loss and hardship as a result of living with demons inside his head.

Children often store trauma away in an inner vault where it continues to haunt them and affect their life choices for decades after the event. This is particularly true when traumatic events are repetitive and ongoing, as can occur when a child is being molested or mistreated within the family context, or when she witnesses the chronic mistreatment of another family member. Feelings of utter helplessness can overwhelm the psyche in such cases, and it is common for children who are trapped in situations of chronic abuse to survive through dissociation—putting the trauma away in a locked section of the brain in order to be able to continue to grow and function normally.

Because of this dissociative process, symptoms of trauma can surface later. Whether triggered by a single overwhelming event or years of abuse, symptoms can occur weeks, months, years or decades after the trauma occurred. This is the reason for the *P* in PTSD—it stands for *post*, as in "after the trauma." Traumatic events can be temporally stuffed in the freezer, so to speak, to be removed and thawed later on, at a time when the child is better able to process them (which may be in adulthood).

On the other hand, children can also become symptomatic immediately following a traumatic event, suffering from *acute stress disorder* (a trauma syndrome that occurs within the month immediately following a traumatic event). After experiencing a robbery in the family home, for instance, twelve-year-old Haley immediately refused to sleep in her own room, had trouble sleeping even when she was not alone, had trouble concentrating in school and began to have panic symptoms on a regular basis starting only days after the unfortunate incident.

If you know that your child has experienced or witnessed a life-threatening event or anything that you think might be a big-T trauma, it is best to have her assessed by a mental-health professional.

However, you cannot always know that your child has been

exposed to a traumatic event. Things happen in the playground, at other people's houses, at school and everywhere else outside your home. In fact, traumatic events also happen within the home without a parent's knowledge. Moreover, some children have been traumatized when they're too young to talk or to describe what occurred. For all these reasons, you won't necessarily be able to intervene in a timely fashion when your child experiences a trauma. However, you can certainly help increase the chances that your school-age youngster will come forward to disclose traumatic events if you are engaged in regular emotional coaching. This technique helps the child become more aware of, and accepting of, her own internal reactions to life events. In addition, you can periodically invite your child to talk out loud about disturbing events she has been exposed to in print, in the media and in her life: "Wow! How did you feel when you saw the picture of all that destruction?" Model the process of emotional disclosure by occasionally describing your own feelings of shock and horror as you hear of tragic and violent deaths on the news and as you encounter your own overwhelming experiences: "I was turning the corner at Elm and Harbord when this truck almost crashed into me! He actually bumped the outer mirror of the car—he was that close. Honestly, I thought, 'This is it! I'm going to die!' My body was shaking for a couple of hours afterward. I finally feel better now." When it's normal to openly share occasional reactions to intensely stressful events, it's just easier for the child to do so too. On the other hand, in homes where such feelings are rarely expressed, children often erroneously conclude that it's best to handle one's confusing, disturbing and overwhelming emotions on one's own.

Besides keeping an emotionally open door, you can also notice and respond to changes in your child's behavior and personality. Pay attention to unusual symptoms like increased fear, insomnia, nightmares, unusual irritability, difficulty concentrating, uncharacteristic poor grades or withdrawal from people. Be curious if your child suddenly develops a strong fear of or aversion to some person, place, thing or activity. Go ahead and *ask* your child what has happened that has caused the sudden bad reaction: "You didn't used to be afraid of going to Maya's house. Did something happen there that upset you?" Even when you think you've figured out what might have happened, and even if it doesn't seem so bad to you, always arrange for a professional assessment if your child's symptoms are intense, disruptive or persistent. Professionals spend years in rigorous training in order to be able to assess and treat trauma, as well as to be able to distinguish between conditions like substance abuse disorders, depressive disorders, PTSD, anxiety disorders, adjustment disorders and other conditions. Your child's symptoms may have a very different meaning than you might be assuming. Getting the right help is dependent on getting the right diagnosis.

If trauma is indeed the culprit behind your child's unsettled mind, body and behavior, it's important to keep in mind that traumatic stress does not generally go away "with time." However, it can often heal completely with the proper treatment. Whether symptoms appear long after an incident as in PTSD or right after the incident as in acute stress disorder, specialized, trauma-specific professional help is required. One such intervention is *eye movement desensitization and reprocessing* (EMDR). EMDR is a professional therapeutic intervention that utilizes bilateral stimulation for the treatment of trauma symptoms and disorders. It has been found to be especially helpful in offering effective (generally permanent) relief from trauma symptoms. Tapping techniques, when carried out by a mental-health professional trained in the treatment of trauma, can also be a highly effective therapeutic modality for trauma symptoms and disorders. Every day, more effective mind-body treatments for trauma are being developed. Talking therapy is generally not considered to be effective for these conditions, as the eradication of trauma symptoms requires a whole-brain approach.

NOTE: HOME TREATMENT IS NOT THE APPROPRIATE INTERVENTION FOR FEARS TRIGGERED BY LIFE-THREATENING OR OVERWHELMING EVENTS OR THOSE ACCOMPANIED BY TRAUMA SYMPTOMS.

EVERYDAY TRAUMAS

Although many children experience big-T traumas, even more experience *small-t traumas*—events that are not life-threatening but generate intensely negative emotions such as humiliation, shame, failure, intense overwhelm and other extremely painful feelings. Although these are called small-t traumas, they are not actually small; they are just not life-threatening. In fact, the events that trigger this kind of trauma may be quite emotionally devastating. For instance, most kids would be negatively affected by something like wetting their pants in class because the teacher refused them permission to leave the room. Although certainly not a life-threatening event, producing a puddle on the floor in a public situation would be devastating for almost any child over the age of seven or eight. The youngster might react by not wanting to return to school, both because of the embarrassment and because of the fear that such an event could happen again. Similarly, a child who has suffered through an excruciating dental extraction may be traumatized enough by the experience to refuse to ever voluntarily sit in a dentist's chair again. Likewise, a youngster who has been punished by an insensitive teacher in front of his peers may not only become avoidant of the teacher but may also hold a lifelong stinging memory of the event.

Fortunately, there are ways for parents to help their children recover from small-t traumas. When home treatment doesn't completely resolve the problem, however, it is extremely valuable to enlist the services of a mental-health professional. Why leave a child with an enduring emotional scar when it is so unnecessary?

HELPING CHILDREN RECOVER FROM BAD EXPERIENCES

Parents help their kids through upsetting experiences all day long. They do so primarily through listening, emotional coaching and problem-solving. Small-t traumas are not just bad experiences, however—they are traumatic experiences. They are the kind of

SARAH CHANA RADCLIFFE

experiences that a child will often remember forever and the kind of experiences that the child never wants to have again. Small-t traumas instill such fear that children will usually do anything to avoid even the possibility of having a similar experience in the future. Although parents can begin their at-home treatment of these kinds of feelings using emotional coaching, they will need to use other tools to complete their treatment.

The trick to addressing the fear that occurs after these kinds of bad experiences is to access the "emotional brain"—the part of the brain that reacts to traumatic events. As we have seen, this is the right brain, home to subconscious thoughts and feelings. Because this is the part of the brain that is having trouble, it is advisable to use left-right brain integration strategies when addressing a child's traumatized feelings. Techniques like Tapping and Visualization will be particularly appropriate for both healing the memory of the event and for restoring feelings of competence and security.

Of course, most parents don't know whole-brain integration techniques and so tend to rely on what they do know: education and problem-solving strategies. The following example shows the limitation of education when it comes to dealing with small-t trauma. When thirteen-year-old Erin started to worry about her parents' health, Mom knew it was because Erin's classmate's dad had died recently after a very short ordeal with pancreatic cancer. (This was a small-t trauma, even though it involved death, because Erin was not particularly close to that classmate and she did not have any connection with any aspect of the experience apart from learning about it after the fact. This was more like hearing a sad story in the news than like experiencing a personal brush with death. The only thing that made it traumatic at all is that it happened to someone the child actually knew.)

When she became aware of Erin's worries, Mom sat down with her and talked to her about statistics, pointing out that there was a much higher chance that Mommy and Daddy would live to old age than die young. Because Erin was feeling so anxious, Mom even arranged for a meeting with their family doctor so that the doctor herself could provide reassuring facts and information. Although Erin intellectually understood everything that everyone was telling her, she just could not turn off her anxious feelings. Her mind sent her scary images both during the school day and also as she was falling asleep at night. She was really worried that something terrible would happen to her parents. It was clear that Erin's emotional right brain—filled with shock, fear and sadness—could not benefit from thinking about the facts of the matter. She needed help in connecting the thinking and feeling parts of her brain. Interestingly, when mind-body, left-right brain strategies are used, factual information can sometimes just seem to slide into place. Mom could help Erin install a healthier thought pattern by combining some EFT Tapping with some Tapping-In. To begin, Mom would start tapping the eight EFT points so that Erin could follow along by copying. Mom would ask Erin to express her fear out loud while tapping. Erin would probably say things like "I'm afraid Daddy will die," "What if Daddy dies too?" and so on. Erin and Mom could continue tapping rounds until Erin says something like "I'm not so afraid anymore." At that point, Mom can ask Erin what her new opinion is. Erin might say something like "Daddy will probably live till he's really old." Then Mom can ask Erin to do three rounds of Tapping-In, tapping slowly and lightly on her left leg then her right leg (three times each) while saying, "Daddy will probably live till he's really old." Here are some common consequences of approaching the problem in this way:

- The information finally sinks in; the child calms down and reverts to her normal self. Fearful rumination ceases and no further action is necessary. (This is what we hope for!)
- Tapping releases a flood of emotion, which continues for a few minutes and then settles; the fear is released, rumination ceases and no further action is necessary. (Parents need to be aware that any kind of Tapping can sometimes lead to a rapid release of feelings; if it resolves quickly, no further action is necessary. However, if the child becomes even more upset instead of calmer, and cannot resolve her

SARAH CHANA RADCLIFFE

feelings, see if you can arrange for a mental-health professional to complete the treatment, using the same or different interventions; it is possible that underlying issues have been triggered by the incident. In other words, the issue may not be as simple or superficial as it might have first appeared.)

- The Tapping makes no difference whatsoever. In this case, experiment with a few other at-home strategies until you find one that brings the child back to her former state of calm. If you can't find one within a couple of days, complete the treatment with professional intervention.

INTERVENTIONS FOR RELEASING FEAR

The interventions that will be most useful in addressing anxious feelings that have been caused by bad experiences are the following:

- providing emotional coaching
- helping the child tell the story of the upsetting event
- helping the child tell the story while Tapping
- helping the child convey his current thoughts and feelings while Tapping
- offering Rescue Remedy or other Bach flower remedies
- helping the child avoid avoidance

HELPING MEGAN GO BACK TO MAYA'S HOUSE

Let's look at how three of these strategies are used when nine-year-old Megan develops a sudden fear of going to her friend Maya's house. In answer to her parents' question "Did something happen at Maya's house that was upsetting?" Megan describes a big fight that occurred there between Maya's fourteen-year-old brother, Dan, and Maya's dad, Henry. Apparently, there was some shouting, swearing and door slamming. This sort of thing never happens in Megan's own home, which made the incident all the more alarming for her.

Emotional Coaching: Megan's dad names her feelings: "That must have been very scary for you. It's upsetting and frightening to hear people—especially big people—yelling at each other, saying bad words and slamming doors!"

Avoid Avoidance: Dad continues: "Maya is a good friend of yours. You're always over at her house, and you've never mentioned anything like this happening before. I know it will be hard on both of you if you can't ever go to her house again. Maybe we can do something that will help you feel comfortable there even though this happened." Dad then goes on to ask Megan questions that will help him formulate the next steps: "Did this ever happen before?" No. "Did anyone get hurt?" No. "Did anyone throw anything or push someone?" No. "Did it go on for more than a minute or two?" No. "Was Maya crying or scared?" No. "Did anyone say anything to you about what happened?" Megan replies, "Yes, Maya's dad told me and Maya that he was sorry for all the noise." Satisfied that this was not a regular or violent occurrence at Megan's playdate with Maya, Dad asks Megan to think of things she can do if such a thing ever happens again. They agree that Megan can call home and ask to be picked up right away if she is ever feeling uncomfortable. She certainly doesn't have to stay there.

Tapping: Now Dad offers to help Megan get the bad feelings and bad memories out of her brain. He guides her through three rounds of the Choices Method of Tapping. The exercise takes less than five minutes. On round one, Dad asks Megan to think about what happened that day and to remember how scary and upsetting it was. Megan thinks about that while she taps the eight Tapping points on her body. On round two, Dad instructs Megan to say, "I know that I can call home and go home if it ever happens again." Megan says this as she taps each of the eight points. On round three, Dad asks Megan to alternate thinking about the scary incident and remembering that she can call home whenever she wants to. He guides her to tap on the first point (at the top of her head) and remember the scary fight. Then he instructs her to tap on the second point (on the eyebrow near the nose) while saying, "I can call home and go home if I am not comfortable." On the third point (at the outer edge of the eye), Megan focuses on the frightening scene, and on the fourth point (under the eye on the eye bone), she focuses on her ability to come home—and she continues to alternate this way for the remaining Tapping points (see Appendix A, page 303, for detailed Tapping instructions for the Choices Method of EFT). After completing this exercise with Dad, Megan feels happy and relieved—and ready to try another playdate at Maya's house.

HELPING REBECCA THROUGH HER FEAR OF DRIVING AFTER SHE HAD TWO CAR ACCIDENTS

Sixteen-year-old Rebecca had been so excited to receive her driver's license. Unfortunately, she had only been driving for one week when she had her first car crash. It wasn't too serious—just a fender bender when she backed up into a car parked behind her. No one was hurt but, of course, there were repairs to be paid for. Nonetheless, Rebecca's parents encouraged her to get "right back into the saddle" and continue driving the family car. Rebecca was shaken but knew that her parents were right. She convinced herself that the accident was a bit of bad luck that could have happened to anyone, and she started driving as soon as the repaired vehicle came back from the shop. Everything was fine for the next several months, but then Rebecca had a second accident when she turned her eyes away from the road for a moment to talk to her friend in the back seat of the car. In that few seconds, Rebecca drove right into a stop sign. Fortunately, no one was hurt, but the police had to be called and charges for careless driving were pressed.

Rebecca was now thoroughly traumatized. "That's it—I'm never driving again," she told her parents. "I'm obviously a threat to myself and everyone on the road." Rebecca's parents didn't want their daughter's driving career to end at this early point in time, but they too were quite anxious. Nonetheless, they knew that they needed to help their daughter get to the point where she would drive again and be safe doing so. They told Rebecca how they felt and they also presented a plan. "You need to build up your skills and your confidence," they told her. "We want you to take a series of extra lessons—there are special advanced driver's skills courses that teach people how to prevent accidents and improve their driving skills far beyond what is normally accomplished in regular driving lessons. When you graduate from that course, you'll have many more skills and much more knowledge; you'll feel a lot better and so will we."

Rebecca really appreciated her parents' emotional and financial support, but she was not willing to get behind the wheel again. Her parents explained that she would have to overcome that initial fear in order to take the driving lessons. They gave her two options: she could try to ease her fear on her own using some self-help strategies or she could make an appointment right away with a mental-health professional. Even if she chose to use the self-help approach first, they warned her that she might still require help from a psychologist who practiced in the area of motor vehicle accidents or traumatic experiences. Rebecca agreed to try the do-it-yourself approach first. Here is what she did:

Tapping: Rebecca used the Tapping technique to revisit both of her automobile accidents, tapping the eight points as she focused her attention on the memory of all the details of each crash. As she tapped the points, she remembered more and more details from the events, including the body memories of shock and fear. She found herself sobbing quietly but continued tapping rounds until all the upset was completely resolved. By the end of the Tapping, she was emotionally drained, but she also felt like the accidents were really over. She had trouble picturing the scenes that had been so vivid in her mind only minutes earlier. Moreover, she could think about what

SARAH CHANA RADCLIFFE

had happened without experiencing any negative emotion at all—a key characteristic of a successful Tapping therapy. (See Appendix A, page 301, for more indications of a successful Tapping intervention.)

Tapping In: Now that the accidents and the feelings they engendered were behind her, Rebecca turned her attention to the idea of taking driving lessons. As she pictured herself driving, she felt "stuck," overwhelmed with uncertainty. She was having trouble seeing herself as a driver. To help herself move into that role, Rebecca used Tapping-In (see Chapter Four, page 110). First, she searched for a memory of a time when she felt very smart and competent, feeling that this would help her remember that she is a capable person. Once she found an appropriate memory, she began tapping bilaterally, left leg, right leg, left leg, right leg, very slowly on one leg and then on the other, as she sat in a chair. As she tapped, she thought of the way she felt when she opened her last report card at school and saw all A's— the feeling of being smart, successful and competent. She Tapped In that feeling, picturing herself with the report card and saying, "I can learn whatever I put my mind to learning," over and over again as she performed the slow tapping. At the end of a few minutes of this activity, Rebecca's confidence had grown, she felt much calmer and knew that she could learn to be a good driver if she put her mind to it. Rebecca finished her session by calling the driving school to set up her first appointment.

HELPING ILANA THROUGH HER FEAR OF GOING TO SCHOOL AFTER BEING BULLIED

Eleven-year-old Ilana White was never a popular child. However, she was smart and talented and kept herself busy with music lessons, art, school projects and reading (she was an avid reader). Ilana always managed to have at least one or two friends in class, and even if they didn't visit much out of school hours, Ilana felt secure with these relationships—until she got to grade five. Something changed that year. For some reason that she couldn't explain, a few kids in the class started picking on her. At first, this came in the form of snickers or the occasional insult. However, the problem quickly escalated, with more and more kids seeming to join the "anti-Ilana" campaign and the behaviors becoming more and more aggressive. Ilana was confused at first but still not deeply rattled—she had her two friends to comfort her. But then these girls started to drift off. They didn't become mean like the others, but they suddenly became unavailable; they weren't around at recess or lunch and they kept a physical distance within the classroom. Ilana could see that they were avoiding her. She thought that they probably didn't want to be associated with a "loser" like her.

Ilana felt increasingly vulnerable and increasingly miserable. Walking home alone after school one afternoon, she was suddenly "swarmed" by a group of her classmates. One grabbed her schoolbag. Another pulled her hat off her head. Someone kicked her lightly in the back of her knees, causing her to topple to the ground. Ilana couldn't really describe what happened next—she just remembers a lot of shouting and laughing and taunting and pushing—and then the children disappeared just as quickly as they had appeared. The young girl was shocked and shaken. She wasn't physically hurt—there were no bruises or cuts—but she was crushed inside. She could barely walk home because of the weakness running through her body. She found her emptied and trampled schoolbag on the sidewalk a few yards ahead, picked it up in a daze and somehow made it to her front door a few blocks farther down the road. When her mother opened the door, Ilana fell in a heap and began sobbing uncontrollably.

After some time, Mrs. White was able to piece together an idea of what had just happened. She called her husband, called the school and called the police. There were steps that needed to be taken to address the issue: Mrs. White was on it. She reassured her daughter: "Don't worry. They won't get away with this behavior. They're a bunch of hooligans, those kids. We're not going to put up with it. I'll see to it that the principal suspends every single one of them!"

The next day, Ilana refused to go to school. Mrs. White understood her daughter's feelings and allowed her to stay home. Meanwhile, she and her husband met with the principal and one of the representatives from the police department and, sure enough, each one of the young culprits was suspended for a week. Moreover, they had to go through a corrective process for the purposes of education and discipline, and the entire class began a formal anti-bullying program taught by the police department. Mr. and Mrs. White were satisfied that the school was taking appropriate action. Ilana couldn't care less. She had no plans to return to her class.

Mrs. White made an appointment for Ilana to talk to a social worker who specialized in bullying, explaining that Ilana refused to go back to school. The social worker met with Ilana and recommended ongoing therapy. The Whites agreed to the idea but were frustrated. How long would their daughter be at home? It would be harmful to miss so much school, but there was no way of knowing how long the therapy would take. They arranged for two appointments a week to speed things along, but every day that Ilana was off school was one day too much as far as they were concerned.

Mrs. White decided to try to speed progress along by taking matters into her own hands. "I understand it's going to take some time for you to recover fully from what happened," she told her daughter. "But I'm not willing to have you stay home from school for the rest of the year! Nor are we moving out of the neighborhood so you can go to a different school—believe me, there are bullies everywhere! So the only choice is for you to recover from this event and heal the fear you have of going back into the class. The therapist is going to help you do all that, and we're also going to help you. However, no matter what, you are going back to school on Monday." Mom was giving Ilana four school days and a weekend to work on getting her courage up to go to school again. Mom knew that continuing to avoid going to school would only increase her daughter's fears—she had to get back there as quickly as possible. Moreover, Mrs. White felt quite sure that the classroom would be safe now and her daughter's attitude would play a large role in how things might unfold over time. Here are the interventions that Mrs. White put into place:

Bach Flower Remedies: As soon as Ilana told Mom what had happened, Mrs. White gave her Rescue Remedy to help address the chemistry of shock and fear that was circulating in her body. Now that two weeks had passed, Mom prepared the following remedy mixture for Ilana and gave it to her four times a day: Star of Bethlehem (for traumatic events), Rock Rose (for terror), Mimulus (for fear of being bullied again), White Chestnut (for replaying the events mentally) and Cerato (for self-consciousness and insecurity).

Tapping: Mrs. White went through the Tapping sequence with her daughter, using a variety of healing choices. Because they were a family that had always turned to God for help in times of need, Mrs. White included this spiritual resource in her statements. Here are some of the statements they tapped on: "Even though mean kids attacked me, I choose to remember that God protected me and I survived without a scratch"; "Even though I don't want to go back into the classroom, I choose to face my fear and move forward in my life"; "Even though I'm afraid of those kids, I choose to find the strength to tell them to leave me alone"; "Even though I have been very badly treated, I choose to remember that I am a person of worth"; "Even though people have been mean to me, I choose to remember that I am a good person and God loves me." (See Appendix A, page 303, for the complete Choices Method Tapping protocol.)

Bibliotherapy: Mr. White went to the local library and, with the help of the children's librarian, picked out a number of books dealing with the subject of bullying. He read all the books to Ilana, discussing the stories and lessons, asking for her thoughts and feelings, sharing his own childhood experiences and so on. Some of the books were informational in nature, explaining what bullying is and how a person should respond to it, and some were stories that illustrated the perspectives of both bullies and victims. Ilana learned a lot—particularly that she was not alone in this experience. She also learned some strategies for dealing with mean kids. Just knowing that this was a common experience made Ilana feel a lot better.

#005 04-13-2019 10:12AM
Item(s) checked out to p15122414.

TITLE: I totally funniest : a middle sch
BARCODE: 39098021834444
DUE DATE: 05-04-19

TITLE: Unleashed
BARCODE: 39098021827547
DUE DATE: 05-04-19

View your account
Go to kpl.org

Self-Defense Training: Mom signed Ilana up for self-defense classes—fortunately, Ilana could start right away. Mr. and Mrs. White felt that this would help empower their daughter, giving her more personal confidence and maybe even a better energy. The parents knew that their daughter's timid nature didn't help matters; Ilana was an ideal victim. Mr. and Mrs. White were hoping that self-defense training would make Ilana look and feel much stronger, building both an inner security and a practical skill.

Emotional Regulation: Mom made it very clear that Ilana was going back to school. The class had already had three modules of anti-bullying classes, and five more were scheduled over the next month. The teacher had hand-delivered a number of personal apology notes to Ilana from children who felt remorse over the way they had treated her. Ilana was starting to wish she could go back to school, but she felt very awkward about the reentry process. She didn't want to be the center of so much attention. She just wanted things to be normal. Mom explained that reentry *would* be awkward for the first day, but things could return to normal quickly if Ilana just acted her normal self. In order to do so, it would help if she could control her breath to help her body stay calm. Mom taught Ilana how to breathe in to a count of four and breath out to a count of four, just focusing on the breath going in and out. Mom asked Ilana to practice this every night before falling asleep and at least two times during the day. She wanted her to be able to do it "on the spot" to stay calm.

Visualization: Mom taught Ilana to use her counting breath to enter a nice, calm state and then to picture things being normal and even pleasant at school. Mom knew that as long as Ilana was picturing images of being bullied, there was no way her daughter would succeed. She asked Ilana to imagine the positive scene several times a day but especially upon awakening (a particularly powerful time for Visualization) and just before going to sleep. Mom warned her, "It may not be perfect right away, but over time, things can change. You keep making that picture in your mind, and I'm sure it will become like that after a while." Ilana knew there was really no other option, so she agreed to use the strategy.

With all of these healing steps in place, Ilana was beginning to recover. By the time Monday came along, she was able to go to school. Even though it was hard, it wasn't impossible. Ilana continued with psychotherapy for a few months, and finally, the entire incident was "in the past" for her. In fact, Ilana grew from the experience (and from the psychological interventions that followed) and was more confident and even happier than before. Although no one wants their child to have unpleasant experiences, parents can keep in mind that sometimes surviving and dealing with the aftermath of difficult experiences can actually help a child develop strengths and hidden resources. In fact, some people, teens included, voluntarily push themselves beyond their perceived limits—doing things like extreme sports or extreme outdoor survival programs—to grow stronger emotional muscles from the experience of mastering severe life obstacles.

HELPING JON GIVE HIS PRESENTATION

Jon had not recovered from the last time he had to speak publicly. He had stood onstage in front of the entire grade, about to give his speech for the school-wide public speaking contest. He had already been selected as the best speaker in his class. Now he was vying for best speaker in the entire seventh grade. The best speaker would go on to compete for best speaker in the school. The only problem was that, looking out at the sea of faces in front of him, Jon suddenly froze. He could not say a word. After several long moments of painful, awkward silence, he turned around and sat down. The next speaker took her turn.

Of course, everyone asked Jon what had happened, and of course, he had no answer. He kept his head down and died a thousand deaths. He vowed never to speak publicly again. Unfortunately, his ninth-grade teacher didn't know or care about all this. She assigned the class the mandatory book reports, to be delivered as part of the combined language/social studies department project. The speeches would have to be read in front of two classes, and Jon was having no part of it. He asked his parents to write a note excusing him from participating. Wisely, they declined and, instead, helped Jon heal his trauma by having him do the following tasks:

Retelling: Dad asked Jon to slowly and carefully describe all the events that had happened during the seventh-grade incident. When Jon was finished describing the events of that day, Dad asked him to tell the story again—nice and slowly. When Jon was finished, Dad nodded his head compassionately and asked him to tell it yet again. In fact, Dad asked Jon to tell the story slowly about twelve times! Interestingly, Jon remembered more and more details as he retold the story. But even more interestingly, the more he told it, the less he cared about it. By the tenth telling, Jon no longer felt humiliated or devastated. By the last telling, Jon thought it was kind of funny. Note that Dad could have chosen Tapping instead of Retelling to help release Jon's trauma. Many fear-fighting strategies are interchangeable; experiment with one and then, if necessary, try another.

Visualization: Dad asked Jon to stand up and look ahead. He was to imagine the kids from two classes sitting in front of him. Dad told Jon to start telling them a story. He was to look carefully at the kids while moving back and forth and using his hands to tell the story in an animated fashion. He should imagine some kids laughing, some talking, some nodding off and some listening intently. Then Dad asked Jon to use the Visualization technique: at bedtime and upon waking, he should use the Relaxation Response (see Chapter Four, page 90) for a couple of minutes and then, while still breathing slowly, picture himself giving the speech. He should imagine the audience as before—some kids laughing, some talking, some nodding off and some listening intently. He should see himself completing the talk and carrying on normally with life.

Bonus Breath: Dad showed Jon how to do the antianxiety Bonus Anti-Panic Breath (see Chapter Four, page 93). He asked Jon to practice it twice daily or more often so that he could use it comfortably right before giving his presentation.

Preparation: Dad took Jon for a two-hour training session on public speaking skills. The one-on-one session taught Jon how to look at his audience, how to hold himself, how to project his voice and how to move while talking. Jon's self-confidence grew tremendously as a result of this preparation, and he felt ready to give the talk.

Rescue Remedy: Dad bought some Rescue Remedy spray for Jon and told him how to use it (see Appendix B, page 315) before giving the talk.

Jon gave his talk successfully. As a result of facing his fear and using strategies to recover from the previous public-speaking trauma, he no longer needed to flee from public-speaking responsibilities. His dad had given him a set of practical tools as well as emotional regulation tools. The traumatic event was now a distant memory with no power to influence his current or future choices.

FAST TRACKS FOR FEARS CAUSED BY A BAD EXPERIENCE

Fastest Fast Track

Take your child or teen to a psychologist who uses specialized treatments for trauma, such as Tapping or EMDR. Treatment for small-t traumas using these therapeutic modalities can be as brief as a session or two. Treatment for big-T traumas may also be brief but generally require a lengthier and more comprehensive treatment plan.

Fuller Program Fast Track

For big-T traumas, take your child to a psychologist who uses specialized trauma treatments such as Tapping or EMDR.

For small-t traumas, begin by addressing the memory of the bad experience using Tapping or Retelling.

Teach your child an emotional regulation strategy like the Bonus Breath, Heart Hold or calming techniques such as Breath, Eye or Ear Focusing. (Only one emotional regulation strategy is required.)

Instruct your child to visualize or rehearse the desired behavior (e.g., "Picture yourself successfully singing your solo.") Optional: use Tapping In to reinforce strengths and resources.

Avoid avoidance. Arrange for your child to engage in the behavior that reminds her of a bad experience. If desired, give your child Rescue Remedy before she engages in the desired behavior. Remind the child to use her tools (Tapping, breathing, visualizing, etc.) as necessary in order to get through the experience.

CHAPTER ELEVEN

Helping Your Child through Fear of Emotional Pain

Fear of loss, pain, embarrassment, rejection, disappointment and failing; fear of parents dying; fear of divorce; fear of dating; fear of inviting friends; fear of taking tests; fear of public speaking; fear of making a mistake; fear of change; fear of separation

In truth, at the root of all fear is the fear of psychological pain—emotional suffering. We're worried that something will *feel bad*. Falling off a tall building, getting trapped in an elevator, being kidnapped, developing a terminal illness, being retraumatized at the scene of a previous traumatic event—ultimately, all of these potential experiences carry with them the threat of very unpleasant emotions. They also carry with them the threat of physical suffering or real-life negative consequences. For instance, some fears center around one's own or one's loved one's death or disfigurement. Some involve penalties, serious loss, deprivation or wounding.

However, there is a certain class of fear in which the total fear—or at least the majority of it—is the fear of *feeling bad*. This is not fear of some negative physical experience—like the fear of getting injured or attacked. Rather, it is fear of a negative emotional experience, such as feeling sad, lonely, inadequate, overwhelmed, rejected or embarrassed. A child or teen can have serious fears of experiences that could result in emotional pain, such as social rejection, doing poorly on a test, failing, doing something humiliating (e.g., wearing the wrong outfit for a social event, or "freezing" when having to talk in front of a group) and so on. These fears can paralyze youngsters, preventing them from trying to date or invite friends over, answer questions in class, try new activities or learn new skills. Many children fear change of any kind—location, activity or routine—because it forces them out of their comfort zone into new, uncharted territories; the unknown is filled with the risk of emotional pain—a missed step can seem to spell disaster.

The fear of emotional pain can be so intense, in fact, that people of every age often say that they would rather die than have to endure it. The fear of public speaking, for example, is greater for most people than the fear of death, as is the fear of the pain of having to continue life without a certain loved one. Indeed, it is precisely because these fears are worse than the fear of dying that they can sometimes lead to suicidal thoughts and behaviors. Some teenagers who have suffered a broken heart have taken their own lives. Indeed, fear of loss may be worse than the feelings generated by loss itself; kids may worry for years that their family will fall apart at some point, suffering more in their anticipatory anxiety than they suffer once their fear is realized. Like loss, failure can be absolutely devastating when it represents a loss of identity, status, position, self-worth or even aspiration. Some kids who have done poorly academically (which can mean anything from having actually failed to having received less than an A+) have been known to take their own lives. Kids who have been severely mocked and mistreated have done the same. Of course, most emotional pain does *not* lead to suicide; this worst-case scenario is worth mentioning only as a reminder that emotional pain is never to be minimized or taken lightly. A broken heart (along with all other sorts of emotional pain) is a very serious, sometimes life-threatening, condition. While this chapter looks at how parents can help their kids negotiate their fears of emotional distress, it is worth repeating that when a child's fear is severe enough to affect his normal functioning (i.e., the child is unable to concentrate on schoolwork, has withdrawn from friends and family or has otherwise ceased to function normally; the child is abusing substances or engaging in other unhealthy strategies in order to cope; or the youngster expresses serious distress or talks about suicide), professional assessment and treatment is necessary.

HELPING TYLER THROUGH HIS FEAR OF HIS PARENTS GETTING DIVORCED

Ten-year-old Tyler is a little boy with a big heart. He is a natural nurturer, great with his little brother and sister and eager to help anyone who needs his assistance. Tyler's strength is also his weakness: his emotional sensitivity leads him to quick tears and easily hurt feelings.

Tyler's parents understand and respect his nature, doing their best to interact with him gently and kindly. However, they are not always able to do the same with each other. Like most couples, they bicker on occasion, and once in a while they even have a full-blown fight. Unfortunately, these moments of conflict cause Tyler great emotional distress. He begs his parents to stop fighting and when they (nicely) tell him that he should just leave the room, he breaks down in tears, crying that he doesn't want them to get divorced. Tyler's folks know that he isn't being manipulative—he is genuinely frightened. Many of his classmates live in separated and divorced families and he knows that things like this can happen. What he doesn't know is that his parents are a happily married, intensely committed couple. Their spats and squabbles are just spats and squabbles—not indications of a marriage on the rocks.

One night, they call Tyler aside, telling him that they want to talk with him about his divorce fears. They begin the conversation by inviting Tyler to describe his worry and fears to them. Giving Tyler the opportunity to really talk about his feelings is an important healing step in itself. Instead of rushing in, after his first sentence, to reassure him that divorce is not a realistic scenario, they let him talk and talk and talk, receiving his words with sympathy and emotional coaching. Their dialogue sounds like this:

Parent: *So Tyler, we know that you get really upset when Mommy and Daddy have an argument. You cry and tell us you don't want us to get divorced. What do you feel when we fight? What happens inside of you?*
Tyler: *I get scared. I don't want you guys to get divorced.*
Parent: *I see. You get worried that our fight means that we will be getting divorced?*
Tyler: *Yes. Mike's parents fought a lot before they got divorced. So did Stephen's parents. They told me that's why they got divorced—too much fighting.*
Parent: *Yes, sometimes people who fight a lot end up getting divorced. So I guess it's pretty scary for you to hear us fight. It makes you think we're going to get divorced.*
Tyler: *Yes. I don't want to live in a house without one of you there. I want you both home every night for supper and bedtime. Mike hardly ever sees his father anymore.*
Parent: *That sounds really awful, really sad. Of course, you wouldn't want that.*
Tyler: *So don't fight anymore, okay?*
Parent: *Well, that's about as likely to happen, Tyler, as the chances of you and your brother, Ryan, never fighting again. In fact, I'll tell you what: if you never get annoyed with Ryan again, I'll never get annoyed with Mommy. Is it a deal?*
Tyler: *No—Ryan is really annoying! That's impossible!*
Parent: *Well, sometimes—not often, mind you—I feel like Mommy is really annoying, and Mommy sometimes feels like I'm really annoying. Family members who love each other sometimes feel really annoyed by each other—that's just the way it is.*
Tyler: *But I don't want you to get divorced.*

At this point in the conversation, Tyler's parents can help him by using the strategy of Moving Fear with Facts. If you recall from Chapter Three, this technique involves offering information that is relevant to the child's fear in a way that is more similar to *education* than to *reassurance*. The conversation continues as follows:

Parent: *We know you don't want us to get divorced and we have no intention of getting divorced. But we think you need to understand a little bit more about marriage and divorce so that you can trust what we're saying. We're going to write a list for you so that you can look at it whenever you start to feel worried. Let's go over each point together: If your parents normally tell you the truth, you can trust them when they tell you they have no intention of getting divorced. Are we normally truthful with you?*
Tyler: *Yes.*
Parent: *Can you trust us when we tell you that we are not headed toward divorce?*
Tyler: *Yes.*
Parent: *Married couples don't get divorced unless something very bad is going on. Having little arguments is not something very bad. Every married couple argues. Nobody is perfect, and people tend to irritate each other a little. Fighting is more likely to lead to divorce when it is frequent, very loud, very insulting (saying really mean things and using really bad words, including swear words), extremely hurtful and, in some cases, violent. Do Mommy and Daddy ever fight like that?*
Tyler: *No.*
Parent: *People who are so unhappy that they want to divorce sometimes look and act unhappy for a really long time. Does either one of us look unhappy a lot of the time?*
Tyler: *No.*
Parent: *Do we look happy?*
Tyler: *Yes.*

Parent: *Couples who are unhappy may not fight, but they also may not want to spend much time with each other. Does it seem like Mommy and Daddy don't want to spend time with each other?*

Tyler: *No.*

Parent: *Do Mommy and Daddy go out alone together every Tuesday night?*

Tyler: *Yes.*

Parent: *Do Mommy and Daddy do lots of things together?*

Tyler: *Yes.*

Parent: *People who end up divorcing often threaten divorce out loud many times before they act on it. Did you ever hear Mommy or Daddy say anything about divorce?*

Tyler: *No.*

Parent: *People who do something very wrong or very unhealthy in marriage make it more likely that there might be a divorce. Some behaviors that might lead to divorce include drinking a lot (being an alcoholic or drug addict), gambling, engaging in illegal activities, immoral activities and so on. Of course, you don't know what Mommy or Daddy might be doing in their private time, but you do know that we are here with you guys every night and every weekend. We don't have too much time to get into trouble. There's no way for you to be sure about this one, but does everything appear to be normal and healthy?*

Tyler: *Yes.*

Parent: *People who have behavioral or emotional problems have a higher chance of getting a divorce. For example, some people refuse to work, some never get out of bed, some are very irresponsible (like never cleaning up or never paying bills), some have anger problems and punch holes in the wall and so on. Do Mommy and Daddy have any of those kinds of problems?*

Tyler: *No.*

Parent: *People who divorce sometimes have more stress*

than they can manage. The ones who divorce under these
circumstances usually don't have good stress management
habits like exercising every day, seeing a therapist, mak-
ing sure they have fun, staying involved with friends and
family, practicing spiritual and religious disciplines and so
on. They are irritable and unhappy because they are not
dealing well with their life stress. You see how Mommy and
Daddy live and you see how we take care of ourselves—do
we seem to be overwhelmed with stress or do we seem to
have good stress-management habits?

Sometimes, parents get divorced even though none
of this stuff is going on and there were no obvious signs
of trouble in the marriage. There are other things—more
invisible ones—that can go wrong in a marriage. However,
it is very, very rare that everything looks really happy and
healthy, and then the parents go and get divorced. I'm
not saying that it can't happen, but just like we don't go
around worrying that a truck is going to drive into our liv-
ing room, we don't need to waste time worrying about and
thinking about that kind of divorce.

Having looked at all this, does it seem to you that
Daddy and Mommy are about to get divorced?
Tyler: *No.*

In most cases, Moving Fear with Facts helps ease and transform
frightened feelings. This happened in Tyler's case. After learning
more about the factors that increase the likelihood of divorce, he
realized that his parents were not "candidates" for divorce. This is
similar to what can happen when a person learns what the various
noises on an airplane mean (e.g., wings opening and closing), what
turbulence is (choppy airwaves) and why airplanes can't fall out of
the sky (the "jello" effect of fast-moving airwaves). Armed with new
information that really addresses their fear, people calm down. Tyler
stopped crying when his parents argued and just went about his own
business. He realized that they'd make up soon and that they really

SARAH CHANA RADCLIFFE

loved each other. Comparing their spats to the ones he had regularly with his brother made him take the whole thing a lot less seriously: "Family members are sometimes annoying, that's all."

HELPING KEVIN THROUGH HIS FEAR OF DATING

Kevin was a "late bloomer." At twenty-one, he was still living at home—a situation that was increasingly common among his college peers. What was not common at his age was that Kevin had never been on a date. Kevin talked to girls in his classes, and he found plenty of them very attractive. But he was intimidated. What if he asked a girl out and she turned him down? He just couldn't take the risk. Apart from this problem, Kevin was a well-adjusted young adult: he was an excellent student who was active in school politics, he had a couple of good friends, he played team sports, and he even held down a part-time job. Although Kevin had always been a cautious kid, he seemed to have overcome his childhood fears. Only this one lingered: the fear of being rejected.

"What are you afraid of, Kevin?" his dad chided him. "Lots of girls turned me down. That turned out just fine, though, because it left an opening for your mom. She said yes and the rest is history. That's why you're here today!" The story didn't particularly inspire Kevin. He didn't want to go through all that rejection in order to find "the one."

Kevin's parents really wanted to help him. They offered to send him on a dating course (he didn't want to go). They offered to send him for counseling (he refused). They brought home some books on dating (he leafed through them, but they had no effect). "I know what I need to do, Mom," Kevin explained. "I just can't do it."

A turning point came for Kevin when two of his good friends got themselves some very nice girlfriends. The boys were busy now with their relationships, and Kevin was having a harder and harder time getting his pals to make some time for him. Couples got together with other couples. There were fewer and fewer unattached guys around for him to socialize with. He knew that he needed a girlfriend of his own if he wanted to have any kind of social life. Kevin reached out to his parents. "I need to get past this," he told them. "I've got to start asking people out. I know intellectually that it's no big deal if someone says no, but my heart starts to go crazy when I just think of asking someone out. I'll go to a psychologist if I have to, but before I do that, do you know of some way I can calm myself down?"

Mom offered two techniques for Kevin to try: the Mindfulness-Yes technique and Visualization. "See which one works best for you," she suggested. "You can even use both of them if you want to. And remember to take Rescue Remedy a couple of times in the hours before you ask someone out."

Kevin started with Mindfulness-Yes (see chapters Four, page 111, and Five, page 145). He sat down, closed his eyes and began to think about asking out the cute girl in his statistics class. He began the exercise:

She'll say no.
Y-e-s.
I'll be humiliated.
Y-e-s.
She'll think it was ridiculous for someone like me to ask
   her out.
Y-e-s.
I'll feel like a fool.
Y-e-s.
I'll feel like sinking into the ground.
Y-e-s.
I won't know what to say.
Y-e-s.
I'll die a thousand deaths.
Y-e-s.
There's no way I'm putting myself through that.
Y-e-s.
But if I don't, I'll never be with anyone.

Y-e-s.
I need to take a chance.
Y-e-s.
Maybe she would agree.
Y-e-s.
Or if she doesn't, I can ask the girl in my economics class.
Y-e-s.
Someone will eventually agree to go out.
Y-e-s.
Maybe someone actually wants to go out with me.
Y-e-s.

Kevin kept going and going with the exercise, allowing his brain to release the fears using this gentle, therapeutic form of acknowledgment of his thoughts and feelings. By the time he was done, he felt pretty optimistic about his chances of getting a date, and he felt much, much more calm when thinking about the process required to make that happen.

Now Kevin added a bit of Visualization to his self-help program. As his mom had pointed out, Kevin had been spending a lot of time using Visualization already—only it was *negative* Visualization instead of positive Visualization. In the back of his mind, he was constantly imagining a scene in which he asked a girl out and she turned him down in a disdainful way. No wonder he was feeling terrified! His mom pointed out that he could intentionally start imagining a more positive scene—one in which a young lady happily agreed to go out with him. Mom gave Kevin instructions for Visualization (see those found in Chapter 5, page 137) and he decided to try it out.

Kevin lay down on the family's big reclining leather chair, closed his eyes and breathed slowly in and out, in and out, thinking the number "one" on the out breath. He continued this way for about eight minutes or so, until he was feeling pleasantly relaxed. Then, with eyes still closed, he imagined that he was looking at a movie screen in front of him. On it, he saw a movie of himself asking out the girl from the statistics class. He purposely generated a positive scene in which the girl flashed a big smile at him and enthusiastically accepted his invitation. He saw himself smiling in return as he asked for her contact information and suggested a time for their proposed date. He flashed forward to an image of himself on the date, laughing, talking and having a great time with the young woman. Just watching the movie made Kevin feel great. After that first run, he watched "reruns" of it every morning before getting out of bed, and every evening as he was preparing to go to sleep, for another week. Then, feeling confident and relaxed, he asked the girl out for real (he didn't even feel the need for Rescue Remedy). As it turned out, she had a boyfriend already and had to decline. However, Kevin felt certain now that he could get a date. He changed the "heroine" of his home movie to the girl in his economics class, watched this movie a few times and then asked her out. This young lady was not only available, but was absolutely delighted to go out with Kevin. In fact, she eventually became his first girlfriend.

For people like Kevin who are fearing rejection, there is another easy trick that helps foster positive imagination: drawing faces. If a youngster is fearing rejection from a crowd (as in a public-speaking situation), she can fill a small page with simple face pictures—each face sporting a very big, accepting, appreciative smile. Indeed, she can fill a number of yellow sticky papers with these faces and stick them to her mirror, her desk, her schoolbooks and the front of her speech papers. When the child's eye falls upon all these smiling faces over and over again for many days, she comes to expect a positive response from her audience. What she's accomplished here is overriding the picture that her mind was previously holding of rejecting faces. Even though she may not have been consciously aware of those sour faces, they were surely present if she was feeling afraid to give her talk. After all, who would be afraid if she genuinely anticipated a delighted response? Those kids who are fearing the rejection of a friend or potential date can just draw one big smiley face and post it all around their environment in the same fashion. Again, the smiling picture says, "Yes, I like you and I welcome your overtures," causing the child's fear to diminish with repeated exposure.

SARAH CHANA RADCLIFFE

HELPING BRADY THROUGH THE FEAR OF HIS PARENTS DYING AND ALEXIS THROUGH HER FEAR OF MOVING

When a child's fear of emotional pain is eased with emotional coaching and Moving Fear with Facts, no further help is needed. However, some kids are not so easily moved out of their anxious feelings. Four-year-old Brady could not be talked out of his fear of his mommy and daddy dying (fear of parents dying is a normal developmental issue that peaks between ages four and six and tends to recede after that period). He would agonize about it every day, particularly at bedtime. Sometimes, he'd get really emotional, crying and begging his parents not to leave him. Brady's folks tried reassuring him that young parents rarely die, and even if they did, he'd always be looked after. This did absolutely nothing to calm Brady down. His folks were really at a loss as to how to help him—until they had to deal with his sister's completely different fear.

Oddly enough, while Brady was worrying about the pain he'd feel if his parents died, his sister, Alexis, was worrying about a more timely issue: the family's upcoming move. The family was moving to a new neighborhood in just a few weeks, and eight-year-old Alexis was feeling very anxious about it. Never great with change, Alexis didn't want to leave her bedroom behind—or her backyard. In fact, she didn't want to part with her house, her street, her neighborhood and, especially, her school. The loss that worried her the most, however, was the loss of her best friend, Paige. How would life continue without Paige? They were in the same class, ate lunch together daily, walked to and from school and practically lived in each other's homes. Alexis was worried that she'd never have another friend like Paige. In fact, she was worried that she wouldn't have any friends at all at her new school.

Mom and Dad let Alexis talk about her concerns without trying to minimize them or cheer her up. They felt bad that she had to go through this, but they knew that the move would be good for the family in the long run. They used emotional coaching, just naming her feelings back to her as she worried out loud. They tried Moving

Fear with Facts, giving her specific tools that she could use in the new neighborhood to help maintain a meaningful connection with Paige and to make new friends as well. They even helped her to take photographs of her room, her house and everything else she held dear and encouraged her to make a scrapbook of all these memories. Although these were all good interventions, they were not enough for Alexis. Like her brother, Brady, Alexis had a tendency to get stuck in dark mental places.

Mom tried the Lego brain intervention with Alexis, showing her that she was building herself a sad and frightened brain (see Chapter Five, page 129). She encouraged Alexis to turn her worries into opportunities by asking "what if" questions like "What if moving meant meeting lots of great new friends?" and "What if moving meant having an even more beautiful bedroom?" and "What if moving meant getting to have lots of new and interesting experiences?" Alexis did work at shifting her thoughts and, as she did so, she felt a little bit better. But her worries still troubled her at night.

Mom gave Alexis some Rescue Sleep—the Bach flower preparation that helps settle the mind (see Chapter Six, page 168). This really helped Alexis—she was able to "turn off" her brain and get a good night's rest. Encouraged by this response to the Bach flower remedy, Mom made a mixture (see Appendix B, page 311) that directly addressed the fears Alexis was feeling. In a mixing bottle she put:

- White Chestnut for obsessively thinking and worrying (noisy brain)
- Mimulus for worrying about the future, anticipating pain
- Walnut for dealing with transitions
- Gentian for negativity, expecting the worst to happen
- Star of Bethlehem for grief and loss

Alexis took 4 drops of the mixture in liquid, four times a day. Within a couple of days, Mom noticed that she was doing better; she was expressing less fear and negativity. About a week later, Mom was shocked to hear Alexis ask if she could help decorate her new

SARAH CHANA RADCLIFFE

room. Alexis was actually getting into the move in a positive way. She seemed a whole lot more optimistic now. The dark cloud around her had lifted. It dawned on Mom that perhaps Bach flower remedies might also help little Brady. She decided to give him this mixture:

- White Chestnut for obsessing (about the possibility of his parents dying)
- Red Chestnut for fear of something bad happening to a loved one
- Mimulus for fear of separation and death
- Rock Rose for feelings of panic

Like Alexis, Brady had an excellent response to the remedies. He simply stopped talking about his parents dying. He was back to himself, a happy, active little boy. Brady's fear would have cleared up eventually on its own, but Mom was happy to cut the heavy, worrying experience short for him. She was happy to have the old, carefree Brady back.

Bach flower remedies can often shorten the course of emotional suffering for children, teens and adults. However, as I previously mentioned, the response to the remedies varies all the way from nonexistent to moderate to "miraculous recovery"—the only way to know how they will work for your child is to try them. Getting a less than ideal response can sometimes result from making a less than optimal choice of remedies—a Bach practitioner may be able to help in such cases.

HELPING CHELSEA CHOOSE HER OWN WARDROBE

Fifteen-year-old Chelsea can't decide what to wear. Ever. Every morning, she approaches her drawers with trepidation, afraid to make a fatal error. Of course, it hasn't helped that her mother has a critical eye. ("Chelsea, those colors don't really work—why don't you wear the blue sweater with that T-shirt instead?") Mom's comments have only served to reinforce her sense of inadequacy, which has a lot to do with Chelsea's innate nature. Her younger sister, Makayla, has no problem ignoring Mom's "helpful advice." ("Why do you *care* what she says?" Makayla asks Chelsea. "You can wear whatever you want!")

Oddly enough, it is Mom who consults a therapist about the matter. "My teenage daughter is so insecure—I'm really worried about her," Mom explains to the counselor as she goes on to describe Chelsea's seeming phobia about selecting her own clothes. In the course of a few sessions of counseling, the therapist helps Mom learn to take a back seat to Chelsea's dilemma. "It will really help her find her own style if you just refrain from making any comments at all about how she looks. Even if her outfit seems bizarre to you, don't say a word. Make clothes a nonissue."

Mom can see the wisdom in this approach. She dutifully follows the doctor's prescription, ceasing to make any comments whatsoever about Chelsea's clothing. Despite Mom's new stance, however, Chelsea still has a lot of trouble. "Please just tell me if this looks okay!" she begs Mom in the morning. Mom has already explained to Chelsea that she is no longer going to be helping her with clothing choices. She has explained to her too that this is for Chelsea's own benefit and, hard as it is, she is going to have to leave it to Chelsea to discover her own taste in clothing. Having said all this, she now simply greets Chelsea's concerns with emotional coaching. For a while, their conversations sound like this:

Chelsea: *Does this match with this?*
Mom: *You're not sure about it.*
Chelsea: *That's right—I'm not sure about it. So tell me,*
does this match or not?
Mom: *You want me to decide.*
Chelsea: *That's right, Mom—I want you to decide. So does*
it match or not?
Mom: *I see that it's hard for you to accept that I'm no*
longer making those choices for you.

Chelsea: *Mom, stop the psychobabble and please tell me. I'm not going out of this house looking like a fool, and you know the answer to this question: Does it or does it not match!*

Mom: *I know you're very frustrated with me, Chelsea, but I can't answer that for you. I hear how frightened you are that you'll make the wrong choice. You seem terrified.*

Chelsea: *I can't believe you're doing this to me! You know I can't decide!*

Mom: *I'm so sorry this is so hard for you, honey. I told you before that I have to do this even if I find it hard to hear your pain. It's the only way you're going to get better. You have to learn that you can survive even if you do make a mistake. That's the only way out of this.*

Although Chelsea is upset with her mom, she also knows in her heart that her mom is correct. In fact, Chelsea really wants to become more confident. She just doesn't know how to get there. Part of her agrees with Mom that having to figure it out independently would be good for her. Part of her just wants someone to take the problem away by becoming her personal shopper.

Meanwhile, Mom has been noticing that Chelsea's fear of looking bad is not exactly diminishing. She decides to try another approach. Mom speaks to Chelsea about the fact that she still holds a lot of fear about making a wardrobe error. She asks Chelsea if she'd like to try a new technique that might bring the fear down a couple of notches. Chelsea is willing to try anything. Mom teaches her how to do *Extreme Tapping*.

Extreme Tapping

This technique involves tapping on all eight treatment points (see Chapter Four, page 115, and Appendix A, page 298) while naming *absolute worst-case* scenarios out loud. The scenarios don't have to be realistic ones—they can be the verbalized fantasies of disaster and catastrophe that worriers can easily generate. These exaggerated horror stories usually stay inside a person's head, managing choices and behaviors from behind the scenes. In Extreme Tapping, the horror stories are invited to come forward and announce themselves. The process of Tapping allows these frightening thoughts and images to slide into the bright light of day without objection. Once there, they tend to quickly resolve.

In the Extreme Tapping technique, points are tapped continuously (tapping round after round without stopping) while every possible imagined bad thing is named and pictured in as much detail as possible. The person stops tapping after a few rounds just to pause and let the energy settle—noticing what thoughts and feelings are happening right then. If there is still some upset or fear, several more rounds are tapped. This process continues until there is no remaining distress.

Note again that if a person were to simply name her nightmares *without tapping,* she would just be reinforcing her worst fears. In Chelsea's case, if she were just to think her extreme anxieties to herself, she'd probably believe them and feel worse than ever. Saying them while tapping, however, is a whole different ball game. Instead of feeling worse, the tapper usually ends up feeling absolutely fantastic (or at least relieved). Here is what Chelsea's Extreme Tapping session sounds like as she taps the points in repetitive rounds:

I'll dress all wrong and make a fool of myself.
Everyone will think I'm such a loser.
They'll point and laugh and run away from me.
No one will ever talk to me again.
I'll lose all my friends.
I will be exposed for what I really am.
Everyone will see how useless I am.
I'll never be able to show my face again.
I'll be so hideous and ridiculous-looking.
My clothes will be ugly and disgusting-looking.

I'll look so awful, no one will have anything to do with me.
People will cross the street when they see me coming,
  because they'll be afraid I'm crazy.
Everyone will see what bad taste I have.
My teachers will fail me because I look so dumb.
I will never be able to leave the house again.

As so often happens, Chelsea feels completely calm after expressing her nightmarish fantasies while tapping on the eight points. With
her nervous system calmed by the tapping, she is able to hear and feel
the ridiculous nature of her worries and is finally able to think straight.
"None of that will happen," Chelsea says to her mom. "Nobody even
cares what I wear. My friends certainly don't. And anyway, they don't
dress amazingly either, and it doesn't bother me a bit. I don't care if I
look less than perfect. Nothing will happen." Chelsea and her mom
are both tremendously relieved.

HELPING SYDNEY THROUGH HER PARENT'S DIVORCE

Ten-year-old Sydney is very, very sad. She has recently learned that
her parents are getting a divorce. In addition to feeling deep grief,
Sydney feels confused and terribly anxious. She doesn't understand
why this has to happen, and she doesn't know what direction her life
is going to take. Where will she live? When will she see her parents?
What will happen to her other relatives—will they still be part of her
family life? She has tons and tons of questions to ask her parents, and
they try their best to answer them. Of course, they themselves are
facing many unknowns. Everything is not yet settled—in fact, they
are just beginning negotiations with their mediator. Dad is moving
into temporary quarters at the end of the month, but it is not clear
where he will end up living once things settle down.

All of this uncertainty and upheaval is taking a toll on Sydney.
She is feeling a terrible heaviness, like her life is ending. "Nothing
will ever be good again," she cries to Mom. "I might as well be dead."

Naturally, Mom is concerned to hear the desperation in her daughter's voice. She feels awful to be putting her through such pain. Yet she understands that there are things she can do to make this difficult passage a bit easier for Sydney. First, she offers the comfort of Parental Presence. "Honey, I know this is so hard for you. Daddy and I are still here and will always be here for you, even if we are not living in the same house. I know your heart is breaking, and I don't want you to go through that alone. You can talk to us as much as you want to about all of this. Feel free to pour your heart out, day or night. Even though we can't change what is happening, we can help you through it."

Sydney is relieved to know that it's okay for her to talk, cry, ask questions, protest, be mad and be sad. Her mom's emotional support helps her to process her emotions. The situation is hard enough already—if she had to bottle up her feelings inside, she feels like she'd explode with the pain.

Fortunately, Mom is also able to provide emotional coaching. Whatever Sydney says, Mom accepts and validates. Mom never corrects her or tries to cheer her up. One day, Sydney says, "I'm so mad at you and Daddy for doing this to me—I hate you!" and Mom doesn't even bother to correct Sydney's disrespectful and inappropriate language. Instead, all Mom says is "Of course you're angry and you have a right to be. Daddy and I are messing up your life right now and there's nothing you can do about it. You're furious at us for taking everything you cherish away from you—part of you hates us for that, and I understand." It's hard to really hate Mom and Dad when they listen to everything you say so compassionately. Sydney immediately apologizes for saying what she said and then just dissolves into tears. Her Mom holds her as she sobs helplessly. Mom understands and stands by her resolve to be there for Sydney's pain.

As the weeks go on, Sydney seems to be sinking into an apathetic state. Mom and Dad have formally separated—that was excruciating for Sydney—and there are lots of changes going on. Furniture and belongings are moving in and out of the house. Mom has lots of appointments and Sydney has lots of babysitters. Nothing is normal anymore. Sydney reiterates her worry to Mom: "My life is over. I can't be happy without you and Daddy living here with me. I don't care about anything anymore." Mom knows that Sydney's feelings are pretty normal considering what is happening in her life. Nonetheless, she asks their pediatrician to make a referral to a psychologist who can assess Sydney for depression and also help her negotiate this difficult period of her life. An appointment is scheduled for a few weeks later. Meanwhile, Mom decides to try to help Sydney with a Visualization exercise.

"Sydney," Mom instructs, "close your eyes. I'm going to count backward slowly from ten down to one—just follow along silently with me. Keep your eyes closed the whole time, and when I'm finished counting, I'll give you more instructions." Mom then counts backward very slowly, in a soft, rhythmic voice. "Now, imagine that there is a movie screen right in front of you. I want you to put a movie there—a movie of your life as it looks right now. Tell me what you see." Sydney describes a scene of chaos: A little girl is sitting on the floor crying while movers are carrying things out of her house. Her father is off in the distance, waving good-bye. Mom tells Sydney she's done a good job making the movie. "Now keep your eyes closed," Mom instructs, "and close that movie screen. Put a new one up, and on that one, make a movie of the little girl a year from now—see what she is doing and what is happening in that scene." Sydney says she sees the little girl still looking sad, but she isn't crying anymore. She's going to school. She's feeling lonely for her old life. Again, Mom praises Sydney's good work. Finally, Mom instructs, "Now we're going to close that screen and put up a new one. On this one, I want you to see the movie of what is happening five years from now, when that little girl is a teenager. Tell me what you see." On the screen, Sydney sees a young lady laughing with her friends, going places and doing things. "Is the girl happy?" Mom asks. Sydney says that she is laughing with her friends, but inside, she is still hurting a little. "That makes sense," Mom says. "A part of her will always hurt a little, but she can still have fun and be happy."

Even though this exercise doesn't have a completely happy ending, Sydney feels a lot better after doing it. It helps her to see that although her pain is front and center right now, it won't always be this way; in fact, life will continue after her parent's divorce. While there is no way to completely eradicate the pain of this important loss, it can come to rest in its rightful place—in a small part of her heart. Life will go on.

Sydney eventually begins her meetings with the psychologist, and they help her continue to come to terms with her grief and anger. Her fears, however, settled to a great extent even before she began treatment. Sydney is taking life one day at a time and worrying far less about what is going to happen next. Although Sydney's parents have decided to part ways, they have made sure to continue to be emotionally and physically present for their daughter, just as they promised. This helps Sydney navigate her new reality successfully, and she goes on to do well in every aspect of her development.

DEALING WITH DAVID'S SEPARATION ANXIETY

Mom knows what's coming. It's the middle of August and school will soon be starting. Five-year-old David is never good with change and he's even worse with separations. Mom still shakes when she thinks about the beginning of the last two years of preschool: David had to be peeled from her so she could leave the school and get to work on time. The scene was traumatizing for them both and probably equally so for all the spectators who watched it for the first few weeks in September. Mom does not want a repeat performance in kindergarten!

Armed with *The Fear Fix* strategies, Mom gets to work. Here's how her plan of attack unfolds:

Bibliotherapy: Two weeks before school is to begin, Mom takes books out from the library and reads bedtime stories to David on the subject of the first day of school.

Emotional Coaching: As Mom reads each story, she highlights the emotions of a little boy who doesn't want to leave his mommy: "Elmo is afraid, isn't he? He doesn't want his mommy to leave him at school with all the other children." Mom names the feelings fearlessly, helping to normalize them and reduce their charge. When David pipes up, "Me too!" she carefully refrains from chiding him or reassuring him. Instead, she simply accepts what he says without alarm. "I know, sweetie. You also don't want Mommy to leave you at school with the children. You're uncomfortable about that, right?" When David agrees wholeheartedly and adds that he is not going to let Mommy leave, Mom offers support and encouragement. She accepts his feeling fully but wants him to know that he may have to modify his behavior. "I know you want Mommy to stay with you. The problem is that the school doesn't let the mommies stay. So Mommy will be going to work and then coming back to get you. I know this is hard for you. I have a special treat for little boys who feel sad and upset and who behave well at the same time. It's important that you let Mommy go to work and that you let the teacher teach the children." Mom is helping David understand the difference between feelings and behaviors. Feeling upset is fine with Mom; screaming, crying and making a disturbance at school is not.

Emotional Regulation and Redirecting Attention: Mom gives David strategies for emotional regulation and Redirecting Attention: "If you feel sad when Mommy leaves, you can cry. Just cry quietly. That will help both you and your teacher. Also, you will feel better faster if you look around for a good toy to play with."

Visualization: In this same two-week period, Mom helps David use a child-friendly type of Visualization. Instead of teaching him to close his eyes and make a picture in his mind, she asks him to look at a picture that she is drawing for him. Mom draws a three-frame scene: in the first frame, a mommy is taking a little boy to school; in the second frame, the little boy is playing with some blocks and trucks in the classroom; in the third scene, the mommy is picking the little boy up from school to bring him home for lunch. Mom draws stick figures and tells the story, but she leaves the faces blank, giving David a crayon and asking him to put a smile on everyone's face. David can see that the story has a beginning, middle and safe ending. The picture sticks in his brain.

Outside Helpers: Knowing that David finds transitions difficult, Mom starts adding the Bach flower remedy Walnut to his beverages during the day. She will continue to add it for the first weeks of school, until David has eased into the new routine.

The night before school, David's little body is wracked with anxiety. He was irritable and fussy the whole day and now, at bedtime, he is all wound up and tense. He says he doesn't know what's bothering him, but Mom is pretty sure she knows. Seeing that David is having trouble settling down to sleep, she makes him a calming cup of warm chamomile tea and adds 4 drops of Rescue Sleep to the cup. She rubs a tiny drop of lavender essential oil on his heart and tucks him into bed for the third time that night. David finally drifts off to sleep.

In the morning, David remembers what's coming. He starts talking about how he's not staying at school. Mom accepts his feelings. "I know, honey. I know. You want to stay with Mommy." Meanwhile, to help calm his obvious fight-or-flight chemistry, Mom adds 4 drops of regular Rescue Remedy to his orange juice and, for good measure, puts a few more drops in the water bottle that she packs in his little lunch box.

Moving Fear with Facts: To help David correct his feeling that his mother is disappearing into the void, Mom tells him her plans for the morning. She has decided to stay home from work that day, as she knows he will be more comfortable picturing her at home. "I'm going home to bake some cookies. You can have some in the afternoon, after school. I'm going to wash some dishes and tidy up the house a bit, and then I'm going to the fish store. After the fish store, I'm coming to get you to bring you home for lunch." All this information is reassuring to David, helping him to know that Mommy is not just disappearing into the universe while he is at school.

Outside Helper: Mom gives David an intangible Outside Helper: a love symbol. Mom takes David's hand and gives his palm a big kiss. "Hold this kiss in your hand, David, and you can also rub it on your heart. That way, Mommy will be with you while you are in school." David likes the idea and closes his fist tightly around the kiss.

Positive Imagination: At school, David starts to get clingy and upset. Mom uses emotional coaching: "I know it's hard, sweetie." She adds a bit of playful imagination: "Look, here's Batman coming to take you into your classroom!" David doesn't see him and wants to know where he is. For a moment in his search, he is distracted, but then he realizes Mom is just pretending. "There's no Batman!" he protests grumpily. Mom acknowledges the truth of that statement but then invites David to pretend with her: "That's true," she says. "But we can pretend, can't we? Let's make a pretend Batman to go into your classroom with you and keep you company while Mommy goes home to clean up and make your cookies." David doesn't say anything but seems to be considering the idea of a pretend companion. He lets Mom walk him into his classroom.

Parental Presence: As Mom bends down to kiss David good-bye, she whips out the picture they drew together. "See, here's the little boy going to school, and here's the little boy just like you in his classroom, and here's the little boy going home. I'll see you soon, sweetie!" Tears well up in David's eyes, but he does not decompose as he did in previous years. Mom refrains from offering reassurance. Instead, she offers quiet Parental Presence, rubbing his hair gently as she stands up and prepares to leave. The teacher comes by just then to show David where he can put his sweater. Mom does not sneak out. Instead, she looks at her son squarely and repeats, "I'll see you soon." Then she leaves.

Sure enough, the morning passes quickly and Mom returns with the promised treat and a big hug. Mom refrains from saying that she missed David (even though she did) because she doesn't want to highlight the sadness of the separation. Instead, she greets him happily with a small hug (so as not to exaggerate the emotionality of the reunion) and quickly offers him his treat. "Say bye and thank you to your teacher, David," she coaches. "Bye," David shouts. "Thank you!"

FRIGHTENING PHILOSOPHIES VS. CALMING CONVICTIONS: GUIDING YOUR CHILD

When it comes to helping children deal with the fear of emotional pain, parental perspectives on life can make a big difference. Emotional pain is a *construct*—suffering that results, to a large extent, from the way a youngster interprets an event. If a student is not accepted into any of the tens of medical schools that he applied to, his pain is *not* a foregone conclusion. It depends very much on what he says to himself at that time, how he understands the world he lives in, what he believes. If he thinks, "That's it—my life is over. If I can't be a doctor, then I don't want to be anything," then, of course, he'll feel intense, crushing pain. If he believes that the rejection letters prove that he is a failure, his feelings of worthlessness can certainly overwhelm him. If he thinks that the one door to happiness and success is now permanently shut, of course he'll be devastated. But why should his head be filled with such destructive negativity? What if his worldview permitted a more positive spin on this turn of events?

In the very same circumstances, another young person might be thinking, "I'll apply again next year and spend this year acquiring an advanced degree that will give me the competitive edge I need. With a master's degree in biological science, I'll certainly get accepted into at least one medical school, and I only need one acceptance!" This student rises to the challenge with faith, optimistic self-talk and a practical plan of action. Throughout his childhood, his parents instilled in him an ethic of "if at first you don't succeed, try, try again." They themselves spoke openly and regularly about the twists and turns of their own journeys and the philosophies that allowed them to persevere. They told him clearly, "There's a plan and a destiny for everyone. A person has to do what he can do, and the rest is up to God."

Of course, each adult has his own worldview and will express optimistic philosophies in his unique way. There are those whose optimism is deeply rooted in spirituality. Within this group, some will call the force behind the scenes "God," while others might refer to "fate," "destiny," "the universe" or something else. Some talk about the soul, a mission and other spiritually-based concepts (as in, "You did everything possible to get into medical school. Obviously, God has different plans for you"; or "You thought you were destined to be a doctor, but it seems you have a different mission in life"). There are also people whose optimism does not stem from a spiritual orientation at all but rather from a psychological one. Members of this group use the language of positive psychology and philosophy when teaching their youngsters how to negotiate life's challenges ("There are many ways to succeed and many roads that can be taken" or "When one door shuts, another door opens"). Whatever the source of their strength and whatever the language they use, people who live with these principles in mind are able to negotiate life's ups and downs much more comfortably and gracefully. They do their best amidst uncertainty and risk, never taking full responsibility for the outcome; they understand that their personal efforts are only part of the picture—the part that they can control. Beyond that, it's a matter of "whatever happens happens." They'll deal with it.

Even when parents live and breathe their own optimistic and courageous philosophy of life, however, they cannot simply hand that protective philosophy over to their child. Nonetheless, they can certainly teach it and model it. Being exposed to a healthy way of thinking, feeling and acting for two developmental decades is definitely good for children. Even genetically vulnerable children (those born with a tendency to feel anxious feelings) benefit from being raised in a more optimistic milieu. The parental message of hope and confidence may not completely eradicate their fears but can help keep them at a minimum.

Parents who hold a lot of anxious, negative thoughts themselves needn't share these out loud with their kids. There is no benefit from offering constant warnings to children about the dangers and disasters lurking around every corner. In fact, instead of offering protection to children, a steady diet of threats to safety and well-being actually harms them. Children can easily acquire a fearful mind-set from openly fearful parents and this "gift" of chronic negativity harms them physically, mentally, emotionally and spiritually. Moreover, when parents worry excessively, children tend not to worry *enough*! As a result, instead of leading safer lives, such children often live in greater danger.

So what should parents do about their anxieties? Hide them? Although silence alone is less destructive than sharing a pessimistic, doomsday philosophy of life, stressed parents can certainly adopt a "fake it till you make it" approach to educating their child. Their personal therapy or use of self-help techniques like the ones found in this book can help rewire their own anxious brains at any age, allowing such parents to become authentically calm and positive over time.

For example, Monica is a woman who worries a lot about her child's future. When young Ethan has problems in school, she panics, thinking that his future will be ruined. Monica works overtime trying to motivate Ethan, educate him, straighten him out. She loses years of sleep. As he grows older, her worries grow with him—the issues are more serious than ever. What will become of him, especially when she isn't there to pick up the pieces? In fact, Monica can call on a variety of strategies from *The Fear Fix*. Here is a small selection with which she can get started:

Build a More Optimistic Brain: Monica can review the Lego brain section in Chapter Five (page 129) for motivation and clarification on how to build a more positively oriented mind-set. She needs to begin to be more selective about which thoughts and images she will entertain, and to accept the challenge of building a more optimistic brain.

Breathwork and Visualization: At night, Monica can use Breathwork, as described in Chapter Four (page 88), and dab a little chamomile essential oil on pulse points, as described in Chapter Six (page 174) and Appendix C (page 317), to improve the quality and duration of sleep. During the day, she can use Breathwork along with Positive Visualization, as described in Chapter Five (page 137), in order to project a happy and successful outcome for her son.

Tapping: Monica can use Tapping, as described in Chapter Four (page 115) and Appendix A (page 298), to release her fears and negative thought processes during her sessions of worry time, as described in Chapter Five (page 144).

Outside Helpers: Monica can take the Bach flower remedies Red Chestnut and White Chestnut, as described in Chapter Six (page 168) and Appendix B (page 310), in order to ease her tendency to worry and ruminate about her child's future.

In other words, *The Fear Fix* strategies can help people of any age to feel calmer, more confident, more optimistic and, ultimately, happier. They can reduce stress and improve mental, emotional and physical well-being. Although they can't take away the challenges of life, fear fixers can certainly help everyone negotiate them in healthier, easier, more comfortable ways.

Becoming less fearful is a process. While a parent is addressing and healing his own anxieties, children are in need of constant support. They can't wait for the parent to work through all of his fears and worries. The good news is that even when a parent still has plenty of emotional baggage to clear out, he can still be an effective guide and coach for his child, giving the youngster the extraordinary gift of a positive life philosophy. The parent can achieve this by doing four simple things:

- refraining from worrying out loud (repetitively predicting negative events) when the child is around

- talking about personal success in calming one's own fear (e.g., "I tried the breathing technique when we drove over the bridge and it really helped! I'm going to use that from now on!")
- routinely greeting the child's fears with acceptance through the use of emotional coaching
- exposing one's child to optimistic philosophies, whether one has personally internalized them or not. For instance, in answer to a child's fear, a parent can say, "We'll cross that bridge when we come to it," even when the parent is just as afraid as the child. "There's always another road," "There's always a silver lining," "The sun will come out tomorrow," "Mistakes are our greatest teachers," and other such pithy sayings have a way of lodging themselves deep in a child's brain, where they can help regulate and soothe anxious feelings throughout life. (By the way, an online search for "optimistic sayings" yields a quick wealth of sayings and sources.) It is powerful to offer such thoughts in the form of books that you give or read to your child, as well as articles and stories that you share at the dinner table concerning great people whose lives and experiences exemplify worthy forms of thought and conduct. Quoting famous, successful and inspirational people is a similar strategy. In other words, parents needn't rely only on themselves in order to impart courageous, hopeful and healthy philosophies; they can draw on the experience, knowledge and wisdom of great human beings spanning the course of history.

Yes, life is full of moment-to-moment risks. We live amidst danger and uncertainty. But we have much to do and little desire to focus on all the things that might go wrong. Our children, too, need to put their energies where they will be productive, leading to lives that are fulfilled, healthy and joyous. To help them accomplish this, we can offer them fear fixers: a ready supply of positive thoughts, ideas and images, a trunk full of practical strategies to calm and support their hearts and minds, and tools for achieving a friendly, compassionate relationship with their frightened and anxious feelings. We can help them march forward with courage, facing and healing their fears along the way. By showing them how to overcome the limitations established by fear, we can swing open the gates before them, releasing them to their fullest and happiest futures.

FAST TRACKS FOR FEARS OF EMOTIONAL PAIN

Fastest Fast Track

Allow your child to talk about her fear of emotional pain, and listen with the intention to accept the fear rather than correct it in any way. Acceptance can help loosen the grip of the fear and also help release it.

Guide your child through the process of fully exploring, expressing and transforming the fear using *any* intervention—Extreme Tapping, Mindfulness-Yes, Speed Journaling and so on—that allows her to fully articulate every possible worst-case scenario. The act of *thoroughly* examining fears of emotional pain very often clears them.

Fuller Program Fast Track

Begin by following the steps in Fastest Fast Track above (emotional coaching and emotional release)

Help your child to consider and imagine positive outcomes, including the possibility of eventually healing from the emotional pain that inevitably occurs in the course of living.

Help your child manage and heal chronic fear of emotional pain by pivoting to positive thoughts (of any kind) when worry arises. Helping the child create positive reframes is an option as well. Instruct your child to choose a brief worry period each day in order to attend to fear of emotional pain using any emotional release technique, until there is no fear left.

Tapping Using EFT (Emotional Freedom Technique) by Gary Craig and the Choices Method of EFT by Dr. Patricia Carrington

EFT, commonly referred to as Tapping, is a form of acupressure for rapidly resolving emotional distress. When a person uses his own fingers to tap on designated parts of the body (specific locations along meridian pathways), he can correct:

- disturbances in bodily functions (e.g., rapid heartbeat, dizziness, muscle tension, nausea, etc.)
- disturbances in emotion (i.e., fear, upset, shock, grief, rage, confusion or distress of any kind)
- disturbances of cognition (i.e., distortions in thinking, such as catastrophizing, black-or-white thinking, jumping to unfounded conclusions, overgeneralizing or generally being irrational)

- disturbances of behavioral tendencies (e.g., strong urges to escape and/or avoid harmless situations, objects, places, etc.)

Let's look at two popular protocols for Tapping. The first is Gary Craig's original EFT. Here are the steps:

1. Name your feeling (e.g., "I'm afraid I'll do poorly on the exam") and rate the intensity of that feeling between one and ten, where ten means that the feeling is extremely strong.
2. Set up the energy system by tapping on the Karate Chop spot (between the baby finger and the wrist on either hand) for a few seconds while saying, "Even though [name your feeling], I completely accept myself." For instance: "Even though I'm afraid I'll do poorly on the exam, I completely accept myself." If you prefer, you can tap on the Karate Chop spot without saying anything at all. It is also possible to skip Step 2 altogether, using it only when the treatment does not seem to be working.
3. Tap the eight treatment points (see diagram on next page) for a few seconds each while thinking about, naming and feeling the frightened feeling.
4. At the end of the round of tapping, take a deep breath in and out and notice what you are thinking and feeling now. Rate the intensity of this feeling between one and ten.
   - If you are at zero, you are finished the treatment.
   - If your number is higher than before, repeat the treatment, making sure to include Step 2.
   - If you are essentially where you started—nothing has really changed—do the same treatment but be sure to do Step 2 if you didn't already do it. If you did do it, then this time use the Tender Spot (see diagram on next page) instead of the Karate Chop spot.
   - If your number is lower than before, repeat the treatment

as many times as necessary till you get to zero. Treatment is also finished if you simply can't think of the fear anymore or can't connect to the feelings at all.

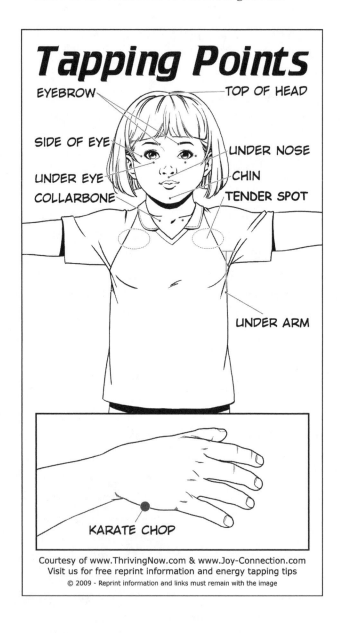

Courtesy of www.ThrivingNow.com & www.Joy-Connection.com
Visit us for free reprint information and energy tapping tips
© 2009 - Reprint information and links must remain with the image

Tapping works deeply on the psyche, affecting all levels of body and mind. I tend to think of it as a form of psychosurgery, as it completely rewires neural pathways. Normally, fears that have been treated with EFT are permanently resolved. After a Tapping session, the most common response is feelings of deep calmness and serenity. However, some people may experience other feelings as well. Here are some common post-Tapping sensations:

- deep exhaustion
- dizziness
- tingling
- giddiness
- tearfulness
- confusion or disorientation

When they occur, these symptoms are harmless and tend to resolve rapidly—often within a few minutes. Sometimes, however, they may last for several hours before quietly dissipating. On rare occasions, some symptoms may last for a few days. In all cases, symptoms are generally accompanied by a profound resolution of the original fear or distress.

Let's look at how Tapping helps sixteen-year-old Lori, who is extremely nervous the night before her big audition for the leading role in the school play. Her body is dysregulated: her heart is beating so loudly she's sure everyone can hear it; her palms are sweaty, her mouth is dry, and she feels nauseated. Needless to say, she can't fall asleep. Her emotions are also running wild: she feels nervous, panicky, agitated and furious with herself for feeling this way. Her thinking is "off" too: she is sure she'll be a big flop, she's thinking that everyone else is more talented than she is (despite all her previous successes in theater) and she is sure that the judges hate her (because one of them didn't smile at her when passing her in the hallway the other day). She begins considering not even trying out for the role.

Fortunately, this young lady already knows how to do Tapping. Instead of continuing to toss and turn fretfully, she decides to use the technique while she's lying in bed (it can be done lying down, sitting up, or standing). After just a few minutes of Tapping, the teenager's body has calmed down completely and is feeling pleasantly relaxed and ready for sleep. The terror and other emotional stress have drained from her body, and her senses have returned: she realizes that she has a fair chance of getting this role, and if she doesn't get it, she will almost certainly attain another major part in the play. She turns over and falls asleep peacefully, looking forward to tomorrow's audition.

Now let's look at Lori's Tapping process as it took place in real time.

To begin with, Lori tunes in to the way she is feeling. She notices her uncomfortable physical sensations, her stressed and anxious feelings and her negative thought process. Putting all this together, she rates the intensity of her fear as a nine on a ten-point scale (zero being "no fear" and ten being "very high fear").

Lori chooses to do Step 2 of the protocol, tapping on the Karate Chop spot while saying three times, "Even though I am so nervous, I completely accept myself." She now proceeds with Step 3, tapping the following eight points with two fingers of each hand (the middle finger and index finger). She could have chosen to do her tapping with just one hand if she preferred to do it that way. Lori pays attention to her frightened thoughts and feelings as she imagines herself at the audition. With this picture in mind, she taps:

- the top of her head
- the eyebrows near the nose
- the outer edge of the eyebrows
- the eyebone directly under the eyes
- the indentation over the lip (under the nose)
- the indentation under the lip (on the chin)
- directly under the collarbone
- on the side of the body, about four inches below the under-

arm for a teen or adult, two or three inches below the under-arm for a child

As Lori is tapping, she silently thinks her anxious thoughts and notes the stress in her body. She's thinking:

I'm going to flop!
I know I won't be chosen—I'm not good enough.
I'll mess it up.
I feel sick just thinking about it.
I'm freaking out.
There are better people than me for this role.
I'm so scared.
I can't do this.
My heart is beating so hard.

At the end of the round of tapping, Lori takes a deep breath in and out, allowing herself to rest for a moment. Then she pays attention to what she is currently thinking and feeling. She still feels afraid and pessimistic but nowhere near as much as before. She imagines herself at the audition again and rates her current level of fear at about a five on the ten-point scale. Lori repeats the protocol a few more times until she is able to rate her nervousness at a zero.

CHOICES METHOD OF EFT

There is another form of EFT called the Choices Method. This method, developed by psychologist Patricia Carrington, involves a positive statement within its structure. Instead of simply focusing on frightening feelings, the child also focuses on a positive strength, resource or intention. Many people prefer this method because the treatment sounds more positive and hopeful. Having used both methods extensively—both personally and professionally—I can say that they both yield the same outstanding positive results. Therefore, using one form or the other is a matter of personal preference. Nonetheless, I would agree with Canfield and Bruner's formulation (as they describe it in their book *Tapping into Ultimate Success*) that it can be helpful to use the original EFT Tapping method described previously to bring intense fear down a few notches before switching to the Choices Method. When a subjective rating of the intensity of the fear is at a six or less, the child can either continue rounds using the regular EFT Tapping or switch at that point, if desired, to the Choices Method.

The way to do the Choices Method is as follows:

1. Name your feeling (e.g., "I'm afraid I'll do poorly on the exam") and rate the intensity of that feeling between one and ten, where ten means that the feeling is extremely strong.
2. Make a positive choice. Write it down or just remember it for now. Choices address the fear in some way. Here are some examples of fears and possible choices:

Examples of Fears and Some Choices

Fear	Choice
Child is afraid of thunderstorms.	Child chooses to remember that she has always been safe inside her house during storms.
Child is intensely worrying about a science test that she's going to have the next day.	Child chooses to remember that she usually does very well on her tests.

Fear	Choice
Child is worried about traveling on her own for the first time.	Child chooses to remember that she knows the steps to take in an emergency and other cases of need.
Child is afraid that her best friend is abandoning her for someone else.	Child chooses to be okay with whatever happens, believing that surprising benefits can come out of any situation.
Child is afraid there might be a spider in the basement.	Child chooses to remember that house spiders are really small and harmless.

3. Tap on the Karate Chop spot (between the baby finger and the wrist on either hand) while naming your feeling and your positive choice.

4. Tap the eight treatment points for a few seconds each while thinking about, naming and feeling the frightened feeling (see the diagram on page 300 for the location of Tapping points). This is round one.

5. Tap the eight treatment points for a few seconds each while naming your positive choice at each point. This is round two.

6. Tap the eight treatment points for a few seconds each, naming the fear at the first point at the top of the head, naming the positive choice at the next point, which is at the eyebrow near the nose, and continuing alternating between the fear and the choice in this way until all eight points have been tapped. This is round three.

7. At the end of round three, take a deep breath in and out

and notice what you are thinking and feeling now. Rate the intensity of this feeling between one and ten.

- If your number is higher than before, repeat the treatment, making sure to include Step 2.
- If you are essentially where you started—nothing has really changed—do the same treatment but be sure to do Step 2 if you didn't already do it. If you did do it, then this time use the Tender Spot (see diagram, page 300) instead of the Karate Chop point.
- If your number is lower than before, repeat the treatment as many times as necessary till you get to zero.
- If you are at zero, you are finished the treatment. Treatment is also finished if you simply can't think of the fear anymore or can't connect to the feelings at all.

If Lori were to use the Choices Method, her self-help intervention might sound like this:

Lori completes Step 1 and then makes a choice. She chooses to "do the best she can and let whatever happens happen." Then Lori begins Step 3: while tapping on the side of her hand (the Karate Chop point), Lori says the following statement three times: "Even though I feel like I'm going to mess it all up, I choose to do the best I can and let whatever happens happen."

Lori then proceeds with Step 4 (round one), naming her fear at each of the eight Tapping points:

I'll be a flop.
I'll freeze on the spot.
They'll kick me off the stage.
It will be my worst performance ever.
I'll make one terrible mistake that will ruin everything.
I'll make a fool of myself.
They'll choose someone else.
I'll be humiliated.

Now Lori moves on to Step 5 (round two), naming her choice at each of the eight Tapping points:

I choose to do my best and let whatever happens happen.
I'll just do what I can do and let whatever happens happen.
I'll let whatever happens just happen.
I'll try out for the part and then let whatever happens happen.
Whatever happens happens.
I'll accept whatever happens.
I'll just do my thing and whatever happens happens.
I'll do what I can do and be okay with whatever happens.

Finally, Lori completes step 6 (round three), alternating between her fear statement and her choice statement at each Tapping point, beginning at the first point (the top of the head) with her fear. The round sounds like this:

Head: *I'm afraid I'll blow it.*
Eyebrows: *I'll do my best and let whatever happens happen.*
Outer eye: *I'll panic and trip all over myself.*
Under the eye: *I'll do what I can do and whatever happens happens.*
Over the lip: *I'll be a miserable flop.*
Under the lip: *Whatever happens happens.*
Under the collarbone: *They won't choose me. They'll choose Stacey or someone else.*
Under the arm: *I'll do my thing and whatever happens happens.*

Lori takes a deep breath in and out, allowing herself to rest for a moment. Then she pays attention to what she is thinking and feeling. She's feeling a lot calmer now, noticing just a tinge of fear left. She imagines herself at the audition again and rates her current level of fear at two and a half on the ten-point scale.

Knowing that it is important to get to zero, Lori starts to do one more set of the three rounds of the Choices Method. As she begins round one, she can still feel a twinge of anxiety. However, by the time she gets to the fourth Tapping point (under her eye), she cannot really feel the fear anymore. In fact, she is having trouble picturing the audition altogether. It doesn't seem important somehow; it feels like the issue is gone. These feelings indicate that the Tapping has done its job and that Lori needn't continue to finish the treatment, even though she has just barely started round one. Since she can hardly think about the audition now, or anything else for that matter, she turns over and goes to sleep.

The next day, she gets up feeling calm and confident and totally ready to perform. Lori's centered emotional state remains with her throughout the audition process. This is a common consequence of Tapping—once anxious feelings have been resolved, they usually stay that way, even though a person often anticipates their return. If a person is really afraid that anxious feelings will return, however, that's no problem: she can simply do EFT or Choices EFT on the issue "I'm afraid that the frightened feelings will return." This strategy normally puts the fear to rest.

"Invisible" Tapping

Actual tapping is not necessary in the Tapping techniques. In public settings, or at other times when you don't want to tap on your body, there are two ways you can do the treatment:

1. Place a finger on the tapping spot while you think of your problem or choice (in other words, touch the tapping point without tapping it). Do the same at each of the eight tapping points.
2. Just think of the tapping spot—*imagine* you are touching it, but don't touch it. Now, think of your problem or choice. Do the same at each of the eight tapping points.

Because energy follows intention and thought processes, invisible tapping works just as well as actual tapping does in Energy Psychology techniques.

Children can also tap on a doll or stuffed animal instead of on themselves. It all seems to work!

Bach Flower Remedies for Children's Anxious Moments

Bach flower remedies address emotional stress of all kinds. By helping to balance negative emotions such as anger, sadness and fear, they are thought to contribute to both mental and physical well-being in people of all ages.

Bach flower remedies are made of water that has been vibrationally altered (flowers are placed in a bowl of water; the mixture is heated in the sun or boiled on a stove; the flowers are then removed and the water is preserved with brandy). Anyone who can safely ingest water and a tiny amount of brandy can safely take the remedies. Pregnant mothers, the elderly, babies and toddlers, sick people, emotionally troubled people, and so on, may all safely use Bach flower remedies. Although Bach flower remedies do not interact with herbs, vitamins, homeopathic preparations or medicines of any kind, anyone taking other forms of treatment should ask their own health practitioner about the advisability of adding Bach flower remedies to their treatment regime.

HOW TO PREPARE AND USE BACH FLOWER REMEDIES

There are thirty-eight Bach flower remedies, each addressing different types of stressed feelings that children, teens and adults are prone to at different times. Although there are Bach remedies to help your child cope with frustration, jealousy, bad or sad moods, depression, low self-esteem, insecurity, explosive anger, impulsivity, lack of motivation, grief, motor and vocal tics, boredom, impatience and much more, only those remedies pertinent to the subject of frightened and anxious feelings will be described in this section. A Bach flower practitioner can prepare an appropriate mixture to help your child through anxious moments (or any other issue), or you can make your own mixture of Bach flower remedies by selecting up to seven of the following remedies to mix together in one treatment bottle as per the directions on page 314.

Bach Flower Remedy	Type of Fear
Aspen	Vague fears, like fear of the dark, fear of ghosts or evil forces, fear of something bad happening (e.g., fear of going to sleep in a dark room)
Cerato	Fear of making the wrong decision; constant need for another's opinion; lack of confidence in one's own choices; feelings of self-consciousness or being judged (e.g., fear of public speaking, fear of picking out one's clothes independently)

Cherry Plum	Fear of losing control or "going crazy"; overwhelming feeling of fear
Crab Apple	Fear of dirt, germs or contamination; feelings of being flawed or ugly (e.g., OCD-type fears of contamination; body dysmorphic disorder or other feelings of being flawed or ugly)
Gentian	When fear is worsened by a tendency to negative thinking and negative expectations
Honeysuckle	Not a fear remedy per se, but useful when a child's separation anxiety is heightened due to feelings of homesickness
Larch	Fear of failing; feelings of inadequacy; lack of confidence in one's ability, especially in comparison to others (e.g., test anxiety, insecurity)
Mimulus	Fear of separation; fear of people, places and things (e.g., dogs, robbers, lightning, etc.); fear of loss (e.g., fear of dying)
Red Chestnut	Fears and worry concerning loved ones (i.e., worry about their health or safety; e.g., fear that parents will die)
Rock Rose	Panic and terror; fears characterized by the fight-or-flight response (e.g., having a panic attack before a performance or test)

Scleranthus	Fear of making a final commitment (accompanied by an endless analysis of the pros and cons, and an inability to decide, but not wanting the opinion of others; e.g., can't decide what college program to undertake); also for mood swings
Star of Bethlehem	Taken with Rock Rose, for fears brought on by traumatic events, shock and grief (e.g., fear of storms that developed after living through a hurricane)
Vine	When fear causes the child to become exceedingly rigid and stubborn
Walnut	Fear of change and difficulty with transitions (as well as to ease all normal transitions, such as first-time experiences, first day of school, going away to camp, etc.); fears brought on by hearing about or seeing disturbing images (e.g., images in books, on the news, in movies, etc.)
White Chestnut	Worrying, ruminating, obsessing (e.g., can't fall asleep at night because of worries, or asks endless questions about the same topic)

Directions for Mixing Bach Flower Remedies

Purchase the desired remedies and two empty mixing bottles (these are 1-ounce glass bottles with a glass dropper, available wherever Bach flower remedies are sold). Follow this recipe:

BACH FLOWER REMEDY MIXTURE

Water
2 drops each desired remedy
1 teaspoon brandy

1. Fill a mixing bottle with water almost to the top, leaving space to add the remaining ingredients.
2. To the water, add the drops of each desired remedy, and the brandy (as a preservative). Place the dropper in the bottle and twist shut. The remedy is now ready to use.

Note: To refill the bottle, empty it completely and rinse the glass dropper thoroughly. Sterilize the glass bottle by boiling it for a few minutes. The bottle is now ready to use again.

Directions for Taking Bach Flower Remedies

Put 4 drops of the remedy from the mixing bottle into a small amount (anywhere from 1 tablespoon to 8 ounces) of hot or cold liquid. Prepare this for your child 4 times a day: in the morning, in the middle of the day, in the afternoon and in the evening. Continue the treatment until the fear is no longer an active concern.

When the fear returns, repeat the above instructions. Over time, the fear should return less and less often and last for shorter and shorter periods until, eventually, it doesn't return at all.

Instructions for Using Rescue Remedy or Rescue Sleep

Rescue Remedy is a premixed Bach flower preparation. In recent years, a few new premixed remedies have appeared on the market, including Rescue Sleep and Rescue Energy. You would take any premixed liquid remedy the same way you would take your own prepared treatment in the mixing bottle: 4 drops in a small amount of liquid, four times a day. Rescue Remedy is now available in other forms as well, such as sprays, pastilles and chewing gum. These are handy to carry in a schoolbag or purse for times of emergency.

Rescue Remedy is used to treat an episode of fear. Unlike the other remedies, it is not used to treat the fear in order to heal the roots of that fear. A child who takes Mimulus for fear of spiders, for instance, will take that remedy off and on over a period of months (or sometimes over a couple of years) until the fear no longer returns. However, if that child is going to spend the summer in a camp cabin filled with spiders, he might bring some Rescue Remedy with him for those occasions in which a spider decides to share his bed. Rescue Remedy would be taken in case of panic following an actual meeting with a spider, or in preparation for a meeting with a spider (in the same way fearful flyers take Rescue Remedy before arriving at the airport, while at the airport and while in flight, if necessary).

Further Notes on Taking Bach Flower Remedies

Having two mixing bottles allows you to prepare a new treatment bottle without having to wait until the first bottle is completely empty. This way, if you cannot immediately boil the first bottle, you can still start the new bottle, boiling the other when you have time.

Bach flower remedies can be dropped into water, milk, chocolate milk, juice, soup, tea, coffee, soda or any other liquid.

For kosher consumers: The Bach flower remedies that are purchased in the store contain brandy that is not certified kosher. However, Rabbi Pesach Eliyahu Falk of Gateshead, England, rules that Bach flower remedies are permissible for treatment purposes. Those who are interested in detailed questions and answers on this subject can visit www.sarahchanaradcliffe.com/bach_flower/.

Aromatherapy for Children's Anxious Moments

Danielle Sade, B.Sc., CAHP
Certified Aromatherapy Health Professional

The practice of aromatherapy is a wonderful, natural way to support your child's health and well-being. Essential oils can be very therapeutic and nurturing. When a child is feeling fear, anxiety, worry, sadness or insecurity, the proper use of essential oils can provide much-needed gentle support and stability.

The following are safe and easy practices that can help a child cope better with feelings of stress and fear.

CALMING ESSENTIAL OILS TO HELP RELIEVE FEELINGS OF ANXIETY AND FEAR

Neroli *(Citrus aurantium)*
Lavender *(Lavandula angustifolia)*

Methods of Application:

- Put 1 to 2 drops of neroli or lavender on a tissue or cotton ball, and ask your child to inhale the fragrance.
- Put 1 to 2 drops of lavender in your child's bath before bedtime.
- Put 1 to 2 drops on a favorite stuffed animal or schoolbag.
- Combine 3 drops of neroli or lavender with 1 tablespoon of jojoba carrier oil (available wherever essential oils are sold) and use it to massage your child's feet before bedtime.

SEDATING ESSENTIAL OILS TO HELP CALM THE MIND AND BODY FOR SLEEP

Roman chamomile *(Anthemis nobilis)*
Lavender *(Lavandula angustifolia)*

Methods of Application:

- Put 1 to 2 drops of lavender and Roman chamomile in your child's bath before bedtime.
- Put 1 to 2 drops of lavender on a tissue or cotton ball. Ask your child to breathe the fragrance in deeply and exhale seven times. Place it underneath your child's pillowcase.
- Put 1 drop of Roman chamomile and 3 drops of lavender in an aromatherapy diffuser (available with instructions for use in health-food stores).
- Combine 1 drop of Roman chamomile and 3 drops of lavender with 1 tablespoon of jojoba carrier oil and use it to massage your child's feet before bedtime.

UPLIFTING AND JOYFUL ESSENTIAL OILS TO HELP RELIEVE STRESS AND WORRY

Orange *(Citrus aurantium)*
Grapefruit *(Citrus paradisi)*

Methods of Application:

- Put 1 to 2 drops of orange or grapefruit on a tissue or cotton ball and ask your child to inhale the fragrance. Place the tissue or cotton ball into the pillowcase.
- Put 1 to 2 drops of orange or grapefruit on your child's stuffed animal or a beanbag. This technique engages your child's senses of touch and smell.
- Put 2 drops each of orange and grapefruit in a diffuser.
- Combine 2 drops of grapefruit and 1 drop of orange with 1 tablespoon of jojoba carrier oil and use it to massage your child's feet before bedtime. Ask your child to imagine the color orange or yellow while smelling these oils.

CALMING AND UPLIFTING ESSENTIAL OIL TO HELP SETTLE FEARS

Mandarin *(Citrus reticulata)*

Method of Application:

- Put 1 to 2 drops of mandarin on a tissue or cotton ball and ask your child to inhale the fragrance.
- Put 1 to 2 drops of mandarin on your child's stuffed animal or other soft toy. This technique engages your child's senses of touch and smell.
- Put 4 to 5 drops of mandarin in a diffuser.
- Combine 3 drops of mandarin with 1 tablespoon of jojoba carrier oil and use it to massage your child's feet before bedtime.

CONFIDENCE-BUILDING ESSENTIAL OIL

Bergamot *(Citrus bergamia)*

Method of Application:

- Put 1 to 2 drops of bergamot on a tissue or cotton ball and ask your child to inhale the fragrance.

- Put 1 to 2 drops of bergamot on your child's stuffed animal or a beanbag. This technique engages your child's senses of touch and smell.
- Put 4 to 5 drops of bergamot in a diffuser.

Note: Since essential oils do have some medicinal qualities—meaning there can be occasional contraindications for use—it is always recommended to consult with a professional aromatherapist before starting to use them in the home.

Danielle Sade, B.Sc., has been practicing and teaching clinical aromatherapy for more than twenty years. She is the director of Healing Fragrances School of Aromatherapy, a certification program for Aromatherapy Health Professionals. See www.healingfragrances.net.

Herbs for Children's
Anxious Moments

Brenna Leah Cashman, BHSc, RHN
Herbal Medicine and Nutritional Counseling

Herbal medicine can help children and teens feel calmer and less stressed. It is easy to use herbs with children—and safe too, as long as gentle herbs are chosen. It can be empowering for parents to discover time-tested remedies that support and nourish the child's nervous system, providing a measure of relief and comfort in a child's anxious moments. Herbs are available at many health-food stores and specialty distributors. Here are some ideas to get you started.

HOW TO USE HERBS

There are various ways to use herbal remedies. Herbs are most commonly available in dried form for making teas. Teas are easy to prepare, and the ritual of preparing and drinking herbal tea can be very soothing in itself. There are quite a few pleasant-tasting teas that children can enjoy hot or cold. However, some kids just don't like tea. Fortunately, herbs are also readily available as liquid tinctures (alcohol extracts). Tinctures are even more convenient than teas, as no preparation is required to take them. Only a few drops are to be taken per dose. The alcohol content can sometimes make tinctures harsh-tasting and less appealing to young children. Glycerites are fluid extracts made from glycerin instead of alcohol. With their mild, slightly sweet taste, they are an excellent option for kids. Herbal syrups—herbs prepared in a sweet-tasting base—are also well received by children and are a particularly good choice when the herbs being used have their own naturally bitter taste.

Herbs can also be used externally. Herbal baths, for instance, are a relaxing and refreshing option for stressed-out youngsters and can be used by even very small children. Herbs can also be gathered into a "sleep pillow" as an aid to relax both body and mind. Here are some herbal recipes that can help kids through their anxious times.

ALL-PURPOSE STRESS-REDUCTION MIXTURE

This mixture of calming herbs helps soothe children, teens and even adults during challenging transitions (moving house, first day of school or camp, changes in the family, etc.) and other stressful events. When a child is worrying or feeling anxious in anticipation of a test or other challenge, this herbal preparation can help take the edge off. To help nourish and support the nervous system, strengthening the youngster's overall ability to deal with stress, try this combination of herbs as a tincture, a tea or a bath infusion.

Oat straw
Chamomile
Skullcap

To prepare as a tea:

1. Mix together in a glass jar the following dried herbs in equal proportions (for example, one half cup of each):

   Oat straw
   Chamomile
   Skullcap

2. Place 1 teaspoon of the mixed herbs in a tea ball or a teapot with a strainer.
3. Pour one cup of boiling water over the herbs.
4. Cover and let set for five minutes.
5. Remove the tea ball and tea is ready to drink.

This can be given to the child once or twice a day during times of stress or pressure.

To use in tincture form:

1. Ask for the tincture oatstraw at your local health food store.
2. The remedy can be dropped directly on the tongue or added to juice, water or other hot or cold liquids.
3. Adults and teenagers can take the dose recommended on the bottle. Children between the ages of 6 and 12 can take half the recommended dose. For children under 6, consult with a professional herbalist for the correct dosage.

To make an calming herbal infusion for the bath:

1. Place two tablespoons of any one of following the dried herbs into a measuring cup or other large container.

   Chamomile
   Lavender
   Calendula

2. Pour two cups of boiling water over the herb.
3. Let sit for 10 minutes.
4. Strain very well, using a mesh tea bag or a fine strainer, so you don't get bits of herbs floating in the bath.
5. Pour the infusion into the bathwater.

SOOTHING TUMMY TEA

Stress, worry and tension often manifest in the body as digestive issues. Some herbs offer wonderful relief for an upset tummy, especially for children. Chamomile is helpful for both nervous system symptoms, such as stress, anxiety, hyperactivity, insomnia and fear, as well as stomach complaints like gas and indigestion. Lemon balm combines well with chamomile and helps to sooth nerves and settle tension in the stomach. Peppermint adds a pleasing taste and helps improve digestion and treat stomach upset. Ginger is another herb that is used for digestive complaints, particularly nausea. Catnip is a calming herb that can also relieve indigestion.

Chamomile
Lemon balm
Peppermint
Ginger
Catnip

You can use either 1 teaspoon of one of these individual herbs, or 1 teaspoon of some combination of them. Pour 1 cup of boiling water over 1 teaspoon of herbs. Allow to steep for about 5 minutes. Cool to a comfortable warm temperature, or serve chilled.

SLEEP SUPPORT TEA

It is not uncommon for a worried child to be a sleepless child. A stressed system makes it hard to relax at night and can result in difficulty both falling asleep and staying asleep. Teas made from the following herbs can be helpful. Ideally, tea should be given to the child one to two hours before bedtime, as part of a relaxing bedtime ritual. An herbal bath made with an infusion of the following herbs can also be part of the bedtime routine.

Chamomile
Catnip
Linden flower
Lavender
Passionflower
Lemon balm
Hops

You can use either 1 teaspoon of one of these individual herbs, or 1 teaspoon of some combination of them. Pour 1 cup of boiling water over 1 teaspoon of herbs. Allow to steep for about 5 minutes. Cool to a comfortable warm temperature, or serve chilled.

SLEEP SUPPORT HERBAL PILLOW

A wonderful comfort for kids who are feeling anxious is an herbal pillow—a small cloth sack stuffed with herbs and set either under the child's regular pillow or just near the sleeping child. An herbal pillow can be a project you create along with your child. Here's what you'll need:

- a piece of fabric for making an approximately 3-by-3-inch pillow
- a sewing needle
- some sewing thread

- some good-smelling herbs, such as chamomile, lavender, catnip, hops or rosemary

Sew the fabric into a pillow shape, leaving an opening in one side. If your sewing skills are basic, you can create a simple square shape. If you are able to do a bit more, children enjoy fun sleep shapes such as a moon, star or heart. Stuff the herbs into the pillow and sew the opening closed. The pillow can be kept on the bed, and volatile oils in the herbs will be released gently into the air as your child sleeps.

HEADACHE REMEDIES

Children and teens may develop chronic headaches as a physical reaction to stress and anxiety. Herbs can be used both to support the nervous system, so as to help prevent or minimize tension in the body, and to treat headache symptoms as they occur. The following herbs are helpful in reducing headache symptoms.

Skullcap
Chamomile
Rosemary
Linden flower

1. Put one or more of the above dried herbs in equal amounts in a glass jar.
2. Place 1 teaspoon of the mixture in a tea ball or a teapot with a strainer.
3. Pour 1 cup boiling water over the dried herbs.
4. Allow to steep for about five minutes.
5. Remove tea ball and serve hot or cold.

For an active headache, drink 1 to 2 cups of tea.

HERBAL SAFETY

Although pharmaceutical solutions for stress and anxious feelings are not prescribed for healthy children, appropriate herbal medicines can be used by almost anyone of any age to help settle and calm mental and physical symptoms caused by worry, panic and fear. However, it is important to keep in mind that herbs do have medicinal characteristics and side effects, and can interact with your child's health conditions and other medicines. While the herbs discussed here are all gentle remedies with a historically proven safety record, it is always recommended to consult with a professional herbalist before starting a new herbal regimen. This is especially important if your child has a health condition or is currently taking other medications. A professional herbalist is familiar with herb-drug interactions and can advise you appropriately. If any adverse reactions occur while taking herbal remedies, discontinue use immediately and consult with your doctor or herbalist.

Once you have ascertained that the herbs you want to use are safe for your child, you can enjoy the simplicity and satisfaction of helping to ease your child's stress in this natural and soothing way. When your child grows up and leaves home, he can continue to draw on the healing qualities of herbs to address stress and anxious feelings throughout life.

Brenna Leah Cashman practises herbal medicine and holistic nutrition in Toronto, Canada. Visit her blog at www.thenutritionist.wordpress.com.

APPENDIX E

Resources

Bartholomew, Sandy Steen. *Zentangle for Kidz!* East Petersburg, PA: Design Originals, 2011.

Benson, Herbert, and William Proctor. *Relaxation Revolution: The Science and Genetics of Mind Body Healing.* New York: Scribner, 2010.

Benson, Herbert, with Miriam Z. Klipper. *The Relaxation Response.* New York: HarperTorch, 2000.

Brantley, Jeffrey. *Calming Your Anxious Mind: How Mindfulness and Compassion Can Free You from Anxiety, Fear, and Panic.* Oakland, CA: New Harbinger Publications, 2007.

Brown, Richard P., and Patricia L. Gerbarg. *The Healing Power of the Breath: Simple Techniques to Reduce Stress and Anxiety, Enhance Concentration, and Balance Your Emotions.* Boston, MA: Shambhalah Press, 2012.

Canfield, Jack, and Pamela Bruner. *Tapping into Ultimate Success: How to Overcome Any Obstacle and Skyrocket Your Results.* Carlsbad, CA: Hay House, 2012.

Childre, Doc, and Howard Martin with Donna Beech. *The HeartMath Solution.* New York: HarperSanFrancisco, 2000. See also www.HeartMath.com and www.HeartMath.org.

Church, Dawson. *The Genie in Your Genes: Epigenetic Medicine and the New Biology of Intention.* Santa Rosa, CA: Elite Books, 2007.

Doidge, Norman. *The Brain That Changes Itself: Stories of Personal Triumph from the Frontiers of Brain Science.* New York: Penguin Books, 2007.

Fournier, Jay C., et al. "Antidepressant drug effects and depression severity." *JAMA: Journal of the American Medical Association,* vol. 303(1): 47–53.

Gerber, Richard. *Vibrational Medicine.* Vermont: Bear & Company, 2001.

Gottman, John, with Joan DeClaire. *Raising an Emotionally Intelligent Child: The Heart of Parenting.* New York: Simon & Shuster, 1998.

Grossman, Marc, and Magic Eye Inc. *Magic Eye Beyond 3D: Improve Your Vision.* Kansas City, MO: Andrews McMeel Publishing, 2004. See also any book in this series, such as *Harry Potter Magic Eye Book* and *Disney's Magic Eye: 3-D Illusions,* as well as any other stereogram (3-D) viewing books by other authors.

Munford, Paul R. *Overcoming Compulsive Checking.* Oakland, CA: New Harbinger Publications, 2004.

Niemi, Maj-Britt. "Placebo Effect: A Cure in the Mind." *Scientific American Mind* (February 2009).

Parnell, Laurel. *Tapping In: A Step-by-Step Guide to Activating Your Healing Resources Through Bilateral Stimulation.* Boulder, CO: Sounds True, 2008.

Radcliffe, Sarah Chana. *Raise Your Kids Without Raising Your Voice.* Toronto: HarperCollins Canada, 2006.

Roberts, Thomas. *The Mindfulness Workbook: A Beginner's Guide to Overcoming Fear and Embracing Compassion.* Oakland, CA: New Harbinger Publications, 2009.

Schwartz, Jeffrey M., and Rebecca Gladding. *You Are Not Your Brain: The 4-Step Solution for Changing Bad Habits, Ending Unhealthy Thinking, and Taking Control of Your Life.* New York: Penguin Books, 2011.

Scott, Trudy. *The Antianxiety Food Solution: How the Foods You Eat Can Help You Calm Your Anxious Mind, Improve Your Mood and End Cravings.* Oakland, CA: New Harbinger Publications, 2011.

Siegel, Daniel, and Tina Payne Bryson. *The Whole-Brain Child: 12 Revolutionary Strategies to Nurture Your Child's Developing Mind.* New York: Delacorte Press, 2011.

ACKNOWLEDGMENTS

I want to thank Brad Wilson at HarperCollins for suggesting this fantastic project. So many children and adults can enhance the quality of their lives by knowing how to deal effectively with inevitable anxious feelings. I have to thank many masters in many disciplines: psychiatry, psychology, medicine, alternative and complementary medicine, and education. Thanks so much to Deena Weinberg for her excellent research assistance. Thanks also to parents and educators Jessie Henry and Shani Tauber for taking time to read the manuscript and offer valuable suggestions. Thank you to the thousands of open-minded clients who have allowed me to introduce both traditional and innovative therapeutic strategies, giving themselves and their children the gift of freedom from fear and giving me the opportunity to learn more and more about the power of the mind, the heart and the human energy system. The journey has been incredibly awesome, and I am truly grateful. Thank-you to my wonderful agent at Westwood Creative Artists, Hilary McMahon, whose gentle vote of confidence and encouragement has always been much appreciated. Thank you to my husband, Avraham, who helps me in everything I do and who has joined me in my work by contributing his professional indexing skills, and thank you to my wonderful family for their constant love and support.

INDEX

Rescue Remedy *(continued)*
  anxiety, 290
  bullying, 262
  car accidents, 173
  fear, 199
  fight or flight, 231, 235
  first-time experiences, 173
  instructions for using, 315
  job interviews, 173
  panic, 240–44
  surgery, medical or dental procedures,
    173
  terrifying events, 173
  tests, 173
  toilet training, 194
  traumatic events, 182
Rescue Sleep, 170, 239, 280, 290, 315
rides. *See* amusement park
rigid and stubborn
  Vine, 313
robbers
  Mimulus, 312
Roberts, Thomas, 92
Rock Rose
  bullying, 262
  fear, 199
  fight or flight, 313
  panic, 170, 191, 193, 210, 223, 231,
    235, 281
  test anxiety, 313
roller coaster, 241–44
Rubik's Cube, 143
rumination, 5, 31, 62, 77, 100, 158, 159,
    177, 223, 254
  White Chestnut, 223

S
scary feelings
  amusement park, 241–24
  dialogue examples, 16–17, 27, 62, 64,
    71–72
  lifestyle factors, 180
  night fears, 208, 210–12, 215–17
  paying attention to, 43

positive imagination, 106–9
redirecting attention, 57, 134–35, 214,
    222
talking to child about, 49
tapping away, 254, 256–57
scenarios. *See* dialogue examples
school, first day of
  Walnut, 313
Schwartz, Dr. Jeffrey, 124, 128
Scleranthus
  indecision, 171, 313
  mood swings, 313
self-consciousness
  Cerato, 170, 262, 311
sensible fear, 1, 183
separation anxiety
  dialogue example, 61–62
  emotional coaching, 288–92
  Honeysuckle, 312
  Mimulus, 170, 206, 281, 312
  PTSD, 247
sexual addiction, 53
shock
  Star of Bethlehem, 313
shyness, dialogue example, 37
Siegel, Dr. Daniel J., 52, 58
singing, dialogue example, 28–29
skin-picking, 5
sleep problems
  Aspen, 311
  dialogue examples, 37–38
  Rescue Sleep, 170
  White Chestnut, 313
snakes, 184
soft eyes. *See* eye focus
soothing strategies, 8–9, 53, 54. *See also*
    breathing
  herbs, 321–27
  locking in, 30
  self-soothing, 32, 79
  stones and crystals, 99, 158–59
  treats, 63
spiders, 4, 109, 184
  dialogue examples, 77–78